# HOW TO BE A
# DOMESTIC GODDESS

Also by Nigella Lawson:

**HOW TO EAT**
THE PLEASURES AND PRINCIPLES OF GOOD FOOD

# HOW TO BE A DOMESTIC GODDESS

## BAKING AND THE ART OF COMFORT COOKING

# NIGELLA LAWSON

Chatto & Windus
LONDON

FOR JOHN, GODDESS-MAKER

Published by Chatto & Windus 2000

1 3 5 7 9 8 6 4 2

Copyright © Nigella Lawson 2000

Photographs copyright © Petrina Tinslay 2000

Endpapers copyright ©
Hulton Getty

First published in Great Britain in 2000 by Chatto & Windus
Random House, 20 Vauxhall Bridge Road, London SW1V 2SA

Random House Australia (Pty) Limited
20 Alfred Street, Milsons Point, Sydney,
New South Wales 2061, Australia

Random House New Zealand Limited
18 Poland Road, Glenfield,
Auckland 10, New Zealand

Random House (Pty) Limited
Endulini, 5A Jubilee Road, Parktown 2193, South Africa

The Random House Group Limited Reg. No. 954009
www.randomhouse.co.uk

A CIP catalogue record for this book
is available from the British Library

ISBN 0 7011 6888 9

Papers used by Random House are natural,
recyclable products made from wood grown in sustainable forests.
The manufacturing processes conform to the environmental
regulations of the country of origin

Printed and bound in Great Britain by
Butler & Tanner Ltd, Frome and London

# CONTENTS

PREFACE vii

A SHORT NOTE ON EQUIPMENT AND INGREDIENTS viii

CHARTS AND CONVERSIONS ix

**CAKES** 2

**BISCUITS** 44

**PIES** 78

**PUDDINGS** 122

**CHOCOLATE** 162

**CHILDREN** 206

**CHRISTMAS** 244

**BREAD AND YEAST** 290

**THE DOMESTIC GODDESS'S LARDER** 332

BIBLIOGRAPHY 364

ACKNOWLEDGEMENTS 366

INDEX 367

# PREFACE

This is a book about baking, but not a baking book – not in the sense of being a manual or a comprehensive guide or a map of a land you do not inhabit. I neither want to confine you to kitchen quarters nor even suggest that it might be desirable. But I do think that many of us have become alienated from the domestic sphere, and that it can actually make us feel better to claim back some of that space, make it comforting rather than frightening. In a way, baking stands both as a useful metaphor for the familial warmth of the kitchen we fondly imagine used to exist, and as a way of reclaiming our lost Eden. This is hardly a culinary matter, of course: but cooking, we know, has a way of cutting through things, and to things, which have nothing to do with the kitchen. This is why it matters.

The trouble with much modern cooking is not that the food it produces isn't good, but that the mood it induces in the cook is one of skin-of-the-teeth efficiency, all briskness and little pleasure. Sometimes that's the best we can manage, but at other times we don't want to feel like a post-modern, post-feminist, overstretched woman but, rather, a domestic goddess, trailing nutmeggy fumes of baking pie in our languorous wake.

So what I'm talking about is not *being* a domestic goddess exactly, but *feeling* like one. One of the reasons making cakes is satisfying is that the effort required is so much less than the gratitude conferred. Everyone seems to think it's hard to make a cake (and no need to disillusion them), but it doesn't take more than 25 minutes to make and bake a tray of muffins or a sponge layer cake, and the returns are high: you feel disproportionately good about yourself afterwards. This is what baking, what all of this book, is about: feeling good, wafting along in the warm, sweet-smelling air, unwinding, no longer being entirely an office creature; and that's exactly what I mean by 'comfort cooking'.

Part of it too is about a fond, if ironic, dream: the unexpressed 'I' that is a cross between Sophia Loren and Debbie Reynolds in pink cashmere cardigan and fetching gingham pinny, a weekend alter-ego winning adoring glances and endless approbation from anyone who has the good fortune to eat in her kitchen. The good thing is, we don't have to get ourselves up in Little Lady drag and we don't have to renounce the world and enter into a life of domestic drudgery. But we can bake a little – and a cake is just a cake, far easier than getting the timing right for even the most artlessly casual of midweek dinner parties.

This isn't a dream; what's more, it isn't even a nightmare.

# A SHORT NOTE ON EQUIPMENT AND INGREDIENTS

You need neither a professionally appointed kitchen nor an expensively stocked larder to bake. Your hands, a bowl and a wooden spoon should see you through most of it, along with a couple of sandwich tins, one or two Springform tins, a loaf tin, a muffin-tray, a pie and flan dish and a rolling pin. A food processor makes life easier for some jobs, but is hardly indispensable. If there is one piece of machinery that does make a baking life more pleasurable, it's a free-standing mixer; I now couldn't live without my KitchenAid mixer, or certainly wouldn't want to. The dough hook makes bread-making a far lighter task (though I would never suggest you give up completely the relaxing routine of kneading by hand), and the other attachments – paddle and whisk – mean that you can let the cake batter be mixed or egg whites whipped while you get on with other things. Unlike a processor, you don't feel excluded from the job at hand; it's thus a very good way of feeling that you're doing it all yourself but with the minimum of effort. Otherwise, a simple hand-held electric mixer is a cheaper alternative. And I cannot do any cooking without a Magiwhisk, sold at any of the below.

As for tins and moulds, I've tried on the whole to use nothing that wouldn't be available at an averagely well-stocked kitchen shop or department store. Should you find difficulties locating any of the fancier pieces – the baby Bundt moulds or siliconware – you should telephone Ecko Bakeware (01291 638 7700) or Paton Calvert (01703 776 458; www.paton-calvert.co.uk) to find stockists near you. And both Lakeland Ltd (01539 488 100; www.lakelandltd.com) and Divertimenti (020 7935 0689; www.divertimenti.co.uk) carry such items as the reusable non-stick baking parchment, along with many of the other pieces of equipment, small and large, used in the book.

None of the ingredients listed should prove troublesome, either. The paste colours I use to tint icing are available from cake-decoration shops, as is gold leaf, other decorative items and a huge range of cookie-cutters. If you can't find what you need near you, Purple Planet will take telephone orders on 020 8969 4119, or you can buy online at www.purpleplanet.co.uk.

I like to use Italian 00 flour in place of ordinary plain flour (it is finer-milled and makes light cakes and desirably elastic pastry) and now that it is stocked at many super-markets, it shouldn't pose problems.

Eggs – organic, free-range for preference – are large unless stated otherwise in the text, and, likewise, butter is unsalted.

If you have any further enquiries, please email me at domesticgoddess@nigella.com.

# CHARTS AND CONVERSIONS

## Oven Temperatures

| gas mark | °C | description |
|---|---|---|
| 1 | 140 | very cool |
| 2 | 150 | cool |
| 3 | 170 | warm |
| 4 | 180 | moderate |
| 5 | 190 | } fairly hot |
| 6 | 200 | |
| 7 | 220 | hot |
| 8 | 230 | } very hot |
| 9 | 240 | |

## Weights

| ounces | grams |
|---|---|
| 1 | 25 |
| 2 | 50 |
| 3 | 75 |
| 4 | 110 |
| 5 | 150 |
| 6 | 175 |
| 7 | 200 |
| 8 | 225 |
| 9 | 250 |
| 10 | 275 |
| 11 | 315 |
| 12 | 350 |
| 13 | 365 |
| 14 | 400 |
| 15 | 425 |
| 16/1lb | 450 |

## Volumes

| fluid ounces | millilitres |
|---|---|
| 1 | 25 |
| 2 | 55 |
| 3 | 75 |
| 4 | 120 |
| 5 | 150 |
| 6 | 175 |
| 7 | 200 |
| 8 | 225 |
| 9 | 250 |
| 10 | 275 |
| 15 | 425 |
| 20/1 pint | 570 |
| 1$^1$/4 pints | 725 |
| 1$^1$/2 pints | 850 |
| 1$^3$/4 pints | 1 litre |

CAKES

# CAKES

Cake baking has to be, however innocently, one of the great culinary scams: it implies effort, it implies domestic prowess; but believe me, it's easy. We've become so convinced that simple food comes out of simple cooking that we're happy to cook elaborate Tuscan suppers – which in reality demand much more than we could ever believe possible – but then baulk at baking a cake, assuming that we don't have the time for all that, that we live a life that doesn't encompass those arcane culinary arts.

If that's how you think, then you're wrong. You know how you make a cake? You mix a few basic ingredients together, stick the mixture in a tin and bake it. And when I say mix, I don't mean mix it yourself, not if you don't want to: I mean process or beat with an electric mixer. How hard can that be?

Too much reassurance can, I know, be troubling in itself. If it's so easy to bake a cake, why is it that you can't? Be honest: I imagine the answer is that you don't often try, or haven't for years. Not all cakes come out perfectly or even the same each time, and not all cakes are equally easy to bake, but if you follow any one of the recipes below, you can be sure it will work. Of course there are always variants in cooking, some more controllable than others, but baking is somewhat different: it's chemistry first, poetry second. That's partly why I came to it late. When you're making a stew, well, you can go your own way, follow instinct, taste, convenience; you couldn't make a cake like this: a cake demands mathematical respect.

Some rules extend beyond the confines of the individual texts. You must remember three basic things: the first is that all ingredients should be at room temperature when you start; the second is that the oven should be at the required temperature when you put in the filled tin; finally, that tin should be of the dimensions specified. (If I'm honest, you can get away with some deviation here, but not too much – and anyway, why make things harder for yourself?)

I've said it's easy to make a cake, but this doesn't convey the depth of achievement you feel on making one. There's something about seeing such elemental change, that flour, butter, eggs, sugar could become this – and more, that you've brought it about – that's so satisfying. Such simple pleasures are not to be underestimated.

# LOAF AND PLAIN CAKES

This is baking at its simplest and most elegant. There's no folderol or fancy footwork: you just feel humble and worthy and brimming with good things.

## MY MOTHER-IN-LAW'S MADEIRA CAKE

I don't know if I ever ate Madeira cake as a child, but just the sight of this golden-yellow loaf with its long crack down the middle makes me feel satisfactorily nostalgic. This recipe, given to me by my mother-in-law Carrie, is the best of any version I've tried. It's just one of those plain cakes you think you can't see the point of, until you start slicing and eating it.

240g softened unsalted butter

200g caster sugar, plus extra for
    sprinkling

grated zest and juice of 1 lemon

3 large eggs

210g self-raising flour

90g plain flour

450g loaf tin, buttered and lined

Preheat the oven to 170°C/gas mark 3.

Cream the butter and sugar, and add the lemon zest. Add the eggs one at a time with a tablespoon of the flour for each. Then gently mix in the rest of the flour and, finally, the lemon juice. Sprinkle with caster sugar (about 2 tablespoons should do it) as it goes into the oven, and bake for 1 hour or until a cake-tester comes out clean. Remove to a wire rack, and let cool in the tin before turning out.

Makes 8–10 slices.

### VARIATION

I love a good old-fashioned seed cake; if you do too, add a couple of teaspoons of caraway to this mixture. For a lemon poppyseed cake, add the juice of another half lemon and a tablespoon or two of poppyseeds. And I once came across an expensive but tempting curiosity: dried strawberries, tiny things harvested by that clever Terence Conran. I upped the liquid to the juice of 2 lemons and folded in 100g of the strawberries. It was a wholly successful experiment.

# EASY ALMOND CAKE

This cake isn't baked in a loaf tin but in a ring mould, preferably a patterned one; and it's a plain cake only in the sense that it isn't filled or iced (though feel free). It's densely almondy and eggily intense. And you know how you make it? You buy a block of ready-made marzipan and put it in the processor along with eggs, flour, sugar, butter and a sprinkle of extracts and blitz.

You could easily use a plain cake tin for this cake but I always use my Springform tube pan (not hard to find) because the particular scent and delicacy of this cake makes it perfect as a dinner-party pudding with a few raspberries in the middle, a few more scattered around the edge and a light dusting of icing powder. When we cooked it for the picture opposite, we couldn't find the right tin (losing essential items is something of a speciality of mine), plus some of it stuck to the tin we did use. I could have cooked it again, but I didn't want to, because these things happen to all of us and I wanted to show it wasn't the end of the world. True, you don't see the moulding as well as you might, if at all, but a quick bit of patching and some judicial sieve-work with icing sugar and it looked fine. Life isn't lived in a lab.

One gentle reminder here: you just will not get the marzipan to ooze into the cake batter if it starts off fridge-cold. In dire straits, I have cubed it and given it a quick whirl in the microwave. And if you wanted to replace the vanilla extract with the zest of an orange, I wouldn't mind in the slightest.

| | |
|---|---|
| **250g softened unsalted butter** | **6 large eggs** |
| **250g softened marzipan** | **150g self-raising flour** |
| **150g caster sugar** | **25cm Springform tube pan or** |
| **1/4 teaspoon almond essence** | **patterned ring mould, buttered** |
| **1/4 teaspoon vanilla extract** | **and floured** |

Preheat oven to 170°C/gas mark 3. Chop the butter and marzipan to make them easier to break down, and put them in the bowl of the food processor, fitted with the double-bladed knife, with the sugar. Process until combined and pretty well smooth. Add almond essence and vanilla extract, process again, then break the eggs one at a time through the funnel, processing again each time. Mix the flour and baking powder and tip down the funnel, processing yet again, and then pour the mixture into the prepared tin, scraping the sides and bottom with a rubber spatula.

Bake for 50 minutes, but check from 40. Then, when the cake looks golden and cooked and a cake-tester or fine skewer (or a piece of spaghetti) comes out cleanish, remove from the oven and leave to cool in the tin before turning out. (This is when you will be feeling grateful if it's the Springform you're using.)

The fact that you could easily get 12 slices out of this is another reason why it comes in useful when you've got people coming for dinner. That it keeps for a good week is another point in its favour; you don't have to be fiddling around with all the courses just before lift-off. And if you don't want to eat raspberries with it, like the rosemary cake it's very good with apples. With this cake, I make a glorious pink apple purée. Either go for apples stewed in blood-orange juice (wonderful around February when the tarocchi are in) which gives a tenderly coral tint, adding a cinnamon stick or $\frac{1}{2}$–1 teaspoon of ground cinnamon, or use red-skinned eating apples and don't peel them before cooking them. In fact, there's no need to core them either, just chop the apples roughly and put them in a pan with some butter, lemon juice, cinnamon or cloves and, if there's some around, a slug of Calvados. Sieve the apples when they're cooked to an utterly yielding pulp, or push them through a food mill. If you want to smarten up the cake-plus-purée deal, then provide a bowl of crème fraîche (with or without Calvados and a little golden icing sugar stirred in) with some toasted flaked almonds on top.

I am not someone who enjoys peeling and depithing oranges at great length, but sliced tarocchi, or ordinary oranges, with a syrup made by reducing equal volumes of juice and sugar to an almost-caramel, would partner an orange-zested version of this almond ring (the zest in place of vanilla) exquisitely.

Needless to say, I also love this cake with a bowl of new season's rhubarb on the side, cooked as if for the rhubarb tart (see p107). And just one further suggestion . . . ice it with chocolate ganache (see p22) or just top with it at the moment of serving so it's still warm and thickly runny, and serve with a bowl of vanilla ice cream with cooled, toasted, flaked almonds sprinkled over (and I suppose you could actually spoon the ice cream into the central cavity, before drizzling over the chocolate ganache and sprinkling over these almonds).

The point of these suggestions is not simply to be interfering and bossy, but to show how cake-baking, which one ordinarily associates with the sort of teas no one eats any more, can be brought to the service of contemporary eating. To call this book 'Baking and the Dinner Party Solution' would not to be too far-fetched. In fact, I will return to this theme later – and see p39.

Serves 10–12.

# ROSEMARY LOAF CAKE

In build, this is much the same as the Madeira cake, but it tastes very different. Don't be alarmed at the idea of using a herb usually associated with savoury cooking: there is something muskily aromatic about it against the sweet vanilla egginess of the cake. And the cake itself works extraordinarily well as part of an elegantly austere pudding. I love it sliced thickly and eaten with cold, stewed apples. Peel, core and chop 3 or 4 large cooking apples, squeeze over the juice of a lemon and an orange, sprinkle with sugar to taste (I'd start off with 2 tablespoons per apple and be prepared to double it) and add a knob of butter. Cook till the fruit is pale and pulpy and leave to cool. If you want to point up the flavours, you could always chuck in a small sprig of rosemary, which you should remove when you're decanting the cold almost-purée to a bowl; but go steadily, we're aiming for subtlety here. I use my stash of rosemary sugar for sprinkling over this cake (just because it's there, really – and see p336) but you can replace it with ordinary or golden caster sugar without a second thought

250g soft unsalted butter
200g golden caster sugar
3 large eggs
210g self-raising flour
90g plain flour
1 teaspoon vanilla extract

needles from a 10cm stalk of
    rosemary, chopped small, but not
    too fine (about 2 teaspoons)
4 tablespoons milk
1–2 tablespoons rosemary sugar or
    golden caster sugar
450g loaf tin, buttered and lined

Preheat the oven to 170°C/gas mark 3. Now cream the butter, adding the sugar when it's really soft, and creaming both together till pale and smooth and light. Beat in the eggs one at a time, folding in a spoonful of the flour after each addition, then add the vanilla. Fold in the rest of the flour – I find a rubber spatula the best tool for the job – and finally the rosemary. Thin the batter with the milk – you're after a soft, dropping consistency – and pour, with some helpful prodding and scraping with your spatula, into the waiting tin. Sprinkle the top with a little sugar before putting it in the oven, and cook for 1 hour, or until a cake-tester comes out clean. Leave to cool on a wire rack, in its tin, and when completely cold, unmould and wrap well in foil till you need to eat it. Like all these sorts of cakes, it keeps well.

Serves 8–10.

# GATEAU BRETON

I came across this recipe for Brittany butter cake in the wonderful Anne Willan's *Real Food*, and as she says, it's really a cross between shortbread and pound cake. Rather like the crostata on p105, it's hard to decide whether it's cake or pastry. I love a stubby slice of this any time, but it does make a perfect, chic ending to a dinner party, too, either with ice cream or fruit, or if you've already had cheese, just with the coffee that follows.

Anne Willan suggests a kneading motion to bring this very sticky dough into shape; I use the dough hook on my free-standing mixer.

Use the best butter that you can find, for this is the plain cake at its simple best, and the taste of each of these few ingredients is crucial.

for the cake:

**223g plain flour, preferably Italian 00**

**250g caster sugar**

**250g unsalted butter, cut into cubes**

**6 large egg yolks**

25cm Springform tin, buttered well

for the glaze:

**1 teaspoon of egg yolk, from your 6**

**1 tablespoon of water**

Preheat the oven to 190°C/gas mark 5. Mix the glaze, and put aside while you get on with your gateau.

Put the flour into a bowl (I never bother to sieve 00 flour because it's so finely milled, but if you're using regular plain flour then do so), stir in the sugar and add the butter and egg yolks.

With the dough-hook attachment of a mixer, slowly whirr till you've got a smooth, golden dough. (If you're making this by hand, make a mound of the flour on a worktop, then make a well in it and add the sugar, butter and eggs and knead to mix.) Scoop this dough into the tin, and smooth the top with a floured hand: expect it to be very sticky; indeed, it should be.

Brush the gateau with the glaze, and mark a lattice design on top with the prongs of a fork. For a reason I am not technically proficient enough to explain, sometimes the tine marks leave a firm, striated imprint (a bit like the scrapy lines that drive Gregory Peck mad in *Spellbound*); at others, as with the cake in the picture, they barely show once the cake's cooked. Bake for 15 minutes, then turn the oven down to 180°C/gas mark 4 and give it another 25 minutes or so until it's golden on top and firm to the touch.

Let it cool completely in the tin before unmoulding it. It'll keep well if you've got a reliably airtight tin. When you come to eat it, either cut it in traditional – though slightly narrower – cake-like wedges or, as I prefer if I'm eating it at the end of dinner, criss-cross, making irregularly sized diamonds.

Serves 8–10.

# DAMP LEMON AND ALMOND CAKE

I love lemon, I love almond, so this for me is cake nirvana. Perhaps it should be in the fruited cakes section, but the citrus element, though intense, just melds with the almonds to give a slab of damp, dense, sharp-toned meltiness. It is a plain cake, but gloriously plain.

If you can, leave this cake wrapped in a double casing of foil for a couple of days before eating it: both its sharpness and its melting dampness will increase in the waiting.

**225g soft unsalted butter**
**225g caster sugar**
**4 large eggs**
**50g plain flour**
**225g ground almonds**

**1/2 teaspoon almond essence**
**grated zest and juice of 2 lemons**
**21–23cm Springform cake tin, lined on**
  **the bottom**

Preheat the oven to 180°C/gas mark 4.

Cream together the butter and sugar until almost white. Beat in the eggs, one at a time, adding a quarter of the flour after each addition. When all the eggs and flour have been incorporated, gently stir in the ground almonds, then the almond essence, lemon zest and juice. Pour the mixture into the cake tin and bake for about 1 hour. I say 'about' only because ovens seem to vary so violently. I've cooked this in one oven when it was finished after 50 minutes; in another when it needed 1 hour and 10 minutes. Whichever, after about 30 minutes you may well find you have to cover it loosely with foil; you don't want the top of the cake to burn. The cake is ready when the top is firm and a skewer, inserted, comes out cleanish: you want dampness, but no battery goo. Take the cake out and let it stand for 5 or so minutes in the tin. Then turn it out on a wire rack and leave till cool.

Then, preferably, wrap well in tin foil and leave it for a couple of days. Push some icing sugar over the cake through a fine sieve or tea strainer when serving. I can't stop myself murmuring 'raspberries' to you, either.

If you do want to make a bigger production of it, then you could do a home-appropriate version of *assiette au citron*. Make the easy, no-churn lemon ice cream that's in *How to Eat* by stirring together the juice of 3 lemons and the zest of 2 with 175g icing sugar. Then, after 30 minutes' steeping time, whip 425ml double cream till soft-peak stage, then whisk in the sweetened lemon juice, zest and all. Turn into a shallow container and freeze till set, letting it ripen in the fridge for half an hour or so before serving.

You could use this cake as the base for the lemon-raspberry plate trifle (p153) in place of the lemon-syrup loaf cake that follows.

Serves 6–8.

# LEMON-SYRUP LOAF CAKE

This isn't, strictly speaking, a plain cake since it has a form of icing, but I can't help feeling that its loafiness counts for a lot. Of course, you could cook this (for slightly less time) in a square, 18cm tin, cutting the syrup-drenched sponge into smaller squares later.

for the cake:
**125g unsalted butter**
**175g caster sugar**
**2 large eggs**
**zest of 1 lemon**
**175g self-raising flour**
**pinch of salt**

**4 tablespoons milk**
**450g loaf tin, buttered and lined**

for the syrup:
**juice of 1 1/2 lemons (about 4 tablespoons)**
**100g icing sugar**

Preheat the oven to 180°C/gas mark 4, and butter and line your loaf tin well. In fact, unless you're using my much-beloved Bake-O-Glide, make sure the lining comes a centimetre or so up the sides of the tin for easier unmoulding later.

Cream together the butter and sugar, and add the eggs and lemon zest, beating them in well. Add the flour and salt, folding in gently but thoroughly, and then the milk. Spoon into the prepared loaf tin and put in the oven. While the cake is cooking, get on with the syrup: put the lemon juice and sugar into a small saucepan and heat gently so that the sugar dissolves.

Bake the cake for 45 minutes, or until golden, risen in the middle (though it will sink a little on cooling) and an inserted cake-tester comes out clean. As soon as the cake is out of the oven, puncture the top of the loaf all over with the cake-tester or suitable implement. Pour over the syrup, trying to let the middle absorb it as well as the sides, then leave it to soak up the rest. Don't try to take the cake out of the tin until it is completely cold, as it will be sodden with syrup and might crumble.

Serves 8–10.

## VARIATION
Double the ingredients for the syrup to make the base for the lemon-raspberry plate trifle (see p153). And there's no reason why you couldn't spike the syrup with some of that glorious Italian liqueur, *Limoncello*. Otherwise, you can use whatever citrus fruit you like. I love Seville oranges, and I'd use them orange per lemon. If you want to evoke the bitter fragrance of this wonderful fruit beyond its short season, then mix the juice of ordinary sweet oranges with lime using, here, 1 smallish or medium-sweet orange and 1 lime, and the zest of both in the cake. See p153 for the lime variant and, if the mood takes you, try a pink-grapefruit version, using the zest of half in the cake and the scant juice of 1 in the syrup.

## FILLED AND ICED CAKES

I used to think that filled cakes were really not for eating as a pudding, that there really was something too nursery-teatime about them, but I am beginning to change my mind. For one thing, I never do tea, or not really. But after a summer lunch, a Victoria sponge filled with cream, fruit and maybe a little good jam, does work. It's a reminder that, when the ingredients are good and the cake tenderly fresh, this is one of the dreamiest combinations in the world. And I say that as someone without a particularly sweet tooth. But then, these cakes don't have to be cloyingly sweet.

Iced cakes, on the other hand, just are sweet, and to apologise for that would be to undermine the whole purpose of making them. And any iced cake is, of course, a birthday cake waiting to be called into service.

## VICTORIA SPONGE

I repeat this recipe from *How to Eat* because I feel this chapter would be incomplete without it. And since I do so many cakes which are basically just a variant of this, it didn't seem right to refer only obscurely to the *ur*-recipe.

Traditionally, jam rather than fruit is used, but unless I've got some very good jam (and the one I do like using is the hands-free raspberry jam on p346), I think adding just a few berries makes a crucial difference. I generally use raspberries with a little raspberry jam, and sometimes strawberries with their matching preserve. My other favourite (and my first choice for sponge drops, see below, p43) is blackberries and blackberry jam, though ever since I found boysenberry jam regularly at the supermarket I often use that, again with either of those berries. At the bottom of the method, I've given yet more fruitful variations.

Although I've listed 200g flour and 25g cornflour because I feel this makes for a lighter, more tender sponge, of course it's perfectly all right to replace these with the customary 225g flour.

for the cake:

**225g unsalted butter, very soft**
**225g caster sugar**
**1 teaspoon vanilla extract**
**4 large eggs**
**200g self-raising flour**
**25g cornflour**
**1 teaspoon baking powder (if using processor method)**
**3–4 tablespoons milk**
**2 x 21cm sandwich tins (about 5cm deep), buttered**

for the filling:
**2–4 tablespoons raspberry or other jam, depending on berries**
**1 punnet raspberries or berries of choice**

**125ml (or simply a 142ml tub) double cream**

for the topping:
**1–2 tablespoons caster sugar**

Preheat the oven to 180°C/gas mark 4. If the tins are loose-bottomed, you don't need to line them, otherwise do.

I always make this basic sponge cake in the food processor, which involves putting in all the ingredients except the milk and processing till you've got a smooth batter. Then pulse, pouring the milk gradually through the funnel till your cake mixture's a soft, dropping consistency. Because I'm clumsy, I habitually make a too-runny mix, but it doesn't seem to matter. Likewise, if your ingredients are too cold you may end up with a batter that looks curdled: this doesn't seem to make any difference in the baking either (though it might get in the way of impressive rising).

If you want to make this the traditional way, cream the butter and sugar, add the vanilla and then the eggs, one at a time, adding a spoonful of flour between each. Fold in the rest of the flour and the cornflour, adding no baking powder, and when all's incorporated, add a little milk as you need.

Pour and scrape the batter into the tins and bake for about 25 minutes, until the cakes are beginning to come away at the edges, are springy to the touch on top and a cake-tester comes out clean. Leave the cakes in their tins on a wire rack for 10 minutes before turning out and leaving to cool completely.

When you're ready to eat the cake, put one layer on a plate, right-way up, spread with jam and scatter the fruit on top. Whip the cream till it's thickened but still soft and spread over the jammy fruit. Sit the other cake on top, and sprinkle over a tablespoon or so of caster sugar.

Serves 6–8.

## VARIATIONS

One variation, which I think I make more often now than the original, is my lemon-mascarpone sandwich cake. I had an early and encouraging success with this at my daughter's first school fête (and see pp235–42 for other bakes for this event). It's very easy to make and the mascarpone brings contemporary tastes to a traditional cake. All you do is replace the vanilla with 1 teaspoon of Boyajian lemon oil (you can get this at selected supermarkets and delis), adding it at the end, just before the milk. For the filling, soften 100g mascarpone in a bowl before spreading it over the top of one of the cakes, and spread 100g of good bought lemon curd over that. Then sit the other cake on top and sprinkle over some golden caster sugar (and you might just as well use it in the cake mix too). If you can't find the lemon oil, just use the zest of

1 lemon and its juice, leaving out the milk, or using the scantest amount if necessary.

There are another two fruity variants I play with. One is a rhubarb version, another a passionfruit one. In both cases, I use a teaspoonful of Boyajian orange oil in the cake. For the rhubarb filling, I stew about 500g rhubarb (or a 400g packet of the cut-down stalks) either using the poaching method (see p107) or with about 100g of sugar and the juice of half an orange in a saucepan on the hob. Since I don't mind if this goes pulpy, I generally go for the stove-top method. Sieve, reserving the juice. When the rhubarb is neither too soggy nor too warm, spread it over one of the cakes and add whipped cream. Reduce the rhubarb juice to an intense syrup, let it cool slightly, and drizzle over the cream. Then sit the second cake on top and sprinkle with caster sugar as usual.

With the passionfruit version, I make a passionfruit fool to lie softly in the middle of the sponge sandwich and a passionfruit glaze to dribble over the top. Mix the spooned-out pulp (seeds and all) of 4 passionfruit with the juice of a scant half lemon and a squeeze of orange, and set aside while you whisk about 100ml double cream with 30g sieved icing sugar till it's forming soft peaks. Just before serving, fold the passionfruit mixture into the cream and scrape it onto the top of one of the cakes. Lightly arrange the second cake over the filling and get on with the glaze. Push the pulp of another 4 passionfruit through a sieve and add to this aromatic liquid the juice of half an orange. Mix to a runny paste with sieved icing sugar – start with 100g and add more orange juice or more sugar as required. Pour over the waiting cake, letting it drip down the sides – I just drizzle it back and forth across the top, and let it run where it will.

For a coffee sandwich, keep the vanilla extract but add, too, 1 tablespoon of instant espresso powder to the flour in the cake mix. Fill with coffee buttercream (see p210, but use espresso powder instead of vanilla) and if you really want to go to town, make double the buttercream, spread it slightly thinner for the filling and use the rest to coat the sides and top of the sandwich, covering the top, or indeed the whole thing, with walnut halves.

Other ideas you might want to bear in mind include the lemon variant of the sponge filled with poached dried apricots or baked plums and crème fraîche – though we're moving into Boston cream pie territory here – or the vanilla version filled with prunes that have been soaked then cooked in Armagnac, placed on one of the cakes, then covered with a crème patissière (see p22) that has been flavoured with brandy rather than vanilla. And when gooseberries are in brief season, stew 100–150g with 1–2 tablespoons of sugar, 1 tablespoon of butter and a couple of tablespoons of elderflower cordial (or, if you've got access to some, a couple of heads of elderflower, which you remove before mushing), then fork to a rough purée. When cool, fold into some softly whipped cream (you're making a gooseberry fool comparable to the passionfruit fool above) and fill a cake which you've made using a tablespoonful of elderflower cordial in place of vanilla. Strictly speaking, you should reduce the sugar to compensate for the sweetness of the cordial, but I like to leave the filling tart, so don't worry too much about the sugariness of the cake.

Boston cream pie

Butterscotch layer cake

Flora's famous courgette cake

Victoria sponge

# FLORA'S FAMOUS COURGETTE CAKE

This recipe was given to me by Flora Woods, who worked in Harrods Waterstone's when *How to Eat* came out, and is now at Books for Cooks. I love being given people's own or family recipes (and if that sounds like an invitation, it's meant to). I like to credit any recipe given to me, not only out of a sense of propriety, but because it makes it all the more interesting. Recipes don't, like Aphrodite, spring fully formed from their author's forehead: to give their provenance is a pleasure and more besides – it's where food and social history merge.

   If courgette cake sounds dodgy to you, think about carrot cake for a moment; this is just an adaptation of that (though if you feel it's safer, don't tell people it's made of courgettes until after they've eaten it). One warning: don't do what I did for the picture (p17), which was to colour the lime-curd filling green. I don't know what got into me, but I got out my colour paste and my probe (a broken instant-read thermometer I use for mixing colours when I ice) and proved in one characteristically rash act that food is better left to its own devices. I decided we could just about live with the menacing green: things do go wrong in cooking and, generally, you can live with them. Still, I've learnt my lesson here, for all of us.

for the cake:
**60g raisins, optional**
**250g courgettes (2–3), weighed before**
   **grating**
**2 large eggs**
**125ml vegetable oil**
**150g caster sugar**
**225g self-raising flour**
**1/2 teaspoon bicarbonate of soda**
**1/2 teaspoon baking powder**
**2 x 21cm sandwich tins, greased and**
   **lined**

for the filling:
**see recipe on p344**

for the icing:
**200g cream cheese**
**100g icing sugar, sieved**
**juice of 1 lime, or more to taste**
**2–3 tablespoons chopped pistachio**
   **nuts**

Preheat the oven to 180°C/gas mark 4.

   If you're using raisins, put them in a bowl and cover with warm water to plump them up.

   Wipe the courgettes with a kitchen towel (but don't peel them), then grate. The coarse side of an ordinary box grater is the best thing to use: anything too fine or too quick can turn them to a wet mush. When you've grated them, turn them into a sieve over the sink to remove excess water.

Put the eggs, oil and sugar in a bowl and beat them until creamy. Sieve in the flour, bicarb and baking powder and continue to beat until well combined. Now stir in the grated courgette and add the drained raisins. Pour the mixture into the tins, and bake for 30 minutes until slightly browned and firm to the touch. Leave in their tins on a rack for 5–10 minutes, then turn out and let cool on the rack until your filling and icing are ready.

If you don't want to make the lime curd for the filling, then just buy a good lemon or lime curd and sharpen with some freshly squeezed lime juice. To make the cream-cheese icing for the top, beat the cream cheese in a bowl until smooth, add the sieved icing sugar, beating well to combine, and then stir in the lime juice to taste. Now get your cakes ready for assembling. Put one cake on the plate and spread with completely cooled lime curd. Put on the top cake and smear it thickly with the cream-cheese icing. If you feel the icings need firming up a little, put the cake in the fridge for a while. Just before serving, scatter chopped pistachios over the top.

Serves 8.

## VARIATION

As an alternative, cook the same mixture in those large (sometimes called 'Texas') muffin tins. When they're cooked and cooled, cut them in half and put the cream-cheese icing in the middle. Pour hot curd over the top, covering each little cake. Put the cakes in the fridge until cold and sieve icing sugar on top just before serving.

Makes 12.

# BUTTERSCOTCH LAYER CAKE

This is the sort of cake that people label 'very rich' but then go on to have three slices with languorous ease. Yes, it is rich, but the gorgeousness is never palate-cluttering or cloying. It makes a comforting pudding after a wintry kitchen supper of something like meatballs or roast chicken and leeks.

To make a coffee-butterscotch cake – as heavenly as it sounds – add a tablespoonful of instant espresso powder to the flour. And it occurs to me as I write this that, for the banoffee bunch, this cake, in its regular, uncoffeed state, would be even more seductive with a few sliced, perfectly ripe bananas in with the filling. But I have to say it does it for me as it is.

for the icing:
**300g caster sugar**
**125ml cold water**
**250ml double cream**
**400g cream cheese at room temperature**

for the cake layers:
**225g unsalted butter, very soft**

**125g light muscovado sugar**
**100g golden (or ordinary) caster sugar**
**4 large eggs**
**225g self-raising flour**
**2–4 tablespoons double cream**
**2 x 21cm sandwich tins, greased and lined with baking parchment**

Preheat the oven to 190°C/gas mark 5 and then get on with the icing. I do this first, since you need to make some caramel and then let it cool. Dissolve the sugar in the water over a low heat, remembering not to stir at all as it will crystallize if you do. When it seems dissolved, turn up the heat and boil until it turns a dark golden colour. This will probably take 10–15 minutes. And try not to be faint-hearted: caramel has to be burnt; it wouldn't be caramel otherwise.

When you've reached that exciting stage, take the pan off the heat and slowly whisk in the cream. It may go a little lumpy but don't panic, it will right itself smoothly enough. When all the cream's in, put the pan back on the heat for a further minute, whisking until smooth and combined. I find one of those little curly wire whisks (sometimes sold as a Magiwhisk) the best tool for the job. Cool, and then put it in the fridge until you need it.

The easiest way to make the cakes is to put all the ingredients except the double cream into the bowl of the food processor and blitz till smooth. (It's for this reason the butter must be very soft before you start.) Scrape down the sides of the bowl, then process again, adding a couple of tablespoons of cream down the funnel with the motor running. Stop and check the consistency of the batter: if it's on the runny (though not liquid) side then stop here; otherwise, add another 1–2 tablespoons of cream to achieve this dropping consistency. If you want to make them by hand, follow the method for the Victoria sponge (p15).

Divide the batter between the prepared tins and bake for about 25 minutes; the cakes are ready when they're beginning to shrink away from the sides of the tin and when a cake-tester or skewer comes out clean. Leave on a wire rack for 10 minutes, then turn out and leave on the rack until completely cooled.

Now for the assembly. Pour the thoroughly cooled caramel into either an American cup measure or into a measuring jug to come up to the 250ml mark. (You'll be using some if not all of the rest to dribble over the iced cake later.) Beat the cream cheese until softened and smooth, then add the cupful of caramel and beat gently to combine.

Put one cake on a plate. Using a rubber spatula or an ordinary blunt knife, roughly spread just under half of the icing over the top of the waiting cake. Place the other cake on top and then roughly ice the top of that cake with what remains in the bowl. Don't feel constrained to use up every last scrap of icing: it tastes almost at its best straight out of a finger-wiped bowl. Using a teaspoon, drizzle some of the reserved caramel over the cake: think Jackson Pollock.

Serves 8.

## BOSTON CREAM PIE

This is not a pie at all but a cake, and apparently the focus of much heated debate by the culinarily concerned of its native land, and although I make up the cake part as if for a Victoria sponge, there are enough differing factors overall to make me feel this deserves its own entry. The story is that, in 1850, the pastry chef at Boston's Parker House Hotel (an American gastronomic hotbed, obviously, since Parker House rolls evidently emanate from here too) had the brainwave of adding a bitter chocolate glaze to a 'Boston pie' – a custardy layer-cake affair – and for some reason the addition of chocolate brought the word 'cream' into play.

This is another of those cakes you could easily use as a pudding. I made it once with the addition of a few halved strawberries in the middle, folded into the crème patissière, and some more dotted about the edge on the plate, and although I prefer it without, I have to report that I was in the minority. And for Valentine's Day, consider going into full-on kitsch mode by making the strawberry version, using cakes baked in a couple of heart-shaped tins.

The idea of making crème patissière might seem daunting if you've not done it before, but it really isn't hard – and remember the flour does stabilize it, so it's nowhere near as tense-making as custard.

for the cake:
**1 batch Victoria sponge recipe (see p14)**
**2 x 21cm sandwich tins, buttered**

for the icing:
**150ml double cream**
**1 teaspoon vanilla extract**
**1 teaspoon unsalted butter**
**150g dark chocolate**

for the crème patissière:
**125ml milk**
**125ml double cream**
**1 vanilla pod or 1 teaspoon vanilla extract**
**3 large egg yolks**
**50g caster sugar**
**15g plain flour**

Preheat the oven to 180°C/gas mark 4 and make the cakes following the recipe on p15. Then pour into the prepared sandwich tins and bake for about 25 minutes, as before, while you make the crème patissière.

Warm the milk and cream in a saucepan along with the vanilla pod split lengthwise. Bring to the boil, then remove from the heat, cover and let stand to infuse for 10 minutes. If you're not using the pod, add the vanilla extract later, when you've combined all the ingredients. In a large bowl, whisk the yolks and sugar until creamy, and then beat in the flour. With the point of a small, sharp knife, scrape the seeds out of the vanilla pod into the milk, and add this warm milk to the egg mixture and whisk until smooth. Pour back into the saucepan and stir or whisk gently over a low heat until the custard thickens. Remove from the heat and let the custard cool by pouring it into a wide bowl and tearing off some greaseproof paper, wetting it, then covering the bowl with it. This stops it forming a skin. Don't put this in the fridge: something goes horribly wrong with the texture if you do, and you want utter, smooth voluptuousness here.

When the cakes are done, sit them in their tins on a wire rack for 5–10 minutes, then turn out and cool directly on the rack. When the cakes and the crème patissière are cool, you can make the chocolate ganache with which you're going to ice this pile-up of gorgeousness. Warm the cream, vanilla extract and butter with the chocolate, chopped into small pieces, and bring to the boil in a thick-bottomed saucepan (I find a non-stick milk pan the best for this), by which time the chocolate should have melted. Remove from the heat and whisk till smooth and thickened. Let cool a little before using, but you want it still runny enough to ice with. Tear off four strips of greaseproof paper or baking parchment, about 8cm wide, and arrange in a square on the plate on which you're serving the cake. Sit one of the cakes on top and spread with cooled crème patissière, then top with the second cake. Dollop spoonfuls of the chocolate icing on top, letting it spread and drip down the sides of the cake.

When the entire confection is cool and set, and you're about to bring it to the table, remove the strips of paper to reveal – aha! – a drip-free plate.

Serves 8.

# COCONUT CAKE

I may have an exaggerated sense of camp or kitsch, but a highlight of this recipe from my point of view is that it uses Malibu. Actually, Malibu is quite useful for baking, since it's hard to come by coconut extract or essence worthy of the name.

But this is also a beautiful cake, pale gold and white and delicately flavoured.

for the cake:

**225g unsalted butter, softened**

**225g caster sugar**

**1/2 teaspoon pure vanilla extract**

**4 large eggs**

**200g self-raising flour**

**25g cornflour**

**1/2 teaspoon baking powder**

**50g dessicated coconut soaked in 130ml boiling water**

**2 x 21cm sandwich tins, buttered and lined**

for the sandwich icing:

**25g dessicated coconut**

**75g soft unsalted butter**

**150g icing sugar, sieved**

**1 tablespoon Malibu**

for the icing:

**2–4 tablespoons Malibu**

**125g instant royal icing**

Preheat the oven to 180°C/gas mark 4 and make the cake by putting all the ingredients in the food processor and blitzing till you have a soft batter. If you want to make it by hand, then proceed as for the Victoria sponge (p15), adding the coconut at the end and leaving out the baking powder. Pour into the prepared tins and cook for about 25 minutes or until ready: not so springy on top as a plain sponge, but still coming away from the edges; a cake-tester, inserted, should come out cleanish.

To make the buttercream icing for the middle of the cake, toast the coconut in a dry frying pan, shaking every now and again, till it's fragrant and golden. Remove to a waiting plate and let cool. Cream together the butter and icing sugar and when you've got a light, smooth paste, beat in the Malibu and then the cold, toasted coconut.

Sandwich the two cakes together with this, and get on with the icing for the top. Using either a free-standing mixer with the flat paddle, or an ordinary bowl and an electric hand-held mixer, beat together 2 tablespoons of Malibu and the royal icing powder (in other words, just follow the packet instructions, replacing the water with Malibu). You may need to add another 1–2 tablespoons of Malibu, but see how it goes. When you've got a smooth, runny but not liquid paste that will ice the top well, pour over the very centre of the cake and let ooze out towards the edge and drip slightly down the sides. Leave to set before cutting and eating.

Serves 8.

# AUTUMNAL BIRTHDAY CAKE

There is no reason on earth why this, adapted from the *Magnolia Bakery Cookbook*, has to be a birthday cake, but since the first two times I made it were for my sister-in-law's and a friend's birthdays in late October and early November, that's how I think of it. In both cases, I put just one (gold) candle on top: better on any number of counts. I know that adorning plates with autumn leaves is not my usual aesthetic, but that's another benefit of using this as a birthday cake: you can allow yourself a little ironic leeway.

for the cake:

**175g butter, softened**
**100g golden caster sugar**
**3 large eggs**
**350ml maple syrup**
**500g self-raising flour**
**175ml hot water**
**2 x 21cm sandwich tins, buttered**
   **and lined**

for the icing:

**2 large egg whites**
**125ml maple syrup**
**125g golden caster sugar**
**¼ teaspoon cream of tartar**
**¼ teaspoon salt**
**1 teaspoon vanilla extract**
**¼ teaspoon maple extract, optional**
**125g pecans**

Preheat the oven to 180°C/gas mark 4.

Beat together the butter and sugar until very pale and fluffy. Add the eggs one at a time, beating in well after each addition, then gradually add the maple syrup to make a smooth mixture. Finally, spoon in the flour alternately with the hot water, beating gently until smooth again. Divide the batter between the two tins, and cook for 40 minutes. A cake-tester, inserted, should come out clean when they're cooked. Let the cakes cool in their tins on a rack for 10 minutes before unmoulding them, then leave them to get cold before you get on with the icing.

Put everything except the pecans and extracts into a glass or metal bowl that fits over a saucepan to form a double boiler. Fill the saucepan with enough water to come just below – but not touching – the bowl when it sits on top. Bring the water to the boil, set the bowl on top and, using an electric hand-held whisk, beat the mixture vigorously for 5–7 minutes. It should stand up in peaks like a meringue mixture. Take the bowl off the saucepan, away from the heat, and add the extracts, beating them in for another minute.

Cut out 4 strips of baking parchment and use to line the cake plate, as explained on p22. Using your dreamy, ivory-coloured meringue, ice the middle, sides and top of the cake. Give the icing a swirly effect rather than smooth, letting the top have small peaks. Chop most of the pecans finely, leaving some pieces larger. Sprinkle over the top of the cake, and throw at the sides.

This cake is best eaten the day it's cooked.
Serves 8.

# BABY BUNDTS

At a blackboard-walled vegetarian café in New York once, I ate a little yoghurty lemony ring-moulded cake and wanted to whip up something similar immediately on my return. I've given you this version not simply because it reminds me of the original inspirational one I ate but because it's the simplest to make. Melting the butter and then proceeding simply by stirring wet ingredients into dry (rather than rubbing butter into flour and so forth) won it for me.

It's getting easier and easier to buy what might once have been recherché baking materials, so I don't feel guilty about suggesting a recipe that requires a tray of mini-Bundt moulds; but if you anticipate problems finding one, see pviii.

for the cakes:
**125ml natural (preferably bio) yoghurt**
**75g butter, melted**
**2 large eggs**
**zest of 1 lemon**
**150g plain flour**
**1/2 teaspoon bicarbonate of soda**
**pinch of salt**

**125g caster sugar**
**1 mini-Bundt tray with 6 moulds,**
**approximately 9 x 4¹/2cm each,**
**buttered or oiled well**

for the icing:
**200g icing sugar**
**juice of 1 lemon**

Preheat the oven to 170°C/gas mark 3.

In a measuring jug, mix the yoghurt, melted butter, eggs and lemon zest. Put the flour, bicarb, salt and sugar into a large bowl. Mix the wet ingredients into the bowl, folding everything in well, then fill the mini-Bundt moulds with the mixture, and cook for 25–30 minutes. When they come out of the oven, leave them to cool a little before turning them out, otherwise they'll break – but don't let them get too cold either, as they will stick. Let them cool on a rack, flat-side down.

To make the icing, sieve the icing sugar into a bowl, and add enough lemon juice to make an icing thick enough to ice the tops and drizzle down like snow-capped peaks.

Makes 6.

## VARIATION
As with all citrus recipes, you can be fairly free with substitutions. Lime is an obvious and beckoning proposition. And you could use orange either as an alternative or along with the lemon (say the zest and juice of a half of each for the cakes and icing respectively) to make a St Clement's version.

# FRUITED CAKES

I haven't gone all quaint and ye olde. I use the word 'fruited' simply to make it clear that what follows is not just fruit cakes – in fact, there's only one here – but all sorts of cakes with fruit in them. For the rest of the more traditional fruit cakes, turn to the Christmas chapter.

## CHERRY-ALMOND LOAF CAKE

I have a nostalgic fondness for this yellow slab punctured by waxy halves of scarlet cherries – the cake we called station cake at home – but this is best with those dark and glossy natural-coloured glacé cherries.

200g natural-coloured glacé cherries
250g self-raising flour
225g butter, softened
175g caster sugar
3 large eggs, beaten

2–3 drops almond essence
100g ground almonds
6 tablespoons milk
23 x 13 x 7cm loaf tin, lined and
    buttered

Preheat the oven to 170°C/gas mark 3. Halve the cherries, wash them in a colander under cold water, then pat them dry, toss them in some flour and shake well to get rid of excess.

Cream the butter and sugar until light and fluffy. Gradually add the beaten eggs and almond essence, then gently fold in the flour and ground almonds. Fold in the cherries and then the milk and spoon the thick mixture into the loaf tin and bake for ³/₄–1 hour, or until a cake-tester comes out clean.

As with all of these sorts of cakes, leave in the tin on a wire rack until completely cooled.

Makes 8–10 slices.

# RHUBARB CORNMEAL CAKE

You can never have too many rhubarb recipes in my book and this cake clamours to be made. It is definitely better in the early days of the rhubarb season just because the breathtaking pink of that first, forced fruit (and, yes, I know it's a vegetable really) makes for a prettier cake. The cornmeal (or polenta, and a few years back no doubt I'd have called this rhubarb polenta cake) helps absorb some of the rhubarb's juices.

The point, too, about this cake is that it is surprisingly versatile. Eat it cold as an orthodox teatime cake, or slightly warm for a pudding after lunch or dinner. For a Sunday-lunch pudding, make a bowl of custard (p134) to go with, to be eaten cold or at room temperature; to turn this into a dinner-party *dolce*, whip up a bowl of divine muscat mascarpone cream, and serve some more honeyed-grape muscat.

| | |
|---|---|
| **500g rhubarb** | **2 large eggs** |
| **300g caster sugar** | **1 teaspoon vanilla extract** |
| **150g plain flour** | **125g unsalted butter, soft** |
| **1 teaspoon bicarbonate of soda** | **250g natural yoghurt, preferably bio** |
| **1/4 teaspoon salt** | **23cm Springform cake tin, buttered** |
| **1 teaspoon ground cinnamon** | **and lined** |
| **155g fine cornmeal (polenta)** | |

Preheat oven to 180°C/gas mark 4.

Wash and dry the rhubarb if necessary (which I rarely find it to be), and then trim, removing any stringy bits, and cut into 1/2cm slices. Put into a glass or china bowl and cover with 100g of the sugar, while you get on with the rest of the cake. Don't let the rhubarb stand for more than half an hour or the sugar will make too much liquid seep out.

Mix the flour, bicarb, salt, cinnamon and cornmeal together. With a fork, beat the eggs with the vanilla in a measuring jug or small bowl. In a large bowl, cream the butter and the rest of the sugar, then gradually add the egg and vanilla mixture, beating while you do so. Then add the flour-cornmeal mixture alternately with the yoghurt. They just need to be combined: don't overmix.

Finally, add the rhubarb together with its sugary, pink juices, folding in to mix, and then pour the speckled batter into the prepared tin. Put in the preheated oven and bake for about 1 hour or until springy to the touch. You may need to cover it with foil after about 40 minutes so that the top doesn't catch. Let cool in the tin on a wire rack for a while before unmoulding.

Serves 8–10.

# MUSCAT-MASCARPONE CREAM

I made this expressly to go with the rhubarb and cornmeal cake, but it is a useful way of giving a little chic spin to any basic cake. It would also be wonderful with Christmas pudding or mince pies.

**2 large eggs, separated**　　　　　　**250g mascarpone**
**100ml muscat**　　　　　　　　　　　**50g icing sugar, sieved**

Whisk the egg whites until stiff but not dry and put aside for a moment. Beat the yolks with the muscat and, when smoothly combined, beat in the mascarpone and icing sugar. Whisk well and then, when you've got a voluptuous, thickening cream in front of you, fold in the egg whites. You can keep this in the fridge, covered, for a day before using it.
Serves 8–10.

## VARIATION

If you wanted to serve this as a pudding in itself, then use 3 eggs, 125ml muscat, 75g sugar and boost the mascarpone to 375g; this should be enough for 4 alpine glasses' worth. Don't forget to put out biscuits for dipping, too.
Serves 4.

# BANANA BREAD

This is the first recipe anyone hesitant about baking should try: it's fabulously easy and fills the kitchen with that aromatic fug which is the natural atmospheric setting for the domestic goddess. There are countless recipes for banana bread: this one is adapted from one of my favourite books, the one I read lying on the sofa to recover from yet another long, modern, stressed-out day, Jim Fobel's *Old-Fashioned Baking Book: Recipes from an American Childhood*. If you're thinking about giving this cake to children, don't worry, the alcohol doesn't pervade: you just end up with stickily, aromatically swollen fruit.

100g sultanas

75ml bourbon or dark rum

175g plain flour

2 teaspoons baking powder

1/2 teaspoon bicarbonate of soda

1/2 teaspoon salt

125g unsalted butter, melted

150g sugar

2 large eggs

4 small, very ripe bananas (about 300g weighed without skin), mashed

60g chopped walnuts

1 teaspoon vanilla extract

23 x 13 x 7cm loaf tin, buttered and floured or with a paper insert

Put the sultanas and rum or bourbon in a smallish saucepan and bring to the boil. Remove from the heat, cover and leave for an hour if you can, or until the sultanas have absorbed most of the liquid, then drain.

Preheat the oven to 170°C/gas mark 3 and get started on the rest. Put the flour, baking powder, bicarb and salt in a medium-sized bowl and, using your hands or a wooden spoon, combine well. In a large bowl, mix the melted butter and sugar and beat until blended. Beat in the eggs one at a time, then the mashed bananas. Then, with your wooden spoon, stir in the walnuts, drained sultanas and vanilla extract. Add the flour mixture, a third at a time, stirring well after each bit. Scrape into the loaf tin and bake in the middle of the oven for 1–1¼ hours. When it's ready, an inserted toothpick or fine skewer should come out cleanish. Leave in the tin on a rack to cool, and eat thickly or thinly sliced, as you prefer.

Makes 8–10 slices.

## VARIATION

I haven't done a tremendous amount of fiddling with this, but I did once make it, for friends who are more chocolate-crazed than I am, by replacing 25g of the flour with good cocoa powder (not drinking chocolate) and adding 100g of dark chocolate, cut up into smallish chunks. And you could just as easily use the chocolate chips sold in the baking aisle of supermarkets.

# MARZIPAN FRUIT CAKE

This may be the only proper fruit cake in this section, but it is my favourite one in the entire world. This is in the first place because it contains marzipan (which I love) and in the second because it doesn't contain any peel (which I hate, or do in its normal, bitter, shop-bought state). Moreover, the dried pears which I've thrown in as well have a fudgy graininess which melds perfectly with the marzipan.

You do have to start this the night before you're baking, but all that means is the marzipan needs chopping and freezing and the fruits need soaking in advance.

150g sultanas

100g natural-coloured glacé cherries, halved

150g dried pears, chopped

100ml white rum

250g marzipan

50g ground almonds

zest of 1 lemon

175g plain flour

100g caster sugar

100g butter

2 large eggs

1 teaspoon orange-flower water

20cm Springform cake tin, buttered and lined bottom and sides, so that the parchment comes a good 10cm above the rim.

So, the night before, mix the sultanas, glacé cherries and pears in a large bowl and cover with the rum. Dice the marzipan and put in the freezer. Leave both to soak and freeze overnight.

When you come to make the cake the next day, preheat the oven to 140°C/gas mark 1. Beat together the almonds, lemon zest, flour, sugar, butter and eggs. Add the drained fruit, orange-flower water and the frozen marzipan. Put the cake mix into the tin, levelling the surface and making a slight indent in the middle to get an even surface when cooked. Bake for 2–2½ hours or until a cake-tester comes out clean. Don't overcook, as it will continue to cook in its own warmth as it cools. But nor should you worry too much about it: there's enough fruit and marzipanny squidge to make sure this golden cake doesn't easily turn dry.

Allow the cake to cool in the tin before rewrapping in parchment and foil to store for about a week. Feed with a little more rum before you wrap for a richer taste if you want (just puncture the top of the cake a few times and slowly dribble a few spoons of rum over). You should also be aware that the wrap-and-keep advice is a counsel of perfection. Last time I made this, two days was the longest I was able to leave it before greedily unwrapping and slicing into it.

Serves 8–10.

# APPLE AND WALNUT CAKE

I got the idea for making this cake from a conflation of two things: the first was reading Anna del Conte's recipe, in her *Secrets from an Italian Kitchen*, for an apple cake made with olive oil; the second was the reproachful remainder of a bottle of walnut oil bought to make some walnut dressing and then left on the shelf with seemingly no further purpose in life. So I thought I'd try making a cake with what I had left, and it worked – well, more than worked.

Since I can't be the only person to have been in this predicament, I pass on the recipe, but with one proviso. The cake is lovely, but in an unfancy, *cucina rustica* kind of a way; walnut oil is expensive: I don't advise you to buy it specially for this cake.

I've marked the walnuts as optional just because the first time I made it I didn't use any – I wanted to eat it as pared down as possible to see how I felt about the walnut oil. If you leave out the walnuts and replace the walnut oil with olive oil (not extra virgin), and the rum with water, you have Anna's delicious *torta di mele*.

100g sultanas

75ml rum

150ml walnut oil

200g caster sugar

2 large eggs

350g plain flour, preferably Italian 00

1 teaspoon cinnamon

1 1/2 teaspoons bicarbonate of soda

1/2 teaspoon cream of tartar

1/2 teaspoon salt

450g Coxes (or other eating apples), peeled, cored and cut into small cubes

zest of 1 lemon

100g walnuts (optional)

20cm Springform cake tin, buttered and floured

Put the sultanas and rum (or water) into a saucepan and bring to the boil, then remove from the heat, letting the sultanas plump up aromatically. Now, preheat the oven to 180°C/gas mark 4.

Beat the oil and sugar together in a bowl, and add the eggs one at a time, beating until it looks like a light mayonnaise. I'd use an electric whisk of some sort here. Add the dry ingredients to the egg mixture, folding with a metal spoon. Then stir in the apples, lemon zest, drained sultanas and walnuts if using. Smooth what will be a fairly stiff batter into the tin and bake for 1 hour, poking into it with a cake-tester or toothpick to check it's done.

Let the cake stand for 10 minutes in the tin on a wire rack, then turn out and leave to cool. Anna advises leaving the cake a day before eating it (I'd wrap it well, once completely cold, in foil first), but I have to admit I love eating it with the warm breath of the oven still faintly upon it.

Serves 6.

# WINTER PLUM CAKE

This is 'winter' cake in the sense of 'out-of-season', or 'store-cupboard'. To be frank, I'd had a tin of red plums in the cupboard for so long I felt I had either to find a way of using it or chuck it out. I'm glad to say that this was the outcome.

The golden unrefined icing sugar here isn't an earnest option but a voluptuous necessity: without it, you won't get an icing of such fudgy beauty, in taste as much as looks.

for the cake:

**567g tin red plums**
**125g self-raising flour**
**1/2 teaspoon baking powder**
**75g ground almonds**
**125g butter, softened**
**125g light brown sugar**
**2 large eggs**

**1 scant teaspoon almond essence**
**20cm Springform cake tin, buttered
  and lined**

for the icing:

**160g unrefined icing sugar**
**1–2 tablespoons hot water**

Preheat the oven to 170°C/gas mark 3.

Drain the plums, then chop and leave in a sieve to drain once more. Mix the flour, baking powder and ground almonds. Cream the butter and sugar, then beat in the eggs, adding a tablespoon of the flour mixture after each one. Beat in the almond essence, then fold in the rest of the flour mixture and the drained, chopped plums. Turn into the prepared tin and bake for about 1¹/₄ hours, though check at 1 hour. When it's ready, that's to say beginning to come away at the sides and so forth, take it out of the oven, leave it in its tin on a wire rack for about 10 minutes, then turn out onto the rack.

When cool, ice with brown-sugar icing, which you make simply by mixing the sieved icing sugar with water till you have a caramel-coloured shiny paste. Pour over the top of the cake to cover thinly, not necessarily uniformly, and leave to drip, here and there, down the sides.

If you want to turn this into a Sunday lunch pudding, serve warm and uniced and make a jugful of custard to pour over (see p134).

Serves 6–8.

# CUPCAKES

Now this really is 'Baking and the Dinner Party Solution'.

At about the time I started getting into top cupcake and fairy-cake mode, ostensibly for children, I noticed that the people who really seemed to get excited by them were the children's parents. I think it's not till you hit 30 that nostalgia is even a remotely comforting option. Since then, I've decided that cupcakes and fairy cakes – by which I mean the plain-bottomed prettily iced cupcakes – are the perfect things to make fordinner. And by this I mean not some shiny tabled, silver-laid grand dinner party but those evenings when you have friends for supper in the kitchen (the only kind of dinner party I know). Give people cheese instead of pudding (or nothing at all: it ain't obligatory) and wheel out these dinky numbers with the coffee and tea. You can make the cakes a day in advance, keep them in an airtight container and ice them later – although since the icing helps keep them fresh you may as well, if you're using a water rather than a butter icing, ice them a day before too and then you'll have nothing to do on the day itself.

I don't normally like teensy-weensy individually portioned things, but cupcakes seem to hit some pre-rational spot and I succumb. But then everyone always does. What follows is not all there is: see also cappuccino and espresso cupcakes on pp198-9, chocolate-cherry cupcakes on p196, dolly-mixture fairy cakes on p215, butterfly cakes on p217, Halloween cupcakes on p216 and Christmas cupcakes on p267.

# FAIRY CAKES

These are so quick both to make and to bake that it really is possible to whip some up for after dinner when you get home from work. On the whole, I leave my fairy cakes plain and unadorned beneath; it's above, when I get to play with colours and flowers and sugar decorations, that a little imagination and artistry comes into play. Not that I can claim much credit, certainly not for the latter: I buy rice-paper roses and sugar daisies and pansies rather than make them. But I like the playing part – choosing the colours, the detail. You can see by the cover of this book that my weak spot is the white-on-white look. (In fact, I've told Hettie, my saviour and right-hand, who's worked with me since this book's inception, that when she gets married she has to let me make her a stacked pyramid of these. Luckily, she's up for it.)

My other favourite – and then I really will leave you to your own devices – is the fifties pistachio-green version (Colourway's food-colouring paste in 'Gooseberry') with the pale-pink rice-paper rose atop.

125g unsalted butter, softened

125g caster sugar

2 large eggs

125g self-raising flour

1/2 teaspoon vanilla extract

2–3 tablespoons milk

500g packet instant royal icing

12-bun muffin tin lined with 12 muffin
  papers

Preheat the oven to 200°C/gas mark 6.

It couldn't be simpler to make fairy cakes: just put all the ingredients except for the milk in the processor and then blitz till smooth. Pulse while adding milk down the funnel, to make for a soft, dropping consistency. (If you do want to make by hand, just follow the method for the Victoria sponge, p15.) I know it looks as if you'll never make this scant mixture fit 12 bun cases, but you will, so just spoon and scrape the stuff in, trying to fill each case equally. Put in the oven and bake for 15–20 minutes or until the fairy cakes are cooked and golden on top. As soon as bearable, take the fairy cakes in their cases out of the tin and let cool on a wire rack. I like my cherry-topped fairies to have a little pointy top, but for all floral and other artistic effects, darling, you need to start with a level base, so once they're cool, cut off any mounded peaks so that you've got a flat surface for icing.

I've specified a whole packet of instant royal icing because the more colours you go in for the more you use, though really 250g should be enough. I make up a big, uncoloured batch, and then remove a few spoonfuls at a time to a cereal bowl and add, with my probe (a broken thermometer, but a skewer is just as good), small dots of colours from the paste tubs, stirring with a teaspoon and then adding more colouring, very slowly, very cautiously until I've got the colour I want (pastel works best here, what-ever your everyday aesthetic). I then get another spoon to spread the icing on each cake (it's important to use a different spoon for icing than for mixing or you'll end up with crumbs in the bowl of icing) and then I leave it a moment to dry only slightly on the surface before sticking on my rose, daisy or whole bouquet of either.

Makes 12.

## VARIATION

To make lavender cupcakes, follow the basic recipe above, but reduce the vanilla to a few drops, about 1/4 teaspoon if you feel like measuring. Half an hour before making up the mixture, put 125ml of milk into a little saucepan with 6–8 sprigs of lavender. Bring to the boil, but just before it starts boiling remove from the heat, cover with foil and leave for 20 minutes. Then strain into a cup and leave for another 10 minutes. Make up the batter as above, using a few tablespoonfuls of lavender milk at the end to loosen the mixture in place of the usual plain milk. Cook as normal and when cool, make up a fairly thick icing by mixing 250g icing sugar, sieved, with more of the lavender milk. Tint it ivory with the colour paste 'Caramel' and place a sprig of lavender on top.

# BURNT-BUTTER BROWN-SUGAR CUPCAKES

It's difficult to explain the wonderful resonant taste that burnt butter has, but think of it as a kind of mouth-filling nuttiness.

for the cupcakes:
**150g unsalted butter**
**125g self-raising flour**
**60g golden caster sugar**
**65g light muscovado sugar**
**2 large eggs**
**1 teaspoon vanilla extract**
**1 teaspoon baking powder**
**2–3 tablespoons milk**

**12-bun muffin tray lined with 12 muffin papers**

for the icing:
**150g unsalted butter**
**250–300g golden icing sugar, sieved**
**1 teaspoons vanilla extract**
**2–3 tablespoons milk**

Preheat the oven to 200°C/gas mark 6 and then get on with burning your butter. Put it in a small saucepan on medium heat, stirring all the time until it turns a dark golden colour. Take the pan off the heat and strain the butter into a bowl or cup, as it will have made a sediment. In other words, this is like clarified butter, but with a smoky note. Let the butter solidify again but don't put it in the fridge; you need it to remain soft for the cupcakes. This shouldn't take long, except in hot weather, in which case leave the preheating of the oven till after the butter's been burnt.

When the butter is solid but still soft, put all the cake ingredients except the milk in a food processor and blitz to a smooth batter. As normal, add the milk down the funnel, pulsing sparingly to form a soft, dropping mixture. And, again, if you want to make them by hand, follow the Victoria sponge method (p15).

Divide between the paper cases, and cook for 15–20 minutes. While the cupcakes are baking, get on with the icing. It's the same procedure for the butter – burn, sieve, solidify – then beat it with half the sugar or enough to make it stiff. Add tablespoons of milk and the remaining sugar alternately to reach a good consistency, and finally the vanilla.

While the icing's still soft, smear messily over the cooled and waiting cupcakes.
Makes 12.

# CARROT CUPCAKES WITH CREAM-CHEESE ICING

I wanted to have some sort of carrot cake here and felt that this cupcake version was the right one. I know carrot muffins have long been in existence but I wanted something luscious and sweet and treaty: a cake not a breakfast scourge. For a reason I cannot quite fathom, these seem to go down particularly well if I bring them out after fish.

for the cupcakes:

**100g light muscovado sugar**

**175ml sunflower oil**

**2 large eggs**

**225g plain flour**

**3/4 teaspoon bicarbonate of soda**

**1 teaspoon cinnamon**

**pinch of salt**

**zest of 1/2 lemon**

**zest of 1/2 orange or 1 satsuma**

**150g (approximately 2 medium) carrots, grated**

**100g walnuts, chopped**

**12-bun muffin tin lined with 12 muffin papers**

for the icing:

**125g cream cheese**

**250g icing sugar, sieved**

**1–2 teaspoons lime juice**

**12 walnut halves**

Preheat the oven to 200°C/gas mark 6.

Beat the sugar and oil together, then add the eggs one at a time. Add the flour, bicarb, cinnamon, salt and zests, then fold in the grated carrot and walnuts. Spoon the mixture evenly into the muffin cases, and bake for 20 minutes. Cool on a rack while you get on with the icing.

Beat the cream cheese in a bowl till smooth and softened somewhat, and then beat in the sieved icing sugar. Squeeze in the lime juice to taste.

When the cupcakes are cool, just smear the icing on top. I find using an ordinary blunt knife works well, and I like to see the knife marks in the icing: these are not meant to be smooth, elegant concoctions. Stick a walnut half in the centre of each iced cupcake.

Makes 12.

# SPONGE DROPS

Sponge drops are not so much cupcakes as saucer-cakes. You make up a very light batter and drop spoonfuls on a baking sheet. Bake them, cool them and sandwich them together with cream, jam and a few berries and you have mouthfuls of heaven. These taste so much better than their school-dinner name evokes: the lightness of the sponge together with the cool fatness of the cream and the juicy sweetness of the berries, and all in such small quantities (and I never thought I'd be grateful for that), make these completely seductive.

for the sponge drops:
**2 large eggs**
**75g caster sugar**
**50g self-raising flour**
**25g cornflour**
**1/2 teaspoon baking powder**
**2 baking sheets, greased or lined**

for the filling:
**150ml double cream, whipped**
**5–6 tablespoons blackberry (or other) jam**
**1 punnet blackberries (or other) berries)**

Preheat the oven to 200°C/gas mark 6.

Lightly whisk the eggs, then add the sugar and whisk again until the mixture becomes pale, creamy and voluminous; I'd use an electric whisk of some sort here. Sieve in the flours and baking powder, and fold them in with a metal spoon. Spoon scant dessertspoon-sized drops onto the baking sheets, leaving room between them so that they can spread. Cook for 5 minutes, then remove them with a metal spatula (you may find a stepped rather than a flat one easier) to cool on a rack.

When they are cool, sandwich them with whipped cream, jam and softly crushed berries.

Makes 8–9.

BISCUITS

# BISCUITS
## Including Scones, Muffins, Pancakes and Small Things

Biscuits are one of the first things we learn to cook when we're little – or at least roll and stamp out, get the feel of, which is just as important – and there seems to be a sense in which we're recapturing some remembered, no doubt idealized, past whenever we make them in adulthood; they still feel like playing. When I want to cook but have no fixed idea of what, and have no actual meal to prepare to justify fiddling about in the kitchen, I often convince myself that there are biscuits that need to be made.

The biscuits here are mostly of the free-form kind: you either spoon them onto a tray or roll them into balls between your hands to shape them. There are exceptions, as you'll see, but the blueprint recipe for cutter-shaped biscuits is in the children's chapter. Their need, I felt, was greater than ours. (And, of course, for chocolate biscuits, see the chocolate chapter.)

I know biscuit-baking may seem a quaintly archaic practice now, but it can make a modern life very much easier. A lot of the recipes that follow can be made to augment a tub of good, bought ice cream to ridiculously great effect. And much easier than making the ice cream and buying the biscuits.

# ROSEBUD MADELEINES

It was the curled-in smallness of these tender sponge biscuits, as well as the fact that they're flavoured with rosewater, that made me name them as I have. I like them with coffee when pudding's been just a plate of cheese, but eat them with whatever and however you want. The dried rosebuds in the picture are obviously not an obligatory ingredient: for me, it's just a *Citizen Kane* kinda thing.

| | |
|---|---|
| **50g unsalted butter, plus 1 tablespoon for greasing** | **45g plain flour, preferably Italian 00** |
| **1 large egg** | **1 tablespoon rosewater** |
| **40g caster sugar** | **icing sugar for dusting** |
| **pinch of salt** | **24-bun mini-madeleine tin** |

Melt all the butter over a low heat, then leave to cool. Beat the egg, caster sugar and salt in a bowl for about 5 minutes, preferably with an electric mixer of some sort, until it's as thick as mayonnaise. Then sprinkle in the flour; I hold a sieve above the egg and sugar mixture, put the flour in and shake it through. Fold in the flour with a wooden spoon and then set aside a scant tablespoon of the cold, melted butter for greasing the tins and fold in the rest along with the rosewater. Mix well, but not too vigorously. Leave to rest in the fridge for 1 hour, then take out and leave at room temperature for half an hour. Preheat the oven to 220°C/gas mark 7.

Generously brush the insides of the madeleine tins with the tablespoon of butter (melting more if you feel you need it) before filling them with half the cake mixture (this amount does 2 batches). About 1 teaspoonful in each should do: don't worry about covering the moulded indentations; in the heat of the oven the mixture will spread before it rises. Bake for 5 minutes, though check after 3. Turn out and let cool on a rack, then arrange on a plate and dust with icing sugar. Repeat with the remaining half of the mixture.

Makes 48.

# COCONUT MACAROONS

These are a very English kind of macaroon, the sort you always used to see displayed in bakers' shops alongside the madelines (those sponge castles dipped in luminous strawberry jam and dredged in throat-catching dessiccated coconut, and so very different from those that inflamed the memory of Marcel Proust). The difference with coconut macaroons is that you need neither to be ironic nor self-consciously retro-cool to enjoy them.

One bit of retail bossiness here: buy shredded, not dessiccated, coconut, otherwise the sugary, fragrant dampness – which is, after all, the whole point – will be lost.

**2 large egg whites**
**¼ teaspoon cream of tartar**
**100g caster sugar**
**30g ground almonds**
**pinch of salt**

**1 teaspoon vanilla extract**
**(or coconut essence, should such be**
**available)**
**250g shredded coconut**
**1 baking sheet, lined**

Preheat the oven to 170°C/gas mark 3.

Beat the egg whites until frothy – no more – then add the cream of tartar and carry on beating, Missus, until soft peaks are formed. Add the sugar a teaspoon at a time and whisk until the peaks can hold their shape and are shiny. Fold in the almonds, salt, vanilla and coconut. The mixture will be sticky but should, all the same, hold its shape when clumped together.

Form into clementine-sized domes, 6–7cm in diameter. Don't make them too flat; they look best if you keep them nicely rounded, but this is really just a matter of personal taste, so follow your own.

Cook for 20 minutes or until they're just beginning to turn golden in parts.

Makes 8 large macaroons.

# PISTACHIO MACAROONS

These are the world's most elegant macaroons. The colour alone, that waxy pale jade, perfectly matches the aromatic delicacy of their taste; and their nutty chewiness melts into the fragrant, soft paste with which they're paired. Of all the recipes in this book, this is the one of which I think I'm most proud: biscuit bliss.

These are perfect at the end of dinner alongside some icing-sugar-dusted raspberries; or alone with coffee, gracefully piled on a plate or cake stand.

for the macaroons:
**75g pistachios**
**125g icing sugar**
**2 large egg whites**
**15g caster sugar**

for the buttercream:
**55g pistachios**
**250g icing sugar**
**125g unsalted butter, softened**
**2 baking sheets, lined**

Preheat the oven to 180°C/gas mark 4.

Grind the pistachios in a food processor along with the icing sugar (this stops them turning into an oily mess), until as fine as dust. Whisk the egg whites until fairly stiff, but not dry, sprinkle the caster sugar over and whisk until very stiff. Fold the whites into the pistachio-sugar dust, and combine gently. Pipe small rounds onto your lined baking sheet, using a plain 1cm nozzle. Let them sit for about 10 minutes to form a skin. Then put in the oven and cook for 10–12 minutes: they should be set, but not dried out.

Remove from the oven and let cool, still on their sheets, while you get on with the filling. This is simple work: grind the nuts and icing sugar in the processor as before; then cream the butter and continue creaming as you add the nut dust. Make sure you have a well-combined soft buttercream. Then simply sandwich the macaroons together.

Makes 20, i.e., 40 sandwiched together.

# SPANISH MACAROONS

I'm not sure I would spend a whole lot of time trying to persuade a Spaniard of the origin of these biscuits, but I call them Spanish because they seem so instantly redolent of that aroma of oranges, almonds and the faintest warm breath of cinnamon that I associate with Spain. Indeed, I have a vague taste-memory of eating macaroons like this when I was in Seville once, and I suppose it was those that I was trying to recreate. I know in my heart of hearts they would be better with blanched almonds which you then grind yourself when you want them, but since I made these with ready-ground nuts and was pleased with them as they were, it seemed honest to leave it that way. If you decide to buy whole almonds to grind, get 500g: they're oilier than the ready-ground, so you need more to get the right consistency.

**425g ready-ground or 500g whole blanched almonds, ground**
**250g icing sugar, sieved**
**zest of 2 oranges**

**½ teaspoon almond essence**
**½ teaspoon cinnamon**
**1 large egg, plus 3 large egg whites**
**2 baking trays, lined**

Preheat the oven to 180°C/gas mark 4.

Mix together the almonds, icing sugar, orange zest, almond essence and cinnamon. In a separate bowl, or wide-mouthed measuring jug, beat the whole egg together with the egg whites. Make a well in the centre of your dry ingredients, then pour and mix in the egg. The mixture will be very sticky, I know, but that's fine.

Form walnut-sized balls by rolling the torn-off pieces of dough between your palms, and place on the prepared baking sheets. It will help if you wet your hands under a cold tap and go back to the sink for degunging and rewetting every now and again as you go along. Apart from making the whole operation less messy, it will make for smoother biscuits.

Cook for 20 minutes, by which time the biscuits should look lightly browned on the surface but won't have lost their sweet and tender chewiness underneath. Cool on a rack.

Makes about 30.

# SWEET AND SALTY PEANUT BISCUITS

If greed alone were the spur and measure, these would be my favourite biscuits. There's something about the contrast between salt and sweet and their crumbly lightness that makes them instantly addictive. They make a seductive partnership with vanilla ice cream: you can do this the elegant grown-up way with bowls of ice cream and a plate of the biscuits; or, my weakness, made up into sandwiches, the nubbly discs clasped round the soft, cold cream.

Two requests: don't use jumbo peanuts and don't use all butter. You need that Trex: quite apart from its trailer-trash charm, it's what makes them light.

**75g light muscovado sugar, plus more for dipping later**
**100g unsalted butter**
**50g vegetable shortening such as Trex**
**1 large egg**
**1 teaspoon vanilla extract**
**175g self-raising flour**
**125g salted peanuts**
**2 baking sheets, lined**

Preheat the oven to 190°C/gas mark 5.

In a large bowl, mix together the sugar, butter, shortening, egg and vanilla. Just beat it together, no ceremony, to combine well. You may find this easiest to do with an electric mixer. Stir in the flour and then the peanuts – and that's your dough done. Now, drop the dough in rounded teaspoons about 5cm apart onto the prepared baking sheets. Oil the bottom of a glass, or brush with melted butter, and dip it into some more light muscovado sugar and then press gently on the biscuits to flatten them.

Bake for 8–10 minutes, by which time they should be cooked through (though remember that biscuits always continue to cook for a while out of the oven), then remove to a wire rack to cool.

Makes about 30.

# RICCIARELLI

I love these beautiful, bone-white Sienese macaroons. They're like soft, chewy, almond lozenges. I know it sounds odd to say use 300g ready-ground almonds or 500g blanched almonds which you then grind yourself, but as with the Spanish macaroons, the drier ready-ground ones absorb more liquid, so you need less. However, these are definitely better when you grind the nuts yourself – and I'm not asking you to do it by hand, but in a food processor for God's sake – so if you can, get them whole and blanched.

You have to start these the day before you want to eat them – not because any drastic action is required, but just because you need to let them dry out before baking them.

| | |
|---|---|
| **2 large egg whites** | **1 teaspoon almond essence** |
| **pinch of salt** | **300g ready-ground almonds or 500g** |
| **225g caster sugar** | **whole blanched almonds, ground** |
| **zest of 1 lemon** | **icing sugar for dusting** |
| **1/2 teaspoon vanilla extract** | 2 baking sheets, lined |

Whisk the egg whites and salt until they're stiff and dry, then gradually whisk in the sugar until you reach a marshmallowy consistency. Now add the lemon zest, vanilla extract and almond essence along with the ground almonds; mix to quite a hard paste.

Shape into small diamonds, dusting icing sugar over your hands to help you form the lozenges if the mixture's a little sticky. Lay on the baking sheets and leave to dry out overnight or for equivalent hours.

Heat the oven to 140°C/gas mark 1 and cook the ricciarelli for about 30 minutes, by which time they should be pale and slightly cracked. When cool, dust with icing sugar and serve.

These keep well in an airtight container.

Makes about 34.

# SNICKERDOODLES

You can't help wanting to cook a biscuit with a name like this. Luckily, these live up to it. They're verging on cakes, but only in the sense that they're neither crisp nor flat; what they taste like, in fact, are oven-baked doughnuts – small, cinnamony, with a drier crumb than the dunkin' sort, and very, very more-ish.

I love these as part of a pudding, with a bowl of warm, spicy, poached or stewed plums (and see the recipe for these in *How to Eat*) and a bowl of cold, sour crème fraîche.

| | |
|---|---|
| **250g plain flour** | **100g plus 2 tablespoons caster sugar** |
| **½ teaspoon ground nutmeg** | **1 large egg** |
| **¾ teaspoon baking powder** | **1 teaspoon vanilla extract** |
| **½ teaspoon salt** | **1 tablespoon cinnamon** |
| **125g butter, at room temperature** | **2 baking sheets, lined or greased** |

Preheat oven to 180°C/gas mark 4.

Combine the flour, nutmeg, baking powder and salt, and set aside for a moment. In a large bowl, cream the butter with the 100g of sugar until light in texture and pale in colour, then beat in the egg and vanilla. Now stir in the dry ingredients until you have a smooth, coherent mixture. Spoon out the remaining sugar and the cinnamon onto a plate. Then, with your fingers, squidge out pieces of dough and roll between the palms of your hands into walnut-sized balls. Roll each ball in the cinnamon-sugar mixture and arrange on your prepared baking sheets.

Bake for about 15 minutes, by which time they should be turning golden-brown. Take out of the oven and leave to rest on the baking sheets for 1 minute before transferring to a wire rack to cool.

Makes about 32.

### VARIATION

Replace 25g of the flour with cocoa to make what we call at home – naturally enough – chocodoodles.

# MAPLE-PECAN BISCUITS

I made these in a flush of excited inspiration with the maple extract I'd bought at the super-deli Dean & Deluca in New York, but since exotic flavourings – and for us, I think this counts as exotic – are more and more available over here, I thought I would include the recipe.

**250g unsalted butter, softened**  
**125g light muscovado sugar**  
**1 teaspoon maple extract**

**350g self-raising flour**  
**35 (approximately 75g) pecan halves**  
**2 baking sheets, lined or greased**

Preheat the oven to 170°C/gas mark 3.

Cream the butter and sugar. When you've got a soft, supple mass, add the maple extract and work in the sifted flour. Roll into walnut-sized balls, and press with the base of a glass that you've lightly oiled (and if you've got some in the house, you could use walnut oil) or brushed with melted butter. Press gently onto the lined baking sheets – leaving a 5cm space round each as they'll spread – and stud each with a pecan half.

Cook for 15 minutes. They start off golden so it's hard to tell if they're cooked just by sight, but lift one up to check it's no longer doughy on the bottom. Remove from the oven, leave for a minute or two on the trays and then transfer to a wire rack to cool.

Makes about 35.

## VARIATION

You can always substitute walnut halves for the pecans, but if you leave them completely nut-free, these are wonderful as cheese biscuits. Yes, they're sweet, but in the same way as digestives are strangely good with both creamy and hard cheese, so these can pair with a pungent blue cheese quite wonderfully.

Lemon gems, Granny Boyd's biscuits (p204) and sweet and salty peanut biscuits (p55)

# LEMON GEMS

My children call these fried-egg biscuits and if you look at the photo you'll see why. But that doesn't convey the desirably acid intensity of their lemoniness. Of course, they are also sweet, but if you use good lemon curd (or make your own), they won't be too sweet: you will get that necesssary contrast between sharp, shining jellied curd, and buttery, sugared dough surround.

**125g Trex, or other vegetable
    shortening**
**125g unsalted butter, softened**
**75g caster sugar**
**1 large egg yolk**
**1 tablespoon lemon juice**
**zest of 1 lemon**

**¹/4 teaspoon salt**
**275g plain flour**
**50g ground almonds**
**25g cornflour**
**6–7 tablespoons lemon curd**
**2 baking sheets, lined**

Preheat the oven to 180°C/gas mark 4.

In a large bowl, beat the Trex, butter and sugar together, then add the egg yolk, lemon juice, zest and salt. Gently fold in the flour in two goes, then the ground almonds and cornflour. Take care not to be too heavy-handed, as rigorous blending will make it very sticky. It veers towards that anyway, so when all's combined, put the dough in the fridge to chill for at least an hour.

Form into balls the size of cherry tomatoes and place the dough 2¹/2 cm apart on your prepared baking sheets. Make an indentation with your thumb in each biscuit, and then cook for 20–25 minutes. They should appear golden and firm.

As soon as they come out of the oven, fill each biscuit with a scant ¹/2 teaspoon of lemon curd. When they're all filled, transfer them to wire racks to cool.

Makes about 40.

# COFFEE AND WALNUT SPLODGE BISCUITS

These are American-style cookies; in other words, just dropped onto the baking sheet free-form. Try to use the instant espresso powder if you can: real coffee or instant coffee granules made up with water change the texture of the dough, and you end up with a slightly too cakey texture (or else a too-weak taste). There is an element of cakiness here, but an entirely desirable one.

250g plain flour

1 teaspoon baking powder

1/2 teaspoon salt

200g unsalted butter, softened

75g caster sugar

60g light muscovado sugar

2 tablespoons instant espresso powder

2 large eggs, beaten

200g walnut pieces

2 baking sheets, lined

Preheat the oven to 180°C/gas mark 4.

Mix flour, baking powder and salt together. In another bowl, cream the butter with the sugars. Add the coffee powder, then, when combined, add the eggs. Stir in the flour mixture and walnut pieces, but don't overmix.

Line a couple of baking sheets with parchment or Bake-O-Glide and, using a tablespoon or a relatively small ice-cream scoop, drop splodges onto them, leaving about 5cm between them as they will spread as they cook.

Bake for 12 minutes, by which time they should be goldenish on top and just firm to the touch.

Cool on a wire rack.

Makes 30 biscuits.

# ITALIAN BISCUITS

This is a rather sweeping description of those shortbready swirls punctuated by glacé cherries that you see everywhere in Italy, mostly sold by weight. Actually, when you do buy them, they can tend towards challenging dryness and sweetness: these are buttery, light and modestly sugared. Don't be put off by the fact that an icing bag is required: piping out this kind of batter is extraordinarily satisfying.

225g unsalted butter, softened
150g caster sugar
1 large egg
zest of ¹/₂ a lemon
350g plain flour

¹/₂ teaspoon baking powder
pinch of salt
approximately 20 natural-coloured
 glacé cherries
2–3 baking sheets, lined

Preheat the oven to 180°C/gas mark 4.

Cream the butter and sugar together until very light, almost moussy (I use my electric mixer for this). When you're happy with the consistency, after about 5 minutes maybe, beat in the egg and lemon zest. Now add the flour, salt and baking powder: this is still easiest in a mixer (flat paddle attached) but not hard by hand. Just go gradually but confidently: you want everything smoothly combined but not beaten within an inch of its life. Remember that it won't be a firm batter; if it were, you wouldn't be able to squeeze it through the nozzle.

Fix a star nozzle into a piping bag and then fill the bag with the mixture and start piping rosettes or, as the Italians often do, rosettes with a tail; this gives you licence to pipe them any way, really, and not to worry about neatness of form. Just leave a good 5cm between each biscuit. Stick a cherry half into the centre of each rosette or at one end of your squiggles, and bake for about 12 minutes. The edges will be just turning gold, but the biscuits overall will still be pale. Transfer to wire racks to cool.

Makes about 40.

## VARIATION
Use a teaspoon of vanilla extract or a few drops of almond essence in place of the lemon zest and – a very un-Italian move, this – use Minstrels instead of cherry halves.

# SAVOURY BISCUITS

## IRISH BLUE BISCUITS

You don't need to use Irish cheese – though Cashel Blue does go particularly well here – nor do you need to worry about getting blue cornmeal if it eludes you (though I did find mine at the supermarket): these biscuits are delicious enough made with 175g of flour and with any robust but crumbly, creamy cheese, blue or otherwise.

**175g Cashel Blue cheese, crumbled**
**100g unsalted butter, softened**
**1 large egg yolk**
**125g plain flour**
**50g blue cornmeal**

**pinch of salt (depending on saltiness
   of cheese)**
**1 beaten egg for glazing (optional)**
**2 baking sheets, lined**

Preheat the oven to 200°C/gas mark 6.

Mix the cheese, butter and egg yolk together and then work in the flour, cornmeal and the salt if you're using, just enough to form a soft dough. Form the dough into a fat disc, wrap it in clingflim and put in the fridge for 30 minutes or so to rest before it's rolled out. Dust a surface with flour (and sprinkle a little blue cornmeal onto it if you'd like) and roll out your cheese pastry to a thickness of about half a centimetre. Cut into whatever shapes you like; I quite like them squarish, but half-moons might be good, given the ingredients. If you're going to eat these by themselves, brush with the egg glaze before putting in the oven; if they're to be served with cheese (and they do go so well with the Cashel Blue of which they're partly made) leave them matt.

Cook for 10–15 minutes, by which time they'll be crisp at the edges and puffy in the middle. Remove to a wire rack to cool.

Makes about 30.

## HOT DISCS

Think of these as a cross between tortilla chips and mini-poppadoms, the sort of biscuits that are perfect for dipping into salsa, hoummos or guacamole. Leave the seasonings out (bar the salt) and you have nineteenth-century Mereworth biscuits, to be eaten with soft cheese or the creamiest, unsalted butter.

Irish blue biscuits

250g plain flour
1 heaped teaspoon salt
1/2 teaspoon cayenne pepper
1/4 teaspoon ground cumin
1/4 teaspoon ground coriander

25g cold unsalted butter, diced
zest of 1 lime, very finely grated
100ml hot milk
5 1/2cm plain round cutter
2–3 baking sheets, buttered

Preheat the oven to 220°C/gas mark 7. Put the flour, salt, cayenne, cumin and coriander in a bowl and rub in the butter as you would for pastry. Add the zest and then gradually pour in the milk until you've got a firm but soft dough. Roll out one half of this as thin as you can: it should look almost transparent and feel like fine cloth. Stamp out as many rounds as you can, transfer them to your baking trays and cook for 5 minutes, though check after 3 1/2. When cooked they will be tinged with brown and wonderfully puffed up. Remove to a wire rack to cool and repeat with the rest of the dough.

Makes about 75.

# OATCAKES

There's something very satisfying about making such good, plain fare as oatcakes – as if you're doing something sober and basic and not entertaining yourself with fripperies.

If you can bring yourself to use lard, please do. Did you know that it is a less saturated fat than butter?

250g medium oatmeal or porridge oats
pinch of salt
1/4 teaspoon bicarbonate of soda
1 tablespoon lard or butter, melted

75–200ml hot water from a recently boiled kettle
1 baking sheet
8cm round biscuit cutter (optional)

Preheat the oven to 200°C/gas mark 6.

Put the oatmeal in a bowl and add the salt and bicarb. Make a well, pour in the fat and, stirring with a wooden spoon, enough hot water to mix to a stiff dough. If you're using oatmeal, you should need about 75ml; with porridge oats you may need as much as 200ml. Knead it for a while to make it come smoothly together, then roll out as thinly as you can. Cut into triangles or rounds, and bake on the ungreased sheet for 15–20 minutes, or until the edges are turning golden-brown and the oatcakes themselves are firm (they'll crisp up on cooling). Remove to a wire rack to cool.

Makes 15–20.

# SCONES AND MUFFINS

## LILY'S SCONES

These are the best scones I've ever eaten, which is quite how it should be since they emanate from one of those old-fashioned cooks who starts a batch the minute the door-bell rings at teatime. Yes, I know they look as if they've got cellulite (see p71) – it's the cream of tartar, which is also why, despite their apparent solidity, they have that dreamy lightness.

**500g plain flour**

**1 teaspoon salt**

**2 teaspoons bicarbonate of soda**

**4¹/₂ teaspoons cream of tartar**

**50g cold unsalted butter, diced**

**25g Trex, in teaspooned lumps (or use another 75g butter)**

**300ml milk**

**1 large egg, beaten, for egg-wash**

**6¹/₂cm crinkle-edged round cutter**

**1 baking tray, lightly greased**

Preheat the oven to 220°C/gas mark 7.

Sift the flour, salt, bicarb and cream of tartar into a large bowl. Rub in the fats till it goes like damp sand. Add the milk all at once, mix briefly – briefly being the oper-ative word – and then turn out onto a floured surface and knead lightly to form a dough.

Roll out to about 3cm thickness. Dip the cutter into some flour, then stamp out at least 10 scones. You get 12 in all from this, but may need to reroll for the last 2. Place on the baking tray very close together – the idea is that they bulge and stick together on cooking – then brush the tops with the egg wash. Put in the oven and cook for 10 min-utes or until risen and golden.

Always eat freshly baked, preferably still warm from the oven, with clotted cream and jam or, my favourite, Thunder and Lightning, which is (as in the picture) clotted cream and black treacle.

Makes 12.

## VARIATION

Add 75g of raisins or sultanas for fruit scones, or, something I'm keen on, use the same amount of dried sour cherries, with or without the finely grated zest of ¹/₂ an orange. To make cheese scones, add 75g of mature Cheddar, grated.

# STRAWBERRY SHORTCAKES

I've long been fascinated by this American pudding, which isn't really a scone so much as a tender, buttery sponge with scone-like properties, split and crammed with strawberries. There's so much dispute, as there always is with traditional recipes, over the right method to make them, serve them, eat them: should they be individual-sized or one huge fat disc? should butter be spread on the tender cut sides while still warm, before the fruit and cream are dolloped on?

I don't intend to enter into the debate – don't feel qualified to anyway – but since I'm a great fan of the methodical-to-the-point-of-obsessive American food magazine *Cook's Illustrated*, I got guidance from its executive editor Pam Anderson's book, *The Perfect Recipe*. I sometimes veer away from it, by using crème fraîche instead of whipped cream, or by using single cream in place of half-and-half (which we don't anyway have here) and I do like to sprinkle a little balsamic vinegar on the crushed strawberries, but in all respects that matter, this is her recipe.

This is what you want to bring out to people by the plateful on a summer's day after lunch in the garden.

for the shortcakes:
**325g plain flour**
**1/2 teaspoon salt**
**1 tablespoon baking powder**
**5 tablespoons caster sugar**
**125g unsalted butter, frozen**
**1 large egg, beaten**
**125ml single cream**
**1 large egg white, lightly beaten**

**1 baking tray, greased or lined**
**6 1/2 cm round cutter**

for the filling:
**approximately 300g strawberries**
**1 tablespoon caster sugar**
**few drops balsamic vinegar (optional)**
**250ml double cream or crème fraîche**

Preheat the oven to 220°C/gas mark 7.

Mix the flour, salt, baking powder and 3 tablespoons of the sugar in a bowl. Grate the butter into these dry ingredients and use your fingertips to finish crumbling the butter into the flour. Whisk the egg into the cream, and pour into the flour mixture a little at a time, using a fork to mix. You may not need all of the eggy cream to make the dough come together, so go cautiously.

Turn the dough out onto a lightly floured surface, and roll gently to a thickness of about 2cm. Dip the cutter in flour and cut out as many rounds as you can. Work the scraps back into a dough, re-roll and finish cutting out – you should get 8 in all. Place the shortcakes about 2 1/2 cm apart on the baking sheet, brush the tops with the egg white, and sprinkle them with the remaining 2 tablespoons of caster sugar. If it helps with the rest of your cooking, or life in general, you can cover and refrigerate them now for up to 2 hours.

Bake for 10–15 minutes, until golden-brown, and let them cool for a short while on a wire rack. Meanwhile, crush half the strawberries with the spoonful of sugar and the few drops of balsamic vinegar if using, and halve or quarter the remaining strawberries, depending on their size. Whip the double cream, if you're using.

The shortcakes should be eaten while still warm, so split each one across the middle and cover with a spoonful of the crushed strawberry mixture, a few halved or quartered strawberries, then dollop some whipped cream or crème fraîche on top, and set the top back on.

Makes 8.

## VARIATION

I love these American-style with passionfruit in place of the strawberries, though if you're going along with this, don't use crème fraîche; you need velvety-smooth, whipped double cream, unpasteurized if possible.

Lily's scones (p67)

# BLUEBERRY MUFFINS

I had always thought that muffins were a lot of fuss about a disappointing nothing. But that, I found, was because they were the industrially produced ones. When you make them yourself – and they are the easiest things in the world to make, which is why you'll find a couple of recipes for them in the children's chapter – they're nothing like as tall and puffy as the ones you see in shops and cafés, and you'll also notice that they've got some interest about them. That dry mass of aerated wodge in cellophane isn't the sort of muffin you want for your breakfast; these are.

If it helps, you can weigh out all the dry ingredients, leave them in a clingfilmed bowl overnight, and measure out the liquids into a jug which you can keep covered in the fridge. That way, you could do all the measuring and close work before you go to bed, then, on getting up, melt the butter, preheat the oven, mix the wet with the dry ingredients, fold in the fruit and dollop them in their cases. In a quarter of an hour, give or take, you will have a kitchen full of baking smells and a plateful of muffins on the table.

75g unsalted butter
200g plain flour
1/2 teaspoon bicarbonate of soda
2 teaspoons baking powder
75g caster sugar
pinch of salt

200ml buttermilk (or 100g yoghurt
    and 100ml semi-skimmed milk)
1 large egg
200g blueberries
12-bun muffin tray lined with 12
    paper cases

Melt the butter, and set it aside to cool for a little. Preheat the oven to 200°C/gas mark 6.

Combine all the dry ingredients in a bowl, and in a measuring jug beat together the buttermilk (or yoghurt and milk), egg and melted butter. Using a wooden spoon and a light hand, pour the wet ingredients into the dry and mix gently to combine. Don't worry about lumps: the important thing with muffins is that the mixture isn't over-worked. Fold in the blueberries, again keeping mixing to a minimum. You could also add orange zest at this point if you wanted. Spoon into the muffin cases – I use an ice-cream scoop and a small rubber spatula for this – and bake for 20 minutes, by which time the muffins should be risen and golden and firm on top. Eat warm or cold as you like: I like warm, broken with fingers and smeared, mouthful by mouthful, with good unsalted butter and blueberry jam.

Makes 12.

# BAKLAVA MUFFINS

I know this sounds like a mad idea, but I came across it in a ringbound book I bought off the Net in the middle of the night called *The Joy of Muffins*. Joy indeed, for what do you know, these taste so good: gooey, crunchy, soft and filling; sticky buns for the slapdash cook.

for the filling:
**100g chopped walnuts**
**75g demerara sugar**
**1¹/₂ teaspoons cinnamon**
**45g butter, melted**

for the muffins:
**210g plain flour**
**2 teaspoons baking powder**
**¹/₂ teaspoon bicarbonate of soda**

**75g caster sugar**
**1 large egg**
**45g unsalted butter, melted**
**250ml buttermilk (or 175g yoghurt and 75g semi-skimmed milk)**
12-bun muffin tray lined with 12 paper cases

for the topping:
**125ml runny honey**

Preheat the oven to 200°C/gas mark 6.

Mix all the filling ingredients together in a small bowl, and then get on with the muffins. In a large bowl, mix together the flour, baking powder, bicarb and sugar. In a wide-mouthed measuring jug, whisk the egg, melted butter and buttermilk (or yoghurt-milk mix). Make a well in the dry ingredients, pour in the liquid and mix lightly and gently, remembering to keep it bumpy rather than going all-out for smooth: anything more than the gentlest handling makes for heavy muffins. Fill the muffin papers one-third full, add a scant tablespoon of filling, then cover with more muffin mixture until two-thirds full. Sprinkle any remaining filling on top of the muffins.

Bake for 15 minutes, by which time they should be golden-brown and ready. Put the muffins, still in their papers, onto a rack and drizzle with honey. You may find it easier to warm the honey a little before pouring.

Makes 12.

# LEMON-RASPBERRY MUFFINS

I think of these more as teatime muffins than breakfast ones, but please don't feel constrained by my prejudices (and it's not often you'll hear me say that).

**60g butter**
**200g plain flour**
**2 teaspoons baking powder**
**1/2 teaspoon bicarbonate of soda**
**150g caster sugar**
**1/4 teaspoon salt**
**juice and finely chopped zest of 1**
**   lemon**

**approximately 120ml milk**
**1 large egg**
**150g raspberries**
**12-bun muffin tray lined with 12**
**   paper cases**

Preheat the oven to 200°C/gas mark 6.

Melt the butter and set it aside to cool. Stir together, in a largish bowl, the flour, baking powder, bicarb, sugar, salt and zest. In a measuring jug, pour in the lemon juice, then enough milk to come up to the 200ml mark (and it will curdle, but that's just fine), then beat in the egg and melted butter. Pour into the dry ingredients and stir briefly; the batter should scarcely be combined. Fold in the raspberries, spoon this lumpy mixture into the muffin cases and bake for about 25 minutes. When cooked, the tops should spring back to your touch. Leave in the pan for 5 minutes to cool slightly, then sit them on a rack to cool for a further 10–15 minutes.

Makes 12.

# PANCAKES

There is something about a pancake, a breakfast pancake, that has domestic goddess stamped all over it.

# JOHNNYCAKES

Johnnycakes are pancakes – or griddlecakes, really – made with the addition of cornmeal, one of the great indigenous American ingredients. I love these eaten sweet with maple syrup or as part of a butch brunch with sausages, bacon and eggs.

150g fine cornmeal or polenta
100g plain flour
4 teaspoons baking powder
2 teaspoons caster sugar

1/2 teaspoon salt
2 large eggs
300ml milk
30g butter, melted

Stir together the dry ingredients in one bowl; in another (big) bowl, whisk the eggs and milk. Then gradually beat in the dry ingredients and when combined stir in the melted butter. Heat an oiled griddle or pan and drop, one by one, tablespoonfuls of the batter on the hot surface to make little pancakes about 6cm in diameter.

After 1–2 minutes, the top of each yellow pool of batter will begin to bubble. Turn over briskly and give a minute or so on the other side before removing to a hot cupboard or moderate-to low oven to keep warm.

This amount makes 30–35 pancakes. This sounds like a lot, but be warned: my two-year-old eats five for breakfast, easily.

## WELSHCAKES

These are somewhere between pancakes and biscuits, and much as I think I don't like dried fruit enormously, I can wolf down plates of these. This recipe comes from the grandmother of a Welsh girl, Heulwen, who helped with my children after my second baby was born. And these were an immensely comforting part of that time.

125g cold unsalted butter, diced
250g self-raising flour
75g caster sugar, plus more for
    sprinkling
1/4 teaspoon ground allspice

100g sultanas
1 large egg, beaten
7 1/2cm crinkled round cutter
smooth griddle or cast-iron frying pan

Rub the butter into the flour as you would if making pastry, then stir in the sugar, spice and dried fruit. Add the egg to make a soft but not sticky dough. Form a disc, cover with clingfilm and leave in the fridge for a minimum of 20 minutes.

Roll out on a floured surface to a thickness of about 3/4cm, and cut out your little cakes; you will need to re-roll and so forth but that shouldn't be problematic. Preheat your unoiled griddle or cast-iron frying pan and cook the cakes for about 3 minutes each side, until golden-brown. Remove to a cold plate and sprinkle with caster sugar.

Makes about 20.

# AMERICAN BREAKFAST PANCAKES

These are those thick, spongy American pancakes that are often eaten with warm maple syrup and crisp fried bacon. I love them with the syrup alone, but if you do want bacon, I think streaky is best: you want a crisp salty ribbon of it here. You can easily cook these pancakes by dolloping the batter onto a hot griddle (smooth, not ridged, side) or cast-iron pan, but I use a blini pan, one of my pet implements.

225g plain flour

1 tablespoon baking powder

pinch of salt

1 teaspoon sugar

2 large eggs, beaten

30g butter, melted and cooled

300ml milk

butter for frying

The easiest way to make these is to put all the ingredients into a blender and blitz. But if you do mix up the batter by hand in a bowl, make a well in the flour, baking powder, salt and sugar, beat in the eggs, melted butter and milk, and transfer to a jug: it's much easier to pour the batter into the pan than to spoon it. I like to leave the batter for 20 minutes before using it; and you may then want to add more milk to the mixture if you're frying in the blini pan, so that it runs right to the edges.

When you cook the pancakes, all you need to remember is that when the upper side of the pancake is blistering and bubbling it's time to cook the second side, and this needs only about 1 minute, if that.

I get 11 blini-pan-sized pancakes out of this, maybe 16 silver-dollar-sized ones on the griddle.

### VARIATION
Sprinkle blueberries onto the uncooked side of the pancake just after you've poured the batter into the pan.

PIES

# PIES

A pie is just what we all know should be emanating from the kitchen of a domestic goddess. Not simply because it is the traditional fare of the kitchen *Koenigin*, but because few things approach it when it comes to inducing that warm, bolstering sense of honourable satisfaction.

The truth is, however, that the less familiar pastry-making becomes, the harder we believe it to be; but all you have to do is make some and then you'll realize that it doesn't require expertise or dexterity beyond your capabilities. And I write as someone who is a clumsy and impatient cook. There is nothing like becoming competent at some hitherto terrifying activity to make one confident. And in cooking, as in everything else, confidence (and competence) breeds confidence. To learn how to make pastry, all I did was make some, and make it again. Then, some time later, again. Suddenly, I found I could do it, more or less without thinking about it. I'd never before considered myself a baker, and so it was particularly satisfying to become this person who turned out pastry and made pies and beautiful tarts.

But like the first kiss, it's the first pie that counts: as soon as I'd whipped it out of the oven and sprinkled sugar over it, I felt suffused with heady satisfaction. This was a real pie: the sort that I thought only women with sensible hands habitually wiped briskly on aprons could make. It changed my culinary self-image instantly. And that's why I am so evangelical now.

Perhaps the greatest joy of pastry-making is that it's mud-pie time; you get floury, sticky, wholly involved. I don't mean by this that you shouldn't use any equipment: I use my free-standing mixer, or processor.

(I need to, indeed, because I nearly always freeze the butter and flour together before combining as this helps you get a more feathery, flaky pastry.) But you still need to use your hands for that last crucial combining, the rolling, and draping into the tin, and the piecing-together of your pie.

Just do it.

Blackberry and apple pie (p118)

# BASIC SHORTCRUST

The basic rule for pastry is that you use half the weight of fat to flour (and I nearly always prefer to make up that fat with equal amounts of butter and shortening and use 00 flour) and use a liquid – egg yolk, orange juice, whatever – to bind it. Throughout this chapter, though, and wherever necessary, I give precise ingredients for the particular recipe, so I give just my method here. What's more, it's foolproof; I was once that fool.

Put the flour in a shallow bowl, add the cold, diced fats and stir gently to coat. Put in the deep freeze – no need to cover – for 10 minutes. As you do so, put your liquid in a bowl or cup with a pinch of salt and transfer to the fridge. Either in a processor or – for choice – in a freestanding mixer with flat paddle, blend the fats and flour until you have a mixture that resembles sandy porridge. Then, gradually process or paddle in the liquid until the pastry is almost coming together. Use your hands now to form it into a disc or couple of discs, wrap in clingfilm and let it rest in the fridge for 20 minutes before rolling out.

# PROCESSOR PUFF-PASTRY

Having discovered the world's most wonderful and hysterically easy Danish pastry (see p327), it occurred to me that the principle would surely apply to the un-yeasted version, that is to say, puff pastry. I tried it: it worked.

**250g strong white flour**
**pinch of salt**
**250g cold unsalted butter, cut into**
 **¹/₂ cm slices**

**squeeze of lemon juice**
**5–6 tablespoons iced water**

Pulse the flour and salt together in the processor, then add the cold butter and pulse 3–4 times; the pieces of butter should still be visible. Turn out into a large bowl and add a squeeze of lemon juice and enough iced water to bind the pastry. Wrap in clingfilm and rest in the fridge for half an hour.

Dust a surface with flour, roll the pastry out into a long rectangle, and fold in three like a business letter. Now turn the folded pastry so that if it was a book the spine would be on your left. Repeat twice more, turning every time.

Wrap again and rest in the fridge for another half-hour before you use it.

This makes enough for 2 x 20–25cm pie bases.

# SAVOURY PIES

## SUPPER ONION PIE

This is just what I want to eat for supper when it's dark early and I'm tired. It is a pie, yes, but not one with pastry that needs rolling out: you just make a cheese-scone dough and then press it over some onions, already softened and aromatic, in the pan.

for the filling/topping:
**4 medium red onions (about 750g)**
**1 tablespoon olive oil**
**1 heaped tablespoon butter (about 25g)**
**3–4 sprigs of thyme, de-stalked, or ½ teaspoon dried thyme**
**130g strong Cheddar cheese or Gruyère, grated**

for the scone dough:
**250g plain flour**
**1 scant teaspoon baking powder**
**1 teaspoon salt**
**100ml milk**
**40g butter, melted**
**1 scant teaspoon English mustard**
**1 large egg, beaten**
**20–25cm cast-iron skillet or 24cm pie dish, buttered**

Preheat the oven to 200°C/gas mark 6. Peel the onions, halve them, then cut each half into 4 segments each. Heat the oil and butter in the pan, then add the onions and cook over a medium heat, stirring regularly, for about 30 minutes; they should be soft and tinged with colour. Season with salt and pepper, and add the thyme. Turn into a pie dish, and scatter 50g of the cheese over the waiting onions. Leave while you get on with the dough topping.

Put the flour, baking powder and salt together in a bowl with the remaining cheese. Pour the milk into a measuring jug, add the melted butter, mustard and egg, mix well and then pour onto the flour mixture in the bowl. Mix to a dough using a fork, a wooden spoon or your hands; it should be quite sticky. Then tip it out onto a work surface and press into a circle about the size of the pie dish. Transfer it to the dish, pressing it to seal the edges.

Put it in the oven for 15 minutes, then turn down to 180°C/gas mark 4 and give it another 10 minutes, by which time the dough should be golden and crisp on top. Let it stand for a couple of minutes, then cover with a large plate and turn upside-down so the plate's beneath and the pie dish on top. Place on a flat surface and remove the dish.

I love this with brown sauce, either home-made (see the domestic goddess's larder, p362) or bought HP.

Makes 6 generous slices.

# PIZZA RUSTICA

Pizza rustica is not a pizza in the way that we've come to understand it, though anyone who's spent time in Italy might well have come across it. The word pizza simply means pie, and this term denotes a deep, pastry-encased creation, stuffed with relatively unfancy ingredients. For a non-Italian, however, these ingredients are at the upper end of the economic scale, and hardly rustica at all, and it's for this reason I thought up my pizza rustica *all'inglese* (see below), though any Italian deli should be able to supply you with the wherewithal easily enough, and increasingly the supermarkets stock what you'll need too. The wonderful Anna del Conte gave me this recipe – from her magnum opus, *The Gastronomy of Italy*. Using a Springform tin rather than pie dish makes the building-up of the pie easy, and the finished, unmoulded creation looks a miracle of proud, golden accomplishment.

for the pastry:

**250g plain flour, preferably Italian 00**

**125g cold unsalted butter, cut into 1cm cubes**

**2 egg yolks**

**2 tablespoons iced water**

**1 heaped teaspoon salt**

**1 tablespoon caster sugar**

**22cm Springform tin, buttered**

for the filling:

**50g luganega or mild pure pork sausage, skinned**

**1 tablespoon olive oil**

**250g ricotta**

**50g smoked provolone, diced**

**125g Italian mozzarella, crumbled**

**50g freshly grated parmesan**

**1/2 clove garlic, chopped**

**2 tablespoons chopped flat-leaf parsley**

**2 pinches chilli powder or crushed dried red chillies**

**100g prosciutto, cut into small pieces**

**100g mortadella, cut into small pieces**

**2 eggs, lightly beaten**

**black pepper**

**1 heaped tablespoon dried breadcrumbs**

for the glaze:

**1 egg yolk**

**2 tablespoons milk**

**pinch of salt**

Put the flour and butter in a dish, and put this dish in the deep freeze for 10 minutes. Stir together the yolks, water and salt in a cup, and put this cup in the fridge. Then, when time's up, tip the flour and butter into the bowl of the processor, add the sugar and pulse to combine: you want a soft crumbly mass, somewhere between sand and porridge oats. Bind with the egg yolks, water and salt, and when it looks like it's on the verge of coming together (you have to stop slightly short of this actually happening), tip the pastry out and wodge it together with your hands. Don't worry, though, if the pastry is

a little too damp: I find one of the miracles of this pre-freezing pastry technique is that it makes it more foolproof on every level. It always seems to roll out well.

Divide into two discs, one somewhat larger than the other, and put both into the fridge to rest wrapped in clingfilm.

Preheat the oven to 200°C/gas mark 6, put in a baking sheet, and get on with the filling. Fry the sausage in the oil for about 5 minutes, breaking it up with a wooden spoon as it cooks, then transfer it to a bowl and let it cool. At which time, add all the other ingredients except the breadcrumbs and mix thoroughly.

Roll out the larger disc of pastry to cover the bottom and sides of the tin, leaving a few centimetres' overhang. Sprinkle the bottom of the now pastry-lined tin with breadcrumbs, and then fill with the hammy, eggy mixture waiting in its bowl. Roll out the smaller disc to make the lid, place it on top of the filled pie, turn over the edges of the overhang to form a border and press down with the tines of a fork.

Just before baking, glaze the pie by brushing over the milky, salty egg, stab it here and there with the prongs of a fork to make steam holes, and place it on the baking sheet in the preheated oven. Give it 10 minutes at this temperature, then turn it down to 180°C/gas mark 4 and bake for a further 45 minutes.

Leave the pie to cool for at least 10 minutes before serving it, but it's at its best after about 25. It's still wonderful at room temperature, though, and I long for leftovers too, eaten standing by the fridge's open door the next day.

Makes 8–10 good-sized slices.

# PIZZA RUSTICA ALL'INGLESE

This recipe comes second, but not in terms of taste or success. To say it's an anglicization of the very Italian pie above isn't quite to describe it, but I did want to preserve the idea of the original, only taking into consideration ingredients that were as easily accessible and familiar to us as the ones in the filling above would be to Italians.

This version makes for a slightly less deep pie, but it's still a comfortingly chunky number. And as with the pie above, it's wonderful cold and can be happily put back in its tin once it is, so it is very easily transportable. Well, picnics don't exist just in the books of Enid Blyton, and this would be so good eaten on a scratchy blanket with lashings of pop.

Since the pastry and method for its preparation and cooking remain the same, as do all other governing injunctions, I'm just giving you the ingredients and method for the filling. By all means use a strong Cheddar in place of the Cheddar and Lancashire below if you want; indeed, make up your own mixture freely to suit yourself, as I did.

200g lean pork

200g streaky bacon (i.e., approximately 150g de-rinded)

125g mild Cheddar

100g Lancashire cheese

250g cottage cheese, drained in a sieve and processed

2 big or 4 small spring onions

1 clove garlic

2 tablespoons chopped parsley

2 eggs, lightly beaten

freshly ground black pepper

1 heaped tablespoon dried breadcrumbs

Mince the pork and de-rinded bacon in a food processor. Render – that's to say melt down – the fat from the bacon rind in a pan (or just use oil), and fry the minced pork and bacon for about 5 minutes. Transfer to a bowl and let it cool slightly, and then add all the other ingredients except the breadcrumbs. Proceed as for pizza rustica.

Makes 8–10 slices.

# SAUSAGE AND SPINACH PIE

Once I had got into making these golden discs, enthused by the Springformed shape and firmness, I wanted to experiment with a number of fillings. This one turned into one of our favourite lunches. Try: you'll see why.

for the pastry:
**as for pizza rustica**
**22cm Springform tin, greased and lined**

for the filling:
**2 medium onions, puréed in a food processor**
**3–4 young sage leaves, chopped**
**2 tablespoons olive oil**
**500g Cumberland sausage, skinned**
**2–3 tablespoons chopped parsley**

**650g spinach, washed, cooked, chopped and drained very well (or 1kg frozen, defrosted)**
**1 tablespoon freshly grated parmesan**
**1 large egg, beaten**
**1 heaped tablespoon breadcrumbs**

for the glaze:
**1 large egg yolk**
**2 tablespoons milk**
**pinch of salt**

Preheat the oven to gas 190°C /gas mark 5, and make up the pastry as for the pizza rustica. Fry the processor-puréed onion and the sage in the olive oil for 5–10 minutes on a medium heat. Add the sausage meat, mashing it with a fork to mix in with the onion, and cook for a further 5 minutes. Take the pan off the heat and add the chopped parsley and spinach and the parmesan. Season with salt and pepper, and add the egg, mixing well.

Now roll out the pastry to line the tin as before, then sprinkle with breadcrumbs, add the filling, cover with pastry, and so on. Curl the pastry edges over to form a neat border around the tin and press the edge with the prongs of a fork. Make a steam hole in the middle and glaze. Cook for about 40 minutes, or until the pie is golden and firm.

Remove from the oven and let stand for at least 10 minutes before cutting into it. Because of the spinach, which tends to continue to ooze liquid when cooling, this pie, as with the one that follows, isn't so good cold. But, in an emergency . . .

Serves 6–8.

# SPINACH, RICOTTA AND BULGAR WHEAT PIE

This started off life as a vegetarian version of the sausage and spinach pie above, though it is in no way an inadequate substitute for the carnivore's version, but rather an entirely seductive alternative in its own right.

for the pastry:
**as for pizza rustica**
**22cm Springform tin, greased and lined**

for the filling:
**100g bulgar wheat**
**1 teaspoon Marigold vegetable stock granules**
**500g spinach, washed, cooked,**
**chopped and drained very well (or 750g frozen, defrosted)**
**450g ricotta**
**3 spring onions, finely chopped**
**zest of 1 lemon**
**pinch of cayenne pepper**
**pinch of dried thyme**
**2 large eggs**
**2 tablespoons parmesan, grated**
**2 tablespoons dried breadcrumbs**

Make the pastry following the method for the pizza rustica, and preheat the oven to 200°C/gas mark 6, slipping in a baking sheet as you do so.

Put the bulgar wheat and stock granules in a bowl and cover with boiling water. Place foil over the bowl and let the wheat soak for 10–15 minutes. Give the spinach another press against the sieve to squeeze out any further wateriness. Mash the ricotta with a fork, and add the spring onions, lemon zest, cayenne, thyme and spinach. Stir in the eggs, parmesan and soaked bulgar (draining first if necessary) and season with salt and pepper.

Roll out the pastry as above, adding breadcrumbs, filling and top; sealing edges, making steam vents and so forth, and bake the pie for 10 minutes before turning the temperature down to 180°C/ gas mark 4 and cooking it for a further 45.

I like this pie best when it has stood for 25 minutes after coming out of the oven. Serves 6–8.

# COURGETTE AND CHICK PEA FILO PIE

We're still in the realm of the Springform here, but it is, nevertheless, a different sort of pie. Quite simply, it's a pie for those of you who don't want to make pastry. I know that you can buy shortcrust not only ready-made but ready-rolled, but that never seems a happy choice to me; buying ready-made filo pastry, on the other hand, is quite simply what you do. (Though, until recently, I was far more frightened of taking the filo sheets from the box than I was of making my own basic pastry.) Correspondingly, I use tinned chick peas, though please feel free to soak and cook the dried ones if you prefer.

I can't claim this as an Iranian creation, but I certainly had the tastes and fragrances of some Iranian dishes in mind.

½ teaspoon cumin seeds

1 small onion or ½ a large onion, finely diced

2 tablespoons olive oil

½ teaspoon turmeric

1 teaspoon ground coriander

3 plump courgettes

125g basmati rice

500ml vegetable stock, or chicken if you prefer

2 × 425g can of chick peas, drained

100g melted butter

200g filo pastry

22cm Springform tin

Preheat the oven to 200°C/gas mark 6 and put in a baking sheet.

Gently fry the cumin seeds and onion in the olive oil until the onion's soft. Add the turmeric and coriander. Dice the courgettes (unpeeled), add them to the onion mixture, and cook on a fairly high heat to prevent the courgettes becoming watery. When they are soft but still holding their shape, add the rice and stir well, letting the rice become well coated in the oil. Add the stock 100ml at a time, stirring while you do so. When all the liquid has been absorbed the rice should be cooked, so take it off the heat, stir in the chick peas and check the seasoning.

Brush the insides of the Springform tin with some of the melted butter. Line the bottom and sides of the tin with ¾ of the filo, buttering each piece as you layer. Leave a little filo overlapping the sides, and keep 3–4 layers for the top. Carefully put in your slightly cooled filling, and then fold in the overlaps. Butter the last layers of filo and scrunch on top of the pie as a covering. Brush with a final coat of butter, and put in the oven for about 20 minutes, or until the filo is golden and the middle hot. Check this by inserting a slim, sharp-bladed knife (or cake-tester). If, when you remove it, it feels hot when you press it against your wrist, the pie's ready.

Serves 6–8.

# STEAK AND KIDNEY PUDDING

You may think that a steak and kidney pudding made with a thick suet crust is not the sort of food you eat. All I can say is cook it and you'll change your mind. When we made this for the photographic shoot, we, to a woman, wolfed it down with what I can only describe as besotted greed.

Contrary to most people's preconceptions, suet gives the crust an almost ethereal lightness. True, this is only the case if it's eaten immediately – any standing around and it seems to seize up and gain thick-set density – but eat fast and it'll still be delicious when you get round to second helpings. I always use vegetable suet, as I don't like eating meat products whose derivation I do not know. The only thing I'd add is that while suet crust is very easy to make, you must make it at the last minute.

As for equipment: life is very much easier if you buy a plastic pudding basin with a fitted lid than if you use a traditional basin and make a pleated foil lid and string handles. You don't need to steam the pudding: you can simply immerse it in a large pan of boiling water.

I often double the quantities for the meat filling, then freeze half, so I'm only a defrost away from another pudding. Traditionally, oysters were added to steak and kidney pud; I thought a little oyster sauce might be an appropriate contemporary adaptation, and it was, rewardingly so. And I happened to find some beer called Oyster Stout which seemed entirely right for it too, but it's hardly essential: any stout in a storm . . .

I always cook the meat filling a day or two in advance: the flavours deepen wonderfully and  the whole thing seems less of a performance.

for the filling:

**2 tablespoons flour**

**1/2 teaspoon English mustard powder**

**500g stewing steak, cut into 2cm pieces**

**250g lambs' kidney, cut into chunks**

**25g butter**

**2 tablespoons olive oil**

**1 medium onion, chopped**

**150g flat mushrooms (i.e., 2 medium-sized), peeled and roughly chunked**

**150ml beef stock**

**150ml stout**

**1 scant tablespoon oyster sauce**

for the suet crust:

**350g self-raising flour**

**1/2  teaspoon salt**

**175g suet**

**1/2 teaspoon English mustard powder**

3-litre plastic pudding basin with lid, both well buttered

The 2 hours of steaming – which involves little activity on your part – seems less of a consideration when separated from the pudding's preparation. So, preheat the oven to 140°C/gas mark 1, season the 2 tablespoons of flour with salt, pepper and the mustard

powder, and put it into a plastic bag along with the steak and kidney. Seal it, and toss everything about to get an even coating of flour.

Warm the butter and oil in a casserole and brown the meat (including the kidney) in batches, removing each to a dish. Fry the onion in the pan, then add the mushrooms and fry them briefly, adding more oil if you need it. Put all the meat back into the casserole and over a medium heat add the stock, stout and oyster sauce. Bring it to the boil, scraping any floury bits off the bottom. Cover with a lid and cook in the preheated oven for 1½ hours. When it's cooked, check the seasoning and put aside to cool.

About 2½–3 hours before you want to eat, fill a large saucepan with water and bring to the boil. When it begins to boil, start making the pastry, and not before. Mix the flour, salt, suet and mustard powder in a large bowl; then, stirring with a wooden spoon, add enough cold water to make a firm dough. Roll out on a floured surface into a large circle, approximately 5mm thick, and cut away a quarter segment from the circle to use later as the lid. Ease the three-quarter circle of pastry into your buttered pudding basin; there should be about 3cm of overhang. Spoon the cold filling in, not letting it come up higher than about 2cm below the rim.

Roll out the quarter segment into a small circle to fit the top and seal it with the overhanging edges. Clip on the basin's buttered lid, immerse it in water or place it in a steamer over water and leave it there for 2 hours, remembering to check water levels occasionally.

Turn the pudding out onto a plate with a good lip, or some sort of shallow bowl: there is a wonderful moment when, like a bulldozed building, your pudding begins to crack and crumple and then cascades downwards; you need to make sure every thick oozy bit of stout, beefy liquid is safely contained.

Serves 6 generously.

## SMALL PIES

I know I have never been much of a friend to the small-portioned, but these are, for all that, lunchtime favourites at my house.

## CORNISH PASTIES

The best Cornish pasties I've ever had were bought from the shop/post office in Helford and then taken, with some crisps, cold beer and a jar of spiced apple chutney (see p357), to be eaten lying on the beach further up the Helford River. We made these shortly after coming back. I really do think you need to use lard, not butter: apart from anything else, Cornish pasties are not fancy French baked goods meant to exude the flavour of expensive butter, and lard gives you the fluttery lightness you need.

for the pastry:
**225g lard**
**500g self-raising flour**
**pinch of salt**
**iced water to bind**
1 baking sheet, lined

for the filling:
**1 tablespoon lard**
**1 small–medium onion, chopped**
**1 large potato (weighing about 250g), peeled, quartered and sliced thinly**

**100g swede (approximately 1/8 of a large swede), peeled, quartered and sliced thinly**
**500g stewing steak, diced fairly small**
**1/4 teaspoon mace**
**1/4 teaspoon English mustard powder**

for the glaze:
**1 large egg, beaten**

First make the pastry following the usual method (see p83).

Preheat the oven to 200°C/gas mark 6 and get on with the filling. Cook the onion, potato and swede in the lard. Add the steak and cook on a medium heat, moving it around to brown the meat evenly. Turn the heat down a little, season with the mace and mustard, and salt and pepper, and cook for about 30 minutes until everything is tender.

Divide the pastry into 4 pieces, and roll each one out into a rough circle about the size of a small dinner plate (23cm); these are going to be fat daddies. Make all the circles before you start filling so that the filled pasties don't go soggy hanging around. Put a quarter of the filling into one side of the circle, brush beaten egg around the edge and fold over to seal the pasty. Curl the edges inwards and then crimp them in a pasty-like fashion. Repeat with the other pasties.

Place the pasties on the baking sheet and brush with beaten egg. Cook for 15 minutes, then turn the oven down to 180°C/gas mark 4 and give them a further 15 minutes.

Eat as soon as you can without burning your tongue (though I love them warm, 15–20 minutes after they've come out of the oven) with apple chutney or brown sauce, or anything else you damn well please.

Serves 4 generously.

# CHEESE, ONION AND POTATO PIES

This is the picnic food of fondest imagination, although actually we eat these for ordinary tea in the kitchen fairly often. I say 'we': that's to say I make them for the children, then snaffle down a couple myself. I love them as much cold as warm, which is why I've suggested you make eight.

The trick, if trick it be, is to use spring onions, which have all the flavour but none of the BO-ey breath of the usual onion, as in cheese & onion, component.

I use Yorkshire pudding tins, with their wide, shallow indentations, for these, and prefer that more English, even rustic, look. But if you wanted to use individual flan tins, of course you could.

for the pastry:

**2 large egg yolks**
**1 heaped teaspoon salt**
**2 tablespoons cold water**
**250g flour**
**35g Trex or other vegetable shortening, teaspooned out**
**90g cold unsalted butter, diced**
2 x 4-bun Yorkshire pudding trays

for the filling:

**500g potatoes (waxy not floury)**
**100g spring onions (about 6) chopped finely**
**125g mature Cheddar: 75g grated, 50g diced**
**2 tablespoons grated parmesan**
**50g Red Leicester, grated**
**2 tablespoons chopped parsley**
**4 tablespoons crème fraîche to bind**

Make the pastry by the usual method (see p83), then halve it, form each half into a disc, wrap in clingfilm and leave in the fridge for 20 minutes.

Preheat the oven to 200°C/gas mark 6.

Meanwhile, peel and dice the potatoes, put them in a saucepan with plenty of cold water and bring to the boil. Boil gently for 5–10 minutes, or until the cubes are cooked but still retain their shape. Drain and leave to cool.

In a large bowl, combine the spring onions, cheeses, slightly cooled potato and parsley. Bind with the crème fraîche and season with salt and pepper. Roll out one of the pastry discs, cut 8 rough circles slightly larger than the indents and push 4 into the first tray to make the bases. Fill each with an eighth of the mixture and put the remaining 4 circles on as lids. Seal the pie edges with the back of a knife, making a little hole in each one. Repeat for the second tray with the other disc and the remaining half of the filling.

Cook for 20 minutes, by which time the pastry should be firm, beginning to turn gold, but still pale, and let the pies stand a little out of the oven in their trays before easing them out of the moulds.

Makes 8.

# SMALL TOMATO TARTS

These, which are so much lighter and fresher than you could ever hope for, are just what I want for lunch when it's warm enough to eat outside, but they'd make an equally good starter for a dinner party. I make the pastry with cornmeal for crispness and to prevent sogginess, but this kind of pastry is quite friable, so I wouldn't want to make a larger tart to cut into wedges – hence my willingness to live with the individual portions. But old prejudices die hard: I'd arrange them all on one large oval dish for people to help themselves rather than plate them up singly in advance.

for the pastry:

**125g flour, preferably Italian 00**
**60g fine cornmeal or polenta**
**1 tablespoon caster sugar**
**1/2 teaspoon salt**
**115g butter**
**25g Trex or other vegetable shortening**
**40–50ml iced water, or enough to bind**
8 individual tart tins (12cm x 2cm)

for the filling:

**495–500g tin chopped tomatoes**
**pinch sugar**
**50g pecorino cheese sliced into thin slivers with a potato peeler**
**15g packet or small handful basil, finely shredded**
**32 (approximately 500g) baby tomatoes, halved around the equator**
**32 black olives in oil, halved**

First make the pastry: pulse the dry ingredients in the processor, then add the butter and shortening, diced into small pieces. Pulse briefly until the mixture resembles coarse bread-crumbs, then add enough iced water to form a dough, pulsing with the gentlest touch to combine. Form into two discs, wrap with clingfilm and refrigerate for 30 minutes.

Roll out one of the pastry discs into a rough square. Cut into 4 squares (each piece should be big enough to fill the small tart case) and drape into the tins, folding the edges inward. Repeat with the other disc of pastry and the 4 remaining tins, and put them back in the fridge for 15 minutes. Preheat the oven to 200°C/gas mark 6, putting in a couple of baking sheets as you do so.

Meanwhile, empty the tinned tomatoes into a bowl, and season well with salt, pepper and a pinch of sugar. To arrange the tarts, put a thin layer of tomato mix, then 3 slices of pecorino cheese on top, then a sprinkling of basil, then 8 tomato halves with 8 olive halves in rows, and finally a grind of pepper.

Cook for 20 minutes on the baking sheets and let the tarts stand a bit, on a rack out of the oven, before you take them out of their tins.

Makes 8.

# SMALL MUSHROOM TARTS

Heady with the success of the tomato tarts, and interested in the custardless quiche, though such, of course, is a contradiction in terms, I started playing with the idea of a mushroom version. There's something rather magnificent in the way these cream-glazed long-sliced flat mushrooms look like silvery sardines as they lie in their polenta pastry case, and something utterly glorious in the intense boskiness of their taste.

for the pastry:
**see the tomato tart polenta pastry, above**
8 individual tart tins (12 x 2cm)

for the filling:
**10g dried porcini, soaked in warm water**
**550g mixed mushrooms, or button mushrooms if that's all that's available**

**75g butter**
**2 cloves garlic, chopped**
**8 large field mushrooms**
**juice of 1 lemon**
**75g parmesan cut into slivers with a potato peeler**
**4–6 tablespoons chopped parsley**
**8 heaped teaspoons crème fraîche**

Make up the pastry as before, and preheat the oven to 200°C/gas mark 6, putting in 2 baking sheets. Drain the porcini and wipe dry before chopping small. Dice the mixed or button mushrooms and fry in half the butter, adding the chopped garlic and porcini. Fry until the mushrooms have softened, then transfer to a bowl.

Slice the field mushrooms into $1/2$-cm slices and fry in the remaining butter for just enough time to soften them. Add the lemon juice and season with salt and pepper. Cook off some of the liquid, then take them off the heat.

Roll out the pastry and line the tins as for the tomato tarts. To arrange the tarts, put a couple of tablespoons of the diced mushroom mixture into each tart, then 2 slices of parmesan, then distribute the field mushrooms on top before adding a sprinkle of parsley and a teaspoon of crème fraîche.

Cook for 25 minutes or until the pastry is golden-brown and the cream has melted. Leave to stand for a few minutes before unmoulding.

Makes 8.

# SWEET PIES AND TARTS

It hadn't quite struck me how varied pudding, pies and tarts were until I embarked on all this; I've got a wonderful gingham-print American book called *Pie Every Day* and sometimes I did feel tempted. But in order not to bombard you with suggestions, I've curtailed my selection here: these are my absolute favourites (for now, at least). Anyway, the whole point is that once you've played around with some of the ideas in this chapter, you will find it easy enough to make substitutions and changes of your own.

## (KEY) LIME PIE

What follows are two versions of key lime pie, although there is little chance of using fresh key limes. You can use bottled key lime juice (or so it's claimed), but I tend to use ordinary limes.

A note on crusts: it's traditional to use digestive biscuits, but I wanted to make a chocolate-based one as well, I suppose in memory of the chocolate lime sweets I ate as a child. If you use chocolate digestives, it's hard to cut the tart once it's been fridged, so I suggest you use ordinary digestives but with a teaspoonful of cocoa added when you mix them with the butter. Ginger nuts work very well, too; and I love using coconut biscuits.

And as far as the filling goes, don't expect a lime pie to be green. It's yellow – though the first pie is slightly greener because of the zest. A really green pie is a dyed pie.

The following seems to be the basic model for a key lime pie; and it's the one in Jane Grigson's monumentally absorbing *Fruit Book*. Don't be put off by the idea of condensed milk. It's essential, and the sourness of the limes totally sees off its temple-aching sugariness.

for the base:
**200g digestive biscuits**
**50g softened, unsalted butter**
**23cm Springform tin**

for the filling:
**5 large egg yolks**
**397g can sweetened condensed milk**
**zest of 3 limes**
**150ml lime juice (of 4–5 limes)**
**3 large egg whites**

Preheat the oven to 160°C/gas mark 3 and put in a baking sheet.

Put the biscuits and butter into the processor and blitz till all's reduced to oily crumbs. Press these into the tin, lining the bottom and going a little way up the sides, and chill in the fridge while you get on with the rest.

You need an electric mixer for this. I always use my KitchenAid, but a hand-held one is fine. Beat the egg yolks until thick, add the can of condensed milk, grated zest and the lime juice. Whisk the egg whites separately until soft peaks form, then fold gently into the yolk mixture. Pour into the lined tin and cook for 25 minutes, when the filling should be firm. It may puff up and then, on cooling, fall, but that's the deal.

Leave to cool on a rack before unmoulding, and chill well.

Serves 6–8.

## VARIATION

This version comes from a friend of Hettie (who works with me), who in turn works for the Nestlé home economics team. Here, cream is used in place of the eggs, and it's not cooked. In some ways, I suppose, it's more like a light, limey cheesecake – and extraordinarily easy to make.

for the base:
**as above**

for the filling:
**juice and zest of 4 limes**
**397g can sweetened condensed milk**
**300ml double cream**

Make your biscuit base and chill it as above, then make the filling. You do this simply by (electrically) whisking all the ingredients together in a large bowl till thick and creamy. Pour into the lined tin and chill in the fridge for a further 30 minutes or until set.

# CROSTATA

This is another recipe from my lovely Anna. I always use blackberry jam and mostly my own home-made stuff (see p348), which is a doddle to make when you just use a punnet of berries, out of which you'll get the exact right amount for the tart below. But, obviously, substitute the jam of your choice.

This is a spongy kind of a pastry, a cake more than a tart. And, as authentically Italian as it is, it is deeply wonderful with a jugful of proper English custard (hot for me). It cheers me up just thinking of it.

| | |
|---|---|
| 75g soft unsalted butter | 1 teaspoon baking powder |
| 150g caster sugar | zest of 1 lemon |
| 2 large eggs | 200g blackberry jam |
| 200g flour, preferably Italian 00 | 20cm high-sided fluted flan tin |
| pinch of salt | |

Preheat the oven to 180°C/gas mark 4 and put in a baking sheet.

Cream the butter and sugar. Beat in the eggs one at a time until the volume has increased moussily. Sift the flour, salt and baking powder, and fold into the egg and butter mixture. Finally, add the lemon zest.

Spoon into the tin, spreading it out to leave a thicker edge of about 2½cm all around. Spoon the jam into the centre, leaving the edge clear. Cook for 35–45 minutes, by which time the pastry/cake will be golden and bouncy-firm. Let it cool in the tin before unmoulding.

Serves 6–8.

## VARIATION

Obviously, as I've said above, the jams can be varied to suit taste and season, but one variation I love is to replace the jam with marmalade and add the zest of an orange along with the lemon. I think a finer rather than coarser cut marmalade is better here; if, as is often the case, it's sweeter than it should ideally be, mix it up first with the juice of half a lime (better than lemon because you get more sharpness for less liquid).

# RHUBARB TART

This is perfect for January, when the new season's forced rhubarb is just in, rosy and budding with its rhubarbiness. (Actually, Marks & Spencer sells exquisite stuff for a few months more.) It's made all the more dazzling by the contrast with the snowy whiteness of the filling beneath. And I like the neatness of this, in shopping terms at least: you need the cream cheese for the pastry, so why not use it as well for the smooth and voluptuous interior? I know it looks as if there's a lot of fat per flour for the pastry, but go with it.

for the filling:
**1kg rhubarb (untrimmed weight)**
**300g caster sugar**

for the pastry:
**150g plain flour**
**1 tablespoon caster sugar**
**1/4 teaspoon salt**
**85g cold unsalted butter, diced**
**85g cold cream cheese, diced**
**2–3 tablespoons cold double cream to bind**

**1 deep 23cm flan tin or shallow 25cm tin**

for the cream-cheese filling:
**200g cream cheese**
**200ml double cream**
**2 tablespoons caster sugar**
**4 tablespoons muscat or rum**

for the glaze:
**6 tablespoons rhubarb juice, reserved from stewing**

Heat the oven to 190°C/gas mark 5.

Trim and cut the rhubarb into 2cm pieces, place in a shallow ovenproof dish (I use a Pyrex dish of about 20cm x 30cm), pour the sugar over the rhubarb and toss it all together so the sugar's well dispersed. Cover with foil and cook for about 45 minutes, or until tender. When you take the rhubarb out, slip in a baking sheet. When the rhubarb's cool, strain it and reserve the juice.

Meanwhile, get on with making the pastry. Using a food processor, mix the dry ingredients, then add the butter and cheese and pulse to make a crumbly mixture. Bind with the cream, pulsing sparingly. Let the pastry rest in the fridge for at least 20 minutes before lining your tart tin. After you've rolled the pastry out and lined the tin with it, put it back in the fridge for another 20 minutes.

Remove from the fridge and line with foil. Fill the pastry case with baking beans (though you could just as well use any dried beans) and put on the sheet in the oven for 15 minutes. Gingerly remove the beans and foil – bearing in mind their heat – and cook for a further 5 minutes or until it's turning golden-brown and is cooked through. Leave to cool on a wire rack.

When you want to assemble the tart (and you can do the steps above a good couple of days in advance, though keep the cooked and cooled flan case in an airtight container), reduce about 6 tablespoons of the juice to a syrup by boiling it robustly in a small saucepan. Don't leave the pan unattended, though, as the juices will become thickly syrupy in a matter of minutes.

Now for the filling: using a whisk, soften the cream cheese, then add the cream, whipping until it has mixed well and thickened slightly. Take care not to over-beat – this must be voluptuous and undulating. Add the sugar and muscat (which is lovely to drink with it, too) or rum, stir to a soft mascarpone consistency, then fill the pastry case with it. Top with the strained rhubarb pieces, then drizzle over your puce-pink glaze. Stand back and admire – then eat.

Makes about 8 slices.


## VARIATION

In late summer, I do a caramelized plum variant of this with about a kilo of plums, halved then roasted for about 15 minutes in a hot oven with a teaspoon each of butter and sugar in every dimpled cavity. When they're cool, I spread them on the creamy filling, boil down the buttery plummy juices that were left behind and pour those over the tart.

# BITTER-ORANGE AND BLUEBERRY TART

Ideally, this should be made with bitter Seville oranges, but since they are available for only one month of the year and ordinary oranges are around all the time, it seems reasonable to have sweet eating oranges as the first choice, adding the juice of a lime in order to reproduce as closely as possible the fragrant bitterness of Sevilles.

I find this easiest to do over a few days; one, because the taste is so much better when the juice and cream and so forth are left to deepen in the fridge for a couple of days, and, two, because then one splits what could be quite an undertaking into a series of small tasks, no one activity taking more than a few minutes.

This is the perfectly balanced pudding: the tangily sharp smooth pale cream offset by the sweet, purple-black beadiness of the berries on top.

for the filling
**juice (200ml) and zest of 1 eating orange and 1 lime or of 2–3 Seville oranges**
**250g caster sugar**
**300ml double cream**
**6 large eggs**

for the pastry:
**90g soft unsalted butter**
**75g caster sugar**

**3 large egg yolks**
**175g plain flour**
**24cm x 6cm fluted tart tin**

for the glaze:
**1 tablespoon arrowroot**
**50g caster sugar**
**2 scant teaspoons orange juice**
**125ml water**
**250g blueberries**

Start with the filling, a couple of days in advance if this suits. In a large bowl or, better still, a wide-mouthed measuring jug, mix the juice with the sugar, add the zest, double cream and eggs, and stir to combine. Cover and chill for 2–3 days in the fridge or leave for a few hours at room temperature.

You can make the pastry at the same time as you mix up the juices and cream or a day or two later. Cream the butter and the sugar together, then add the yolks one at a time. Stir in the flour to form a soft dough, then form into a fat disc, wrap in clingfilm and rest in the fridge for half an hour. Preheat the oven to 180°C/gas mark 4 and put in a baking sheet. Roll out the pastry to fit the flan tin and line, pushing gently down so that it lies flat at the bottom, leaving a little overhang. Put back in the fridge for a further 20 minutes to rest again.

Roll a rolling pin over the top of the flan case to cut off excess pastry neatly. Line the tin with foil or crumpled baking parchment and fill with baking beans. Put the tin in the oven for 15 minutes, then remove beans and foil or parchment and give it another 5–10 minutes, until the bottom has dried out. Transfer to a wire rack to cool a little and turn the oven down to 170°C/gas mark 3.

Strain the liquid mixture into the pastry case to remove the zest, put back on the sheet in the oven and cook for 45 minutes. (You may find this easier – if more long-winded – if you sieve the mixture into a jug and pour from this into the pastry case already on the sheet in the oven with the rack pulled out.)

When the tart's cooked – and it should be firm on top but with a hint of a wobble underneath – remove to a wire rack and let cool. Unmould and transfer to the serving plate.

To make the glazed blueberry topping, combine the arrowroot and sugar in a small saucepan, then stir in the juice and water. Put the pan on the heat and bring to the boil, stirring all the time: it should turn clear pretty soon. Take it off the heat and add the blueberries, then spoon the now-glossy berries over the waiting tart. Leave to set for about 10 minutes.

Serves 8.

# BAKED SUMMER-FRUIT TART

I keep the word 'baked' in the title simply to distinguish it from a fruit tart, which comprises a squidgy filling of crème patissière with fresh berries on top. Here, you make a custard, pour it into a partially cooked pastry case, tumble fruit on top and put it in the oven for a few minutes to set into a harmonious whole. I've used crème fraîche for the custard because I wanted an edgy note to counterbalance the sweetness of the glazed fruits.

for the pastry:
**175g soft unsalted butter**
**150g caster sugar**
**6 large egg yolks**
**350g flour, preferably Italian 00**
**1 high-sided 25cm flan case**

for the custard:
**8 large egg yolks**
**125g caster sugar**

**600ml crème fraîche**
**zest of 1 orange**

for the glazed fruits:
**225g summer fruits – blackberries, raspberries, redcurrants and blueberries**
**4 tablespoons of blackberry jam**
**2 tablespoons water**

Make the pastry up a few days in advance if you're the sort of person who's soothed by this strategy. Cream the butter and sugar, and then add the yolks one by one, beating after each addition. Fold in the flour gently until the dough comes together. Form into a disc, wrap in clingfilm and put in the fridge for at least 2 hours.

Preheat oven to 190°C/gas mark 5 and put in a baking sheet. Roll out the pastry and line the tart case, leaving an overhang of about 3cm. Rest again in the fridge or freezer for 20 minutes, then roll your rolling pin over the top of the flan case to cut off excess pastry. Bake blind – that's to say, lined with foil and filled with dried beans – for 15–20 minutes. Then remove foil and beans and bake for another few minutes to dry the base out. Half fill a sink with cold water (for salvaging nearly-splitting custard later, in the unlikely event it may be necessary). Whisk together the yolks and sugar until they are pale and creamy. Warm the crème fraîche in a saucepan, and then whisk it into the yolks and sugar, adding the orange zest. Put everything back into the saucepan, and return to the heat, stirring constantly until it becomes thick. This will only happen gradually, so be patient and keep the heat quite low. Pour the custard into the cooked pastry shell, and top with the mixture of summer fruits. Put the tart back into the oven, lightly covered with foil, for 10 minutes. Uncover the tart and cook for a further 5 minutes.

Put the jam and water into a small saucepan and warm. Using a pastry brush, lightly coat the summer fruits with the glaze. Leave to cool for a little. Whichever way you cut it, this is *good*.

Serves 8–10.

# BLACK AND WHITE TART

I apologize for the slightly eighties ring to the title, but I can't help myself. You could use any berries here, but I made this to wallow in the sheer beauty of the blackberries and whitecurrants of the last summer of the last century. And before you start mewing to yourself about the difficulties of unearthing such rare treasures, I should tell you that Sainsbury's regularly stocks them in season. This is one of the easiest tarts you could make: a cheesecake base, the filling a mascarpone cream, and the berries dropped like gleaming gems – jet and moonstone – on top.

for the base:

**250g digestives, roughly broken**

**75g unsalted butter, melted**

**25cm fluted flan tin, 3 1/2cm deep**

for the filling and topping:

**1 large egg, separated**

**75g caster sugar**

**500g mascarpone**

**squeeze of lime or lemon (to taste)**

**1 tablespoon tequila or white rum, optional**

**400g blackberries**

**100g whitecurrants**

Put the biscuits in the processor and blitz to crumbs. Then, motor running, add the melted butter down the funnel. Tip into the flan case and, using your fingers, press onto the base and up the sides. Put in the fridge while you get on with the creamy filling-cum-topping.

Whisk the egg white until stiff but not dry and set aside for a moment. Beat the yolk with the sugar until thick and pale; you may think there's too much sugar to make a paste, but persist: it happens. Add the mascarpone, beating till smooth, then the lime or lemon juice and the rum, if using. Fold in the egg white and pile and smooth this mixture into the prepared flan case. Arrange the blackberries and whitecurrants on top, but loosely. You should, for ease of eating, remove most of the stalks and stems, but I like to leave some still on for beauty's sake.

Serves 8.

## VARIATION

You can alter the fruit as you like, and certainly don't feel constrained to stick with berries. The best and freshest peaches are wonderful, as are figs, and in winter you could soak and cook dried figs or apricots, arrange the fruit on the cream, then drizzle over some reduced cooking liquid.

# BLACKBERRY GALETTE

This is really a free-form pizza-like tart, which I made for the first time while we were doing the photography for this book. We happened to have some polenta pastry left over and some spare blackberries in the fridge and I, suddenly rebelling against the planning and rule-following necessary to get all the food photographed, played around. This was the result. And really, you could use any fruit. I'd stick with the polenta or cornmeal pastry only because nothing soaks up the fruit's juices better without going soggy.

for the pastry:
**60g plain flour**
**30g polenta/fine cornmeal**
**1 scant tablespoon caster sugar**
**¼ teaspoon salt**
**50g cold butter**
**15g (1 tablespoon) vegetable shortening**
**1-3 tablespoons iced water or enough to bind**

**1 baking sheet, lined**

for the filling:
**1 punnet blackberries (approximately 150g)**
**approximately 3 tablespoons caster sugar**
**3 heaped tablespoons crème fraîche, plus more to serve**

In a food processor, pulse the dry ingredients, then add the butter and shortening diced into small pieces. Pulse briefly until it resembles coarse breadcrumbs, then add enough iced water to form a dough, pulsing gently to mix. Form it into a disc, wrap in clingfilm and put in the fridge to rest for about 30 minutes.

Preheat the oven to 190°C/gas mark 5. Roll the pastry out into a rough circle, transfer to the baking sheet and scatter blackberries on top, leaving a good 7cm margin round the edge. Sprinkle with 1–2 tablespoons sugar, to taste, then dollop with crème fraîche. Sprinkle a further tablespoonful of sugar over, dampen the edges with water, then wrap them over themselves to form a knobbly, ramshackle rim and put in the oven for about 20 minutes or until the pastry is cooked through.

Serves 6.

# DOUBLE APPLE PIE

I don't want to nominate favourites, but even so, I have to say this is a pie I am ecstatic about – perhaps because it's so far removed from what I've spent my life cooking.

The notion of putting Cheddar in the pastry of an apple pie is not a new one  but I was pleased all the same to see how well it worked. I've used a Springform tin (learning a lesson from the pizza rustica, above), which makes this a good, hefty, sliceable pie.

The double-apple element – Coxes to hold their shape, Bramleys to make for an appley-velvet background – does entail quite a bit of work, but it isn't difficult work, just moderately time-consuming. Anyone who's hanging about the house claiming to want to help should be handed a vegetable peeler and an apple corer without delay.

for the pastry:
**50g cold unsalted butter, diced**
**50g Trex or other vegetable**
  **shortening**
**250g self-raising flour**
**50g finely grated Cheddar**
**1 large egg**
**iced water to bind**
**pinch of salt**
**22cm Springform tin**

for the filling:
**750g Bramley apples (about 3 large),**
  **peeled and cored**
**1kg Cox apples (about 10), peeled,**
  **cored and cut into eighths**
**80g unsalted butter**
**pinch of ground cloves**
**good grating of nutmeg**
**2 large eggs, beaten**
**100g caster sugar**

Make the pastry in a food processor as normal: pulse the butter and Trex into the flour until it looks like crumbs. Leaving the mixture in the bowl, put the grating blade in and process the cheese into the crumb mixture. Replace the normal blade, and add the egg, iced water and salt  to bind. Turn the pastry out and press it into two discs, one slightly smaller than the other. Wrap each in clingfilm and put them in the fridge to rest for at least 20 minutes.

Preheat the oven to 200°C/gas mark 6, putting in a baking sheet. Slice the Bramleys into small chunks and fry in half the butter until they become soft and begin to lose their shape. Add the cloves and nutmeg. Tip the apple mush into the food processor, and purée, pulsing so as not to make it too like baby food. Add about three-quarters of the beaten egg and all of the sugar and pulse again to mix. Fry the Coxes in the other half of the butter and cover them to help them cook a little. Cook for about 10 minutes: they should be tender but still holding their shape.

Roll out the larger disc of pastry and line the tin with it, letting it hang over the sides. Pour in the puréed mixture, and then push the Cox pieces into the purée to coat them. Roll out the smaller disc of pastry to form the top. Lay over the pie, and curl the edges inwards, crimping them to seal. Decorate with any leftover pastry if you wish, and brush with the remaining egg as a glaze. Cook for 15 minutes, then turn the oven down to 180°C/gas mark 4 for a further 30 minutes. Sprinkle with caster sugar when it comes out of the oven.

Let it cool a little before unmoulding (it will, anyway, slice better when it's not piping hot). And although it tastes like the sort of pie that should be eaten cold, don't leave it hanging around too long or the wonderful pastry will start to sog and wilt.

Serves 8.

## BLACKBERRY AND APPLE PIE

This otherwise traditional English pie also uses cornmeal in the pastry, to soak up the liquid given off by the blackberries when cooking. Otherwise I love this pretty much uninterfered with. The apples come from the tree in my garden and I use the leaves as a template for the decoration on top.

I like a jugful of cream with this, but ice cream seems to be everyone else's favourite whenever I've made it. Traditionally, though, it should be eaten with some creamy, vanilla-scented, eggy custard.

for the pastry:
**65g cold unsalted butter, diced**
**60g Trex, teaspooned out**
**200g self-raising flour**
**50g fine cornmeal**
**2–4 tablespoons salted iced water or enough to bind**
**squeeze of lemon juice as needed**
**20cm shallow pie plate**

for the filling:
**650g Bramley apples (2 medium)**

**60g unsalted butter**
**125g caster sugar**
**1 tablespoon rosewater**
**1/2 teaspoon ground cinnamon**
**3 scant tablespoons cornflour**
**325g blackberries**

for the glaze/topping:
**1–2 tablespoons milk**
**1–2 tablespoons caster sugar**

Make the pastry according to the usual method (see p83) then form into two discs, one slightly smaller than the other. Cover with clingfilm and rest the pastry in the fridge.

Preheat the oven to 190°C/gas mark 5, remembering to put a baking sheet in at the same time. Peel, core and slice the apples. In a saucepan, melt the butter and add the sugar, rosewater and cinnamon, then cook the apples in the pan for about 3 minutes;

remove them to a dish with a spatula. Pour the caramelly juices into a measuring jug and whisk in the cornflour to form a paste.

Line the bottom and sides of the pie dish with the bigger disc of pastry, and put the apples and blackberries into the pie. Pour over the cornflour-butter mixture, stirring gingerly to cover all of the fruit without tearing the pastry. Roll out the smaller disc of pastry, dampen the edges of the pie with water, and put the pie lid on top. Crimp the edges, either by hand or using a fork, to seal. Decorate the top with any pastry scraps, made artistically into leaves, or stamped out into miniature apple shapes with cutters, or whatever takes your fancy.

Glaze with milk and cook for 30 minutes, by which time the still slightly knobbly top should be golden. Sprinkle with caster sugar when it comes out of the oven, and leave for about 15 minutes before cutting into it.

Serves 6.

## PEACH CREAM PIE

This is one of the first pies I made in my early baking days: it's plain, but with just enough goo to make one feel that in some way it's a stolen treat – and a way of letting daylight into those long, cold, fruitless wintry days.

For this filling – fragrant and eggy – I use an ordinary packet of dried peaches from Sainsbury's, which I soak and then cook to ensure honeyed tenderness (though you can leave out the soaking and just cook for a bit longer if you really haven't got time). They are then bound with a light, creamy custard.

for the pastry:
**pinch of salt**
**juice of 1 orange**
**250g self-raising flour**
**125g cold unsalted butter, diced**
**yolk of 1 large egg**
**iced water to bind**
**milk to glaze**
**1–2 tablespoons sugar for sprinkling**

**22cm pie plate**

for the filling:
**250g dried peaches, soaked for at**
    **least 6 hours in 500ml water**
**6 tablespoons single cream**
**1 tablespoon strong honey**
**1 large egg, beaten**

I like self-raising flour for fruit pies, but plain works just as well. If you're making the pastry in advance you may as well use plain flour, as the leavening agent in the self-raising will have fizzled out by the time you use it. Dissolve the salt in the orange juice and set aside in the fridge. Put the flour and the diced butter in a bowl and put this bowl in the freezer for 10 minutes. I am assuming you're using a food processor to make the pastry, in which case after the 10 minutes are up, put the very chilled flour and butter in the bowl of the mixer and process until you have a mixture that resembles the flat crumbliness of oats. Add the egg yolk, give a quick whizz, and then add the salted juice and whizz further. If the pastry hasn't come together, add ice-cold water, teaspoon by teaspoon, till it does. The minute it starts to clump, take it out of the machine, divide in two, and press into a couple of discs. Cover with clingfilm and put in the fridge for 10 minutes.

Put a metal sheet in the oven and preheat to 200°C/gas mark 6. Put the soaked peaches, with their water, in a saucepan, cover and bring to the boil. Let boil for 5 minutes, and then drain, reserving the liquid. Set the peaches aside, pour the liquid back into the pan, boiling it down until you have about 3 tablespoons of syrupy peach juice. Then cut each peach slice in half lengthways.

Roll out one of the pastry discs and use it to line a 22cm pie plate (not a dish, which would be too deep); I use a Jane Asher one with a hole-punched base, which helps prevent sogginess. Dampen the edges with water, but don't cut off the overhang yet. Fill with drained peach slices, mounding slightly in the centre. Stir the cream and the honey into the peach juice, add to the beaten egg and pour the mixture over the fruit. Roll out the other disc of pastry and cover the pie. Cut off overhang, and pinch all along the rim with your finger and thumb to crimp. Using a sharp knife, cut four slashes in the centre of the pie to let steam escape. Dab some milk over to glaze and put on the sheet in the oven.

After 20 minutes, turn down to 180°C/gas mark 4 and cook for another 30–35 minutes. You may need to cover loosely with foil about halfway through to prevent it burning, but remove the foil for the last 5 minutes.

Take the pie out of the oven, put on a rack and sprinkle with a tablespoon or two of sugar. Leave for about an hour before eating.

Serves 6–8.

# REDCURRANT MERINGUE PIE

In *How to Eat* I gave a recipe for a rhubarb meringue pie. There is just something about the fragrant acerbity and sweet, crispy-tipped soft meringue that makes you realize what an oven is for. This pie, I hope, will do the same. Strangely, redcurrants are not used much in cooking, but their intense sourness allied to that rounded exaggeration of flavour is just what you need to stop even the joyfully sweet from cloying. I've made a hazelnut crust because this nut and this fruit were born to be together.

for the pastry:

**100g plain flour**

**25g ground hazelnuts**

**15g caster sugar**

**75g softened unsalted butter**

**1 large egg yolk**

**1 tablespoon iced water or more to bind**

21cm high-sided fluted tart case

for the filling:

**250g redcurrants**

**30g unsalted butter**

**100g caster sugar**

**3 tablespoons orange juice**

**2 large egg yolks, beaten**

**3 tablespoons cornflour**

for the topping:

**2 large egg whites**

**120g caster sugar, plus 1 teaspoon for sprinkling**

**1/4 teaspoon cream of tartar**

Make the pastry in a food processor, in the usual way (see p83), then wrap and rest in the fridge for 20 minutes. Roll out and line the tart case, making the sides come just a little way over the edge of the tin. Rest again in the fridge until the filling is ready. Preheat the oven to 190°C/ gas mark 5, putting in a baking sheet at the same time.

Heat the redcurrants, butter, sugar and orange juice in a saucepan for 3–5 minutes; it should become syrupy but the fruit should remain whole. Take off the heat and add the beaten yolks and cornflour. Put the fruit mixture into the cold, uncooked tart tin. Place in the oven on the ready-heated baking tray and cook for 20 minutes.

Meanwhile, whisk the egg whites until fairly stiff, and gradually add half the sugar. When stiff, satiny and glossy, add the remaining sugar and cream of tartar, folding it in with a metal spoon.

When the tart has had its 20 minutes, dollop the meringue on top, sealing the edges well. Sprinkle with a teaspoon of caster sugar, and put back in the oven for a further 10 minutes, or until the meringue is golden and crisp.

This is good eaten half an hour after it's come out of the oven, but for me it's best of all eaten late at night at room temperature.

Serves 6–8.

PUDDINGS

# PUDDINGS

When I was a restaurant critic, I was once teased for talking about 'the pudding' and then proceeding to describe some elaborate, light and most definitely unpuddingy French confection. But pudding is the word I stick to: can't help it and don't want to. Regardless of style or substance, if it's intended for the last, sweet course, it's pudding in my book. That's not to say that several of the recipes elsewhere in this book couldn't also be made and served up as pudding; indeed, given that we no longer eat tea to any convincing degree, the chances are most of them will end up that way. (That's if you don't count the stand-up breakfast comprising wolfed-down leftovers stashed overnight in the fridge.)

On the whole, I take the line that you do not have to make pudding: the French have always bought their pâtisserie from those who really know how to do it. But in fact there is a good, lazy reason to cook pudding: unless you go out of your way to choose something complicated, the chances are that the process will not be difficult, and the reward gratifying. Quite apart from that essential sense of private satisfaction, people really do seem far more impressed by a home-made pudding, however simple, than they would be by the most lovingly produced main course. You know I'm not a cook-to-impress kind of a girl, so my point isn't so much that you can luxuriate in the astonished admiration of your friends by cooking pudding, but you can thereby lessen the culinary load all round.

Do you know how easy it is to make a steamed sponge? You just bung all the ingredients in a processor, blitz and scrape into a pudding bowl and then sit the pudding bowl in boiling water for a couple of hours. In that time, you are required to do nothing, except maybe for the odd topping-up from the kettle so the pan doesn't boil dry. In other words, this is the easy option, the comforting one – for cook and cookee. What more do you want?

# BLUEBERRY BOY-BAIT

When I saw this title, I had to make it. I came across it in a wonderful book by Christopher Kimball, the editor of *Cook's Illustrated* magazine in the States, called *The Yellow Farmhouse Cookbook*. The recipe has just the provenance you want it to have: it was devised by a Chicago teenager for the Pillsbury $100,000 Recipe & Baking Contest 1954. (She came second in the junior division, incidentally.)

Now, the actual recipe didn't quite do it for me – though it's true I didn't test it out on its own terms. I wanted something different, something more luscious and perhaps something more English. My version, then, goes like this: aromatic custardy sponge, sweet gooey fruit and meringue, sugar-crisped – boy-bait Brit-style. And the proof of the pudding . . .

for the base:

**150g fresh breadcrumbs**

**40g unsalted butter, plus more for greasing dish**

**575ml full-fat milk**

**2 teaspoons caster sugar**

**zest of 1 lemon**

**5 large egg yolks (and keep the whites for the topping)**

**1¼ litre oval or round dish, buttered**

for the blueberry filling:

**325g blueberries**

**100g caster sugar**

**2 tablespoons plain flour, preferably Italian 00**

**2 tablespoons lemon juice**

for the meringue topping:

**5 egg whites**

**125g caster sugar, plus extra for sprinkling**

To make the breadcrumbs, simply process some stale good white bread to rubble. Preheat the oven to 160°C/gas mark 3 and put in a baking sheet.

Heat the milk and butter in a saucepan until hot but not boiling. Stir in the breadcrumbs, sugar and lemon zest, take off the heat, and leave to steep for 10 minutes. Beat in the egg yolks very thoroughly and pour this bread-thickened custard into your greased dish. Bake for 20–30 minutes, until it's firm on top but still with a hint of wobble underneath. Let it stand for a few minutes to let the top form a skin while you get on with the blueberries.

Put the fruit, sugar, flour and juice in a saucepan, and stir to coat. Heat to a robust simmer and cook until you've got a thick jammy sauce, stirring every now and again to prevent it catching. You should still have plenty of whole blueberries visible. Take this off the heat and set aside while you make the meringue topping.

Whisk the whites until stiff but not dry, then add half the sugar, a spoonful at a time, whisking as you do so. Fold in the remaining sugar with a metal spoon. Pour and scrape the cooked blueberries onto your set custard base, spreading evenly. Then dollop over the meringue topping, making sure you seal the edges well so that no dark syrup bubbles up and seeps out. Make peaks with the back of a spoon, sprinkle with a little caster sugar and put back in the oven for a further 20 minutes or until the meringue is burnished and crisp. Underneath, however, it will still be desirably yielding.

Serves 6–8.

## RHUBARB GRUNT

This is another American inspiration. A grunt is like a cobbler or a slump: at its most basic, fruit stewed in the oven with a scone-like topping. Here it is made with cream in place of butter; I'd never come across it before and I doubt it's traditional, but it is gorgeously light and tender, and ridiculously easy to knock up. This version comes from *The San Francisco Chronicle Cookbook*, contributed by the illustrious Marion Cunningham.

for the filling:
**650g rhubarb cut into 2–3cm pieces**
**200–250g caster sugar depending on
  preference (and sourness of fruit)**
**50g unsalted butter cut into small
  pieces, plus more for greasing dish**
**20 x 30cm shallow ovenproof dish,
  greased**

for the topping:
**150g plain flour, preferably Italian 00**
**3 tablespoons golden or ordinary
  caster sugar**
**1/2 teaspoon salt**
**250ml double cream, whipped**

Preheat the oven to 190°C/gas mark 5 and, as with all puddings which could possibly bubble up and spill over the oven floor, put in a baking sheet.

Spread the chopped rhubarb over the bottom of the dish, sprinkle with the sugar, coating evenly, and dot with butter. For the topping, sift the flour, sugar and salt into a mixing bowl (but don't bother to sift if you're using 00 flour). Gently stir in the cream, making a sticky dough. Spread this mixture over the fruit in handfuls, covering the top evenly. Bake for 45 minutes, or until the fruit is bubbling – it's easiest to judge this if you're using a Pyrex dish – and the top is golden.

Serve with cream, ice cream or custard: there just isn't a bad way to eat this.
Serves 6–8.

# PLUM AND PECAN CRUMBLE

There is absolutely nothing wrong with a plain crumble, but having given several suggestions for them in *How to Eat*, I reckoned it was better to offer you here the two crumbles I do most often when I've got people coming for dinner. This plum and pecan crumble (which can just as easily be made with walnuts) is comfortingly autumnal. If you want, use ordinary white sugar in place of the demerara; all I do urge is that you use self-raising flour, not the normally stipulated plain.

for the filling:

**approximately 1kg plums**

**30g unsalted butter, plus more for greasing**

**2–4 tablespoons light muscovado sugar, depending on sourness of fruit**

**1 scant tablespoon cornflour**

**20cm round pie dish, buttered**

for the crumble topping:

**150g cold unsalted butter, diced**

**250g self-raising flour**

**150g demerara sugar**

**200g pecans, some chopped finely, others left larger or whole**

Preheat the oven to 190°C/gas mark 5 and put in a baking sheet.

Halve the plums and put them cut-side up in the dish. You may find you don't need all of them, but squeeze in as many as will fit comfortably. Dot with the butter, sprinkle with the sugar and put, uncovered, in the oven for about 20 minutes. I know it's not normal to cook the base of a crumble first, but I find plums need a head start. You want the fruit's juices to have run a little and the fruit itself to be moving towards tender.

While the plums are cooking, make the crumble topping (or you can make this in advance if you prefer). Rub the butter into the flour, either with your fingers or in a free-standing mixer with the flat paddle. I find the processor makes the crumb a little too fine and you want texture, not Caribbean sand, here. But what you can do to make this better is finish off by rubbing the mixture through your fingers for a while – soft pad of thumb fluttering against soft pad of index or first three fingers – to clump up some of the topping. Fork the sugar and nuts into the crumble mixture, and set aside for a moment.

When the plums have had their time in the oven, pour some of the liquid into a little bowl in which you have placed the cornflour. Stir to a paste, then stir into the plum dish. Now add the crumble topping, pressing down lightly around the edges. Put the crumble back on the baking sheet in the oven and cook for 25 minutes or until the crumble is cooked and speckled golden-brown.

Eat, for choice, with custard.

Serves 4–6.

# GOOSEBERRY-CREAM CRUMBLE

If the above is essentially autumnal, this is an early-summer delicacy. Gooseberries are around for such a short time that it's always good to make use of them when they are in season. Do substitute the elderflower cordial I suggest with some elderflower heads if you have them. Put them in a pan with the fruit and sugar, heat till hot, and leave to steep for 20 minutes or so.

The first time I made this, I wanted to make a crumble which provided its own sauce. The first version, while it tasted wonderful, had too much of this eggy, elderflower-scented custard: on serving, the topping subsided into the fruit-studded sauce below. I'm not really a presentation queen, but I do see that a knobbly sludge isn't the most attractive sight, however good it might taste. So I fiddled and fiddled to come up with a recipe that would deliver on sauce but not fail on style. Be my guest . . .

for the crumble:
**175g cold unsalted butter, diced**
**200g self-raising flour**
**6 tablespoons light muscovado sugar**
**5 tablespoons vanilla sugar**
**pinch of salt**

for the filling:
**750g gooseberries**
**125g caster sugar**
**1 tablespoon plus 1 teaspoon**
**    elderflower cordial**
**1 large egg**
**5 tablespoons double cream**
**1 pie dish, approximately 20cm**
**    diameter, buttered**

Preheat the oven to 190°C/gas mark 5, and slip in a baking sheet to catch drips later.

Make the crumble topping by rubbing the butter into the flour and then forking in the sugars (see method above). Put the crumble mixture in the fridge while you get on with cooking the fruit.

If you can be bothered, top and tail the gooseberries. Put them into a pan with the sugar and the tablespoon of elderflower cordial and heat till just bubbling. All you really want to do is break down the skins slightly, so after a minute's gentle seething, remove from the heat.

In a measuring jug, beat together the egg, yolk, teaspoon of elderflower cordial and cream, and pour into the pan of gooseberries, stirring to combine. Now pour this into the prepared dish and leave to sit for one minute before piling the crumble mixture on top. Put on the baking sheet in the oven and cook for 30–40 minutes, until cooked and golden-brown.

You need nothing to accompany this, save perhaps a bottle of Frontignan.

Serves 4–6.

# GIN AND TONIC JELLY

I love jellies and one of the wonderful things about them is that they are so simple to make. This has a definite kick and unarguable elegance: what better food to emanate from the modern woman's kitchen?

I remind you again of the necessity, in my book, of using leaf gelatine, since it is about a thousand times easier than the powdered sort.

300ml plus 50ml water
300g caster sugar
zest and juice of 2 lemons
400ml tonic water (not slimline!)
250ml gin
8 sheets of leaf gelatine

2 punnets whitecurrants or 3–4
   punnets raspberries, optional
1 teaspoon icing sugar if using
   raspberries
1 1/4 litre jelly mould, lightly greased
   with almond or vegetable oil

Put the water and sugar into a wide, thick-bottomed saucepan and bring to the boil. Let boil for 5 minutes, take off the heat, add the lemon zest and leave to steep for 15 minutes. Strain into a measuring jug, then add the lemon juice, the tonic water and the gin; you should have reached the 1,200ml mark; if not, add more tonic water, gin or lemon juice to taste.

Soak the gelatine leaves in a dish of cold water for 5 minutes to soften. Meanwhile, put 50ml of water into a small saucepan and bring to the boil. Remove from the heat, squeeze out the gelatine leaves and whisk them in. Pour some of the gin and lemon syrup mixture into the saucepan and then pour everything back into the jug. Pour into the mould and, when cold, put in the fridge to set. This should take about 6 hours.

When you are ready to unmould, half-fill a sink with warm water and stand the jelly mould in it for 30 seconds or so. Clamp a big flat plate over the jelly and invert to unmould, shaking it as you do so. If it doesn't work, stand it in the warm water for another half-minute or so and try again. If you've used a dome mould, surround the jelly with whitecurrants (Sainsbury's sells them in summer, as do many greengrocers'), or fill the hole with them if you've used a ring mould. Raspberries are just as good, but dust these with icing sugar – it sounds poncey, but it makes the pale-jade glimmer of the jelly and the otherwise-too-vibrant red of the fruit come together on the plate. The white-currants should be left to glimmer, opal-like, without interference.

Serves 8.

## VARIATION
To make a vodka and lime jelly, simply substitute 6 limes for the 2 lemons and use vodka in place of the gin.

# STEAMED SYRUP SPONGE

Even though this pudding takes 2 hours to cook, that isn't as awkward as it sounds. You can assemble it all very quickly, and if you're serving it for a dinner party on a working day, just get started the minute you get in, before you've even taken your coat off, and then you should have no problems about timing.

Not being particularly good with my hands, I don't go in for all that foil-pleating farrago: I just use a plastic pudding basin which is manufactured for the purpose and comes with its own lid which fits. (Don't put either bowl or lid in the dishwasher, however, or the next time you use it it won't.)

I cannot tell you how glorious this is: light beyond words, feathery textured and comfortingly, not cloyingly, sweet. I know steamed sponges are so out of favour as to be, generally, beyond consideration now, but please do yourself a favour: cook it, eat it and then tell me . . .

for the sponge:

**175g very soft unsalted butter, plus
   more for greasing**

**175g self-raising flour**

**175g caster sugar**

**3 large eggs**

**zest of 1 unwaxed lemon and juice
   of 1/2**

**3 tablespoons milk**

for the syrup base/topping:

**250g golden syrup**

**juice of other 1/2 lemon**

**1 3/4 litre pudding basin with lid**

Put the kettle on, then put the butter, flour, sugar, eggs, lemon and milk in the food processor and whizz together, adding a little more milk if the mix is too thick (it should be a thick, pouring consistency).

Pour the boiling water into a large saucepan which has a lid (the water should come about half to two-thirds of the way up the side of the pudding basin when in) or into the base of a steamer. Put it on the heat. Meanwhile, butter the pudding basin, put the golden syrup in the bottom of it and stir in the lemon juice. Pour the sponge mixture on top of the syrup and put on the plastic lid, remembering to butter it first. Then put the pudding basin into the saucepan, put the lid on the saucepan, and that's it. The pan should keep just boiling, with the lid on. The important thing is that it shouldn't boil dry. Keep some water hot in the kettle to pour in when necessary.

I know one is supposed to put the basin on a saucer in the pan, but the rattling noise it makes drives me mad, and the pudding doesn't seem to suffer for being untriveted. Let it cook for a minimum of 2 hours, more won't matter. When it's ready, remove (I don't bother to make a handle out of string, but use two spatulas to lift it out

of the boiling water) and let rest for a couple of minutes, no longer. Turn out with great aplomb onto a large plate with a sauce-saving lip.

The usual trio of suggestions holds good here: cream, ice cream, custard. If custard, think of flavouring with lemon zest, not vanilla.

Serves 6–8.

## VARIATIONS

The variation I do most – and chiefly because it is my father-in-law's favourite – is a marmalade sponge. Replace the golden syrup with 275g best marmalade and stir into it not lemon juice but 2 tablespoons of orange juice, replacing the lemon zest in the sponge above with the zest of ½ an orange.

And any other jam could go below, but in most cases I'd then flavour the sponge with a teaspoon of real vanilla extract instead of zest.

# CUSTARD

No chapter on puddings should leave out a recipe for custard. The only problem really is a fear of it splitting. Feel the fear, and cook it anyway. But first, half-fill the sink with cold water so that if you think the custard's about to split, you can plunge the pan into the sink and whisk like fury.

**1 teaspoon vanilla extract or 1 vanilla pod**
**500ml single cream**

**5 large egg yolks**
**1 tablespoon caster sugar**

If you've got a vanilla pod, cut down its length so that the seeds will be released, and heat it in a pan with the single cream till nearly boiling. Take off the heat, cover and leave to steep for 20 minutes. If you're not using a pod, put the cream and vanilla on the heat, and beat the yolks and sugar together in a bowl. When the cream's warm, pour it over the sweet yolks, beating all the while. Pour the uncooked custard back into the rinsed-out and dried pan and cook over a medium heat, stirring constantly, until the custard's thickened. Ten minutes should do it, unless you're being very timorous and leaving the flame too low. When the custard's thickened, plunge the pan into the cold water in the sink and whisk it for a minute or so. You can eat it straight away, or if you want to make it in advance, reheat later in a bowl over a pan of simmering water.

Serves 4.

# APPLE-SYRUP UPSIDE-DOWN PIE

I include this here and not in the pie chapter mainly because you need to eat it hot and because I find it useful as a very easy way of turning a supper of leftovers into something a little more heart-warming. The pastry element is just a scone dough, which requires the minimum involvement on your part.

for the fruit:

**30g unsalted butter**

**4 Granny Smiths or other eating apples, peeled, quartered and cored**

**100g walnut (or pecan) halves**

**8 tablespoons golden (or maple) syrup, plus extra for serving**

**20cm shallow pie dish, buttered**

for the scone dough:

**250g plain flour**

**15g caster sugar**

**pinch of salt**

**1 scant teaspoon baking powder**

**40g unsalted butter**

**1 large egg, beaten**

**100ml full-fat milk**

Preheat the oven to 220°C/gas mark 7, putting in a baking sheet.

Melt the butter in a pan, and gently fry the apples, curved side down, for about 10 minutes. Put the walnut halves in the pie dish flat side up. Pour over the golden syrup, and then arrange the fried apples curved side down. Leave it for a moment while you get on with the dough.

Put all the dry ingredients into a bowl. Cut the butter into cubes and rub into the flour mixture until it resembles coarse breadcrumbs. Make a well in the centre, pour in the milk and egg all at once, and mix to a soft dough. Using your hands, press the dough into a circle roughly the size of the pie dish and then place it over the fruit, taking care to seal the edges well against the edges of the dish. Bake in the oven for 15 minutes, then turn it down to 180°C/gas mark 4 for 10 minutes, by which time the top should be crusty and golden.

Let it sit out of the oven for a minute or so, and then place a large plate with an outer rim or lip over the top of the pie, and with one swift action (and wearing oven gloves: the dish will be very hot of course) turn it out onto the plate. It is best to do this over the sink as the syrup will be very hot and runny. Spoon about 3 tablespoons of syrup over the pie, and adjust any stray bits of apple or walnut that may have come off. If you want, and I resolutely do, put a jug of warmed syrup on the table for people to add when eating, as well as some single cream in another jug.

This sort of pastry becomes stodgy on cooling, so time it to be ready no more than 10 minutes before you'll be wanting to eat it.

Serves 6–8.

# RED-GOOSEBERRY CLAFOUTIS

A real clafoutis, that vanilla-scented, dense batter pudding studded with fruit, is made with cherries. But that poses problems, the first being that the sour cherries that should punctuate the sweet billowy batter are not available over here (unless you've got a tree of your own). The second is that, traditionally, even if you lay your hands on the correct cherries, you should not stone them. Most people, however, would find it difficult to eat a pudding studded with unpitted cherries; and if you do stone them, you lose some of that desirable, bitter-kernel taste (although a bit of Kirsch thrown over the pitted fruits might help). I have made it with the stoned sour cherries you can find bottled in tall glass jars from Poland, but by the time they have sat around in their syrup they tend to lose their edge, too. I wouldn't rule them out, though, particularly since the version here, made with red, or dessert, gooseberries is really only a possibility in midsummer. Red gooseberries, which I've only recently come across, are now easier to find than the tougher-skinned, bitter green ones and are still sour enough to provide the juicy contrast you're after here.

| | |
|---|---|
| **1 tablespoon butter** | **1 teaspoon vanilla extract** |
| **350g red gooseberries** | **300ml double cream** |
| **6 large eggs** | **300ml full-fat milk** |
| **100g plain flour, preferably Italian 00** | **icing sugar for dusting** |
| **75g caster sugar** | **20cm diameter pie dish (I use a** |
| **1/2 teaspoon orange-flower water** | **stainless-steel one for this)** |

Preheat the oven to 190°C/gas mark 5, putting in a baking sheet at the same time. When it's reached temperature, grease the pie dish with the tablespoonful of butter and throw in the gooseberries. Put in the oven for 10 minutes.

Make the batter the easy way: put all the remaining ingredients into the food processor and blitz till smooth and combined. When the gooseberries have had their 10 minutes, pour the batter over them, put the dish back on the sheet in the oven and cook for 35 minutes, by which time the pudding will be just set in the middle and golden-brown and puffy at the edges. Indeed, all of it will be gloriously risen when you take it out, but it will have sunk – and that's just the way it goes – by the time it's at optimum eating temperature, about 20 minutes later. Dust with icing sugar before bringing it to the table.

And boy, does it make a good breakfast tomorrow.

Serves 4–6.

# MUSCAT RICE PUDDING

By providing this recipe for a slightly souped-up rice pudding, I am emphatically not suggesting that the basic, plain version is in any way deficient, but this muskily ambrosial pudding really is mellow heaven. And it's wonderful too with a dollop of the muscat jelly – coriander-seeded infusion and all – on p352. Perfect dinner-party comfort food.

**500ml full-fat milk**

**500ml double cream**

**50g caster sugar**

**pinch of salt**

**3 tablespoons unsalted butter**

**150g arborio rice**

**250ml muscat**

**fresh nutmeg to grate over**

**1 1/2 litre hob-proof casserole**

Preheat the oven to 150°C/gas mark 2.

Combine the milk, cream, sugar and salt in a measuring jug. In a casserole dish – and I use an age-old battered enamel oven casserole of my mother's – melt the butter over a medium to low flame, add the rice and stir well to coat, then throw in the muscat (much as you would wine in a risotto). Stir well and let the syrupy liquid bubble away for a couple of minutes. Then pour in the milk mixture, stirring while you do so. Let it all come back to a gentle bubble, stir well again and grate over some fresh nutmeg.

Put in the oven and cook for 2 hours, though check after 1½ because the depth of your dish and the nature of your oven may make a significant difference. The rice should have absorbed the liquid, but still have a voluptuous creaminess about it. Remove and let cool for at least half an hour before eating.

Serves 6–8.

# CALVADOS SYLLABUB

Syllabub is one of those ethereal, dreamy confections which seem at odds with the description 'pudding'. But this scented, whipped cream, piled up to swell cloudily out of its container, is a perfect way to end dinner and gloriously easy to boot.

| | |
|---|---|
| **8 tablespoons dry cider** | **juice of 1 lemon** |
| **2 tablespoons Calvados** | **300ml double cream** |
| **¼ teaspoon ground cinnamon** | **4 cinnamon sticks (optional)** |
| **4 tablespoons caster sugar** | **4 x 150ml glasses** |

Put the cider, Calvados, ground cinnamon, sugar and lemon juice in a bowl and stir until the sugar's dissolved. Keep on stirring as you gradually pour in the cream. Now, using a wire whisk or an electric one at low speed, whip the syllabub until it is about to form soft peaks. It should occupy some notional territory between solid and liquid – you're aiming for what Jane Grigson calls 'bulky whiteness' – so be careful not to let the cream become too thick or, indeed, to go further and curdle.

Spoon the syllabub into the glasses (and those you see here were bought by my maternal grandparents on their honeymoon in Venice) and puncture each semi-solid mound with a cinnamon stick, just as a Flake is plunged into a scoop of ice cream. If that's just a little too frou-frou for you (and I quite understand), simply dust the uneven tops with the merest haze of ground cinnamon.

Serves 4.

# OM ALI

I first ate this at Ali Baba, an Egyptian restaurant in London to which I was taken by Claudia Roden, about 10 years ago. How I remembered it, when I came to cook it myself, was as a kind of Egyptian bread-and-butter pudding; certainly, the idea is the same. Filo pastry is buttered and baked, then layered with nuts and dried fruit in a dish into which you pour cream-enriched sweetened milk before baking it again.

It looks beautiful – the white, the gold, the amber, the green – and it tastes just how you might imagine it would: light, comforting, fragrant. And, like most of the puddings here, it's extremely easy to make. I cook it in a dish made by Calphalon called an Everyday Pan, mainly because it's graceful, unfancy and it looks the part, but any normal-sized (approximately 20cm) pie dish should be fine.

**200g filo pastry**
**100g butter, melted, plus some for greasing**
**60g sultanas**
**75g dried apricots, diced small**
**75g flaked almonds**
**50g pistachios, chopped**

**50g pine nuts**
**1 litre full fat milk**
**300ml double cream**
**100g caster sugar**
**fresh nutmeg**
**2 baking sheets**
**20cm pie dish**

Preheat the oven to 150°C/gas mark 2

Paint the filo sheets with melted butter and crumple loosely like wet rags, dividing them between the baking sheets. Cook for about 20 minutes until they turn crispy and golden.

Now turn your oven up to 240°C/gas mark 9. Butter the dish you're using and crumble the filo pastry into it to cover the bottom, then sprinkle the sultanas, apricots and nuts on top, and continue layer by layer until all is used up. Heat the milk, cream and sugar in a saucepan, and bring to the boil. As soon as it's come to the boil, pour over the filo and fruit layers, grate over some fresh nutmeg and then put the dish back into the oven for 10–15 minutes. The top should be lightly browned, burnished and billowed up with the heat. Leave for a few minutes before spooning into small bowls.

Serves 6–8.

# PROFITEROLES, MY WAY

I couldn't write a book with this title without including a recipe for profiteroles. These, however, are not your usual profiteroles: they're stuffed with a burnt-sugar custard and have a toffee sauce poured over them. I haven't done this to be fancy, but simply because they're monumentally impressively better that way.

I am not going to pretend that making profiteroles is a completely effort-free exercise – there's an amount of fiddly preparation – but you can make it easier by cooking the little choux buns the day before you need them and keeping them, once cooled, in an airtight tin or Tupperware. And you can make the burnt-sugar custard earlier on in the day, and keep it covered with wet baking parchment (but don't, unless it's the highest, hottest summer, put it in the fridge).

for the profiteroles:
**200g plain flour, preferably Italian 00**
**350ml water**
**150g unsalted butter, diced**

**pinch of salt**
**4 large eggs, beaten**
**2 baking sheets, oiled**

Preheat the oven to 200°C/gas mark 6.

Sieve the flour. Put the water, butter and salt in a decent-sized saucepan on the hob and heat until the butter's melted and the water's begun to boil. Take the pan immediately off the heat (you don't want the water to evaporate at all) and beat in the flour. Use a wooden spoon for this and don't worry about how lumpy or how unyielding it is, just keep beating until it comes smoothly together. Put the pan back on the heat for just long enough to finish this process off, about a minute or even less, until the dough begins to come away from the sides of the pan to form a smooth ball.

Now beat in the eggs: and you can do this either by hand (not difficult but you'll need muscle power) or by machine. So, either turn the dough into a mixing bowl and add spoonfuls of egg as you continue to beat with your wooden spoon, or turn it into the bowl of a food processor fitted with the double blade and gradually pour the eggs through the funnel while blitzing until you have a smooth, gleaming dough, soft enough to pipe but still stiff enough to hold its shape. You may not need all of the eggs, so go carefully. Using a 2cm plain nozzle, or just a spoon, pipe little rounds onto the oiled baking sheets and bake for about 15 minutes until golden and crisp. Remove to a cooling rack and pierce each profiterole with a pin, to let the steam out and prevent them going soggy.

for the custard filling:
**250ml milk**
**250ml double cream**
**6 large egg yolks**
**100g caster sugar**

**30g plain flour, preferably Italian 00**
**1 teaspoon vanilla extract**
**2 tablespoons caster sugar**
**2 teaspoons water**

Warm the milk and cream in a saucepan. While you're waiting, beat the yolks and sugar until creamy, and then whisk in the flour. Stir the heated milk into the egg mixture and whisk until smooth. Pour back into the saucepan and stir or whisk gently over a low heat until the custard thickens. Add the vanilla and set aside. Then burn your sugar by putting the sugar and water in a little pan and turning the heat to high, letting the sugar and water turn to a dark brown caramel. Using a Magiwhisk for preference, though a fork would do, beat the custard as you pour in the molten liquid. When it's combined, pour into a bowl and let cool, placing a wet piece of greaseproof on the top to prevent a skin forming.

for the toffee sauce:
**6 tablespoons light muscovado sugar**
**4 tablespoons caster sugar**

**100g unsalted butter**
**300g golden syrup**
**4 tablespoons (60ml) double cream**

Put all the ingredients except for the cream into a saucepan, bring to the boil and let bubble away for 5 minutes. Put to one side to cool a little while you assemble your profiteroles.

Get out a large shallow bowl. Fit an icing bag with a small plain nozzle and fill with the cold burnt-sugar custard. Fill the profiteroles by splitting them with a small knife, inserting the nozzle into each one, and squeezing. As you fill them, arrange them in a loose pyramid in the bowl. Pour over some sauce to cover lightly about halfway through, and then again when your entire pyramid has been assembled. You should think of using half of your sauce-pot. The toffee will harden slightly, shining on top of the egg-yellow profiteroles. Just before you eat, add the cream to the remaining sauce and reheat, letting it bubble away for a few minutes. Decant to a warmed jug and stick a ladle into it so that people can pour their own. This sauce reheats easily, by the way.

Serves 8–10.

## VARIATIONS
The easiest variation is the expected one: fill the profiteroles with some whipped cream and pour over them chocolate ganache, which you make by bringing 350ml double cream and 350g best dark chocolate, chopped into little pieces, to the boil in a milk pan. Whisk till thick and smooth, let cool a bit, then pour over the cream-stuffed profiterole pyramid.

# PISTACHIO SOUFFLÉS

Normally I hate the individually portioned, the mealy-mouthed ramekin of professional practice. But I make exceptions. I've made pistachio soufflé in one large dish and loved it, but you just don't get that perfect ratio of heat-singed exterior and tender interior unless you use dishes with a small diameter.

I have a particular love for pistachios, their scent, their fragrant, delicate taste, that clean eau-de-nil colour, those romantic, *Arabian Nights* associations. The square of dark chocolate, hidden dark and melting within, is the soufflés' killer secret. Don't ruin it by announcing it beforehand.

Lindt Excellence is a good chocolate to use here, because it comes in bars already scored with squares exactly the right size to be pressed into a ramekin (and it's generally stocked by supermarkets and sweet shops). This picture was taken in a huge, cold studio in the dead of winter. I promise you that they rose higher, as yours will too.

30g soft unsalted butter, plus extra
  for greasing soufflé cups
60g caster sugar, plus extra for
  dusting soufflé cups, plus 1 tablespoon for the egg whites
20g plain flour
150ml full-fat milk
4 large eggs separated
100g pistachios (peeled weight),
  ground

2 drops almond extract
1/2 teaspoon vanilla extract
1/2 teaspoon orange-flower water
5 large egg whites
pinch of salt
6 x 10g squares, or similar, good
  dark chocolate
icing sugar for dusting over
6 x 250ml ramekins or soufflé dishes

Preheat the oven to 200°C/gas mark 6 and put in a baking sheet. Use a little butter to grease the insides of the ramekins and then tip in a little caster sugar, swirl about to cover, and tip out the excess.

Put the flour in a saucepan and add a little milk, just to blend. Then, stirring (I tend to use one of those little Magiwhisks here, but a wooden spoon would do fine as long as you're patient), add the rest of the milk and 60g sugar. Whisk over a medium heat until it comes to boiling point, then whisk for 30 seconds and take off the heat, by which time it should be very thick. Let it cool a little, then add the yolks, whisking in one at a time.

If you're making this in advance, beat in half of the butter and dot the rest on the top to stop a skin forming; otherwise just beat in all the butter now.

Add the ground pistachios, the almond and vanilla extracts and the orange-flower water, and mix in well. Then, whisk all 5 egg whites together with the salt until soft peaks form. Sprinkle over the tablespoon of sugar and then carry on whisking until thick and glossy.

Lighten the mixture with some – up to a quarter – of the whites. Don't be afraid of this: just splodge them into the saucepan and stir briskly. Now fold in the rest of the whites, gently but purposefully.

Pour 1cm of the mixture into each ramekin, then lie chocolate pieces on top and pour over the remaining mixture. Open the oven and as quickly but unhurriedly as possible, arrange the dishes on the heated baking sheet. Immediately, turn the oven down to 180°C/gas mark 4 and cook for 12–15 minutes, when the tops will be scorched gold and risen high above the ramekins' rims. Remove from the oven, dust with icing sugar and serve absolutely at once. But one note of reassurance: you can open the oven door to see that the soufflés are cooked and risen; they won't fall just because you've got the temerity to check on them.

## CHESTNUT ICE-CREAM MERINGUE CAKE

Three layers of meringue, sandwiched with and topped by chestnut ice cream, covered with grated chocolate, then frozen: it sounds kind of fancy, doesn't it? Let me tell you that it's one of the easiest recipes in the book. The contrast of textures is wonderful because for some reason which I can't quite fathom meringue doesn't freeze. That's to say, even straight out of the freezer it tastes as if it's at room temperature, with its normal texture. This, then, is a useful template for any sort of ice-cream cake you'd want to make. Chocolate meringues (see the gooey chocolate stack on p185) layered with chocolate ice cream would indeed be fabulous: but making chocolate ice cream is a more long-winded process than this no-churn chestnut one culled from Shona Crawford-Poole's *Iced Delights*. You could always use a good bought one, I suppose.

But not but what – as my stepfather always used to say – this is just right as it is, so there's no onus on any of us to search anxiously for substitutions.

for the meringue layers:
**6 egg whites**
**300g caster sugar**
**2 teaspoons cornflour**
**1 teaspoon  wine vinegar**
**1/2  pure vanilla extract**
**3 baking sheets, covered with baking**
  **parchment**

for the ice cream:
**3 tablespoons rum**
**500g tin sweetened chestnut purée**
**600ml whipping cream**
**100g icing sugar**
**20g best dark chocolate to grate over**

Preheat the oven to 150°C/gas mark 2.

Make the meringue layers first: whisk the egg whites until soft peaks form, then add the sugar a spoonful at a time as you carry on whisking. When you have a quarter of the sugar left, stop whisking and fold in the remaining sugar with a metal spoon. Finally, fold in the cornflour, vinegar and vanilla.

Draw 3 x 21cm circles (use a Victoria sandwich tin and draw round it) on separate pieces of baking parchment and place on baking sheets. Divide the meringue equally between the 3, making flat discs. Don't get too nervous about handling: I've been brutally clumsy with this, to no detrimental effect. Cook for 1 hour, then turn the oven off, leaving the meringue discs to cool in the oven.

When the meringues are cold – and there's no reason why you can't make them days in advance – get started on the ice cream. You won't believe how pathetically low-effort this is. First, combine the rum and chestnut purée to make a smooth paste. Second, whip the cream and sugar to form soft peaks, and then fold into the chestnut and rum. This smooth mixture is your (unfrozen) ice cream.

To assemble the cake, put one meringue layer on a lipless plate and spread with one-third of the ice-cream mixture. Repeat with the remaining layers of meringue and the remaining ice-cream mixture. Then, on top of the final third of ice cream, grate over the chocolate. I suggest a Microplane grater for this.

Freeze the cake uncovered until it has set, then cover with clingfilm and keep frozen until you need it. This is a fabulously rich pudding: even greedy people like me can't manage more than a modest slice.

Serves 12–14.

# TRIFLES

I came to trifle relatively late in life, which is probably just as well. The three trifles that follow have very little in common with each other, but I feel they have equal claim on your attention.

The first, if not a traditional English trifle, is at least based on one and divinely so. The second is in some sense a tiramisu spin-off; if you have ever tried the white tiramisu in *How to Eat* you will know what I mean. Now, the third trifle I am excitedly pleased about. I came up with it a couple of summers ago: it was hot, I was hot, and I wanted to make something like trifle but lighter, sharper, less formal. The version I came up with is a modern, deconstructed trifle; the idea pared down to essentials. I have no favourites really, not when it comes to eating, but I can't help having a special maternal fondness for this, my own baby.

Trifles do need a certain amount of attention, but this can be spread over days if that makes life easier. Most satisfying, trifles are best when they're the fruitful result of leftover-inspired innovation. Use any stale cake lying around and create harmoniously, accordingly.

## CHERRY TRIFLE

As with all trifles, it's hard to specify quantities: really you need to think of layers rather than amounts, but I can see that doesn't help much with the shopping list. The quantities below were enough to fill — just — a glass bowl such as you might expect to use for trifle: you can see from the picture. Otherwise, I tend to use a rather unsuitable terracotta dish with a capacity of about 2½ litres.

for the trifle:
**135ml brandy**
**1 vanilla pod, cut into lengths**
**300ml full-fat milk**
**300ml whipping or double cream**
**8 large egg yolks**
**75g caster sugar**
**8 trifle sponges (1 packet)**
**approximately 100g best cherry jam**

**750g cherries**

for the topping:
**3 tablespoons flaked almonds**
**500ml double cream**
**1 tablespoon sieved cherry jam**
**juice of ½ lemon**
**1 tablespoon water**

First, make your vanilla-brandy infusion to flavour the custard later. So, in a small saucepan, bring 60ml – about 4 tablespoons – of brandy and the chopped vanilla pod to the boil, and then let it bubble away for 2 minutes. Remove from the heat and leave to cool.

Fill the sink with cold water, and get on with the custard: warm the milk and cream in a saucepan. In a bowl, whisk together the yolks and sugar, then beat the warm milk and cream into the yolks. Put everything back into the washed-out saucepan and, stirring or whisking constantly, keep on a low heat until it thickens. With this many yolks, it won't take long. But if you think there's any sign of imminent splitting, plunge the pan into the sink of cold water and beat like mad with a Magiwhisk till all danger is averted.

When the custard's thick, take it off the heat, stir in the brandy-vanilla infusion and set aside, covered with wet greaseproof, till cold.

Split the trifle sponges and sandwich with the cherry jam and line a bowl (preferably glass) with them. Pour over the remaining 75ml brandy and now, holding them over the sponges in the bowl for profitable juice-catching, stone the cherries. Boring work, time-consuming certainly, but not difficult. When all the cherries are stoned and in, pour over the cooled custard, cover with clingfilm and rest in the fridge for 24 hours, or at least 12.

When you're ready to eat, or almost, toast the almonds in a dry pan for a few minutes till golden and aromatic, then turn onto a cold plate to cool. Whip the double cream till thick but still soft, and pile it over the custard in the bowl. Put the sieved cherry jam, lemon juice and the tablespoonful of water into a little pan and bring it to the boil, letting it bubble away till you have a runny red syrup. Take the pan off the heat to let it cool down slightly, then scatter the almonds over the trifle and drizzle over the jam syrup.

Serves 10–12.

# PASSIONFRUIT, MASCARPONE AND MERINGUE TRIFLE

I have a weakness for anything with passionfruit, but this at least uses my weakness to good effect. You may as well let an obsession work for you. I don't for one instant expect you all to rush out to Gerry's in Soho to get a bottle of Passoa, though it is the most divinely camp liqueur you could ever come across. Cointreau is what I suggest if you have neither my sense of kitsch nor worrying extravagance. (Although, since my Passoa was a present, I actually have no idea how much it costs. Believe me when I say it doesn't taste expensive.) I'm not going to suggest an alternative fruit, but do substitute whatever you'd like. And, if you cannot find Savoiardi, you can use 16 (2 packets) trifle sponges.

for the soaking liquid:
**15 passionfruit**
**2 limes, peeled and chopped**
**1 tablespoon golden icing sugar**
**approximately 400ml Cointreau or**
   **Passoa**

for the trifle:
**juice of 1 lime, reserving skin**
**2 large egg whites**

**2 large egg yolks**
**125g caster sugar**
**750g mascarpone**
**12 meringue nests, bought or**
   **home-made**
**approximately 16 Savoiardi biscuits**
   **(2 packets), or trifle sponges**
**12 passionfruit**
glass dish or somesuch, measuring
   32 x 25 x 6cm

Put the passionfruit pulp, seeds and all, into a food processor or blender with the limes and icing sugar, pulse a couple of times and then strain the liquid into a measuring jug. You should have about 200ml: make up the quantity to 600ml with Cointreau or Passoa.

Rub round a bowl with the skin of your juiced lime, then whisk the egg whites until stiff. Set aside for a moment. Beat together the egg yolks and sugar, preferably with an electric mixer. They will be a thick paste at first, but add the lime juice, keep beating, and the mixture will become like mayonnaise. Gently fold in the mascarpone and then the beaten egg whites. Take half of your meringue nests and crumble them into the mascarpone mixture, saving the rest to crumble on top afterwards.

Dip the Savoiardi one at a time into the passionfruit liquid, then arrange them in a large, shallow dish. Pour in any remaining juice. Spread the mascarpone mixture over the top, covering the biscuits evenly. Cover with clingfilm and leave in the fridge for a day or so.

Just before before you sit down to the meal at which you're going to eat this, crumble the remaining meringues on top and spoon the scooped-out pulp of the passionfruit, including the seeds, over it.

Serves 14–16.

# LEMON-RASPBERRY PLATE TRIFLE

This, as I've already buttonholed you about, is a deconstructed, pared-down version of the original: sliced lemon-syrup cake sprinkled with raspberries, topped with syllabub and then scattered with almonds. It's simple, and it's perfect.

For the lemon-syrup loaf itself, see 'Cakes', p13, but double the amount of syrup stipulated: you want the cake drenched, not merely doused. In fact, you need only half the cake, but as you can't actually make half a cake, there will be some some left over – hardly a problem. If you want to make enough for 10 or 12, simply use the whole cake, and double the topping ingredients, below.

| | |
|---|---|
| 2 tablespoons flaked almonds | 300ml double cream |
| 8 tablespoons dry sherry | 1 lemon-syrup cake with double syrup |
| 4 tablespoons caster sugar | (see page 13) |
| 1/4 teaspoon rosewater (optional) | 2 punnets raspberries |
| juice and zest of 1 lemon | |

Put the flaked almonds into a dry frying pan and put over a medium to high heat to toast them. When they're golden and aromatic, remove to a plate and set aside to cool.

Mix the sherry, sugar, rosewater and lemon juice and zest in a bowl large enough to take the cream when whipped. I find the best way to grate the lemon zest is by using a Microplane fine grater: this way the peel's tender and shredded enough not to need straining later. Leave for an hour if you've got it, or else give it a good stir and make sure the sugar's dissolved fully. Slowly, while whisking by hand, add the double cream. Then – for ease – switch to an electric mixer and beat till airy and floppily bulky.

Slice half the cake onto a large oval plate, or one of whatever shape and size looks about right to you, and then empty out the punnets of raspberries on top. Flop over the syllabub and scatter the toasted almonds on top. Perfect for pudding outside on a summer's evening.

Serves 4–6.

## VARIATION
Make the syrup cake with lime instead of lemon and replace the raspberries with a paw-paw, deseeded, peeled, sliced and spritzed with lime. Make the syllabub with white rum instead of the sherry and 2 passionfruit in place of the lemon, and instead of topping with flaked almonds, just scoop out the beady pulp of 2 or 3 passionfruit.

# CHEESE BLINTZES

The cheese blintz is a wonderful thing: a pancake cooked on one side only, filled with a mixture of curd cheese, lemon zest, vanilla and egg yolk, folded into a parcel and then fried in butter before being splodged with some cold sour cream and perhaps some bitter fruit sauce. This is the traditional way, as eaten by generations of central Europeans; it comes originally, I think, from Hungary, but as with all dishes that are part of Jewish culinary culture, it's hard really to give an accurate provenance.

This version is changed only moderately. I've added some cream cheese to the curd, to make for a less grainy filling, and I've baked the pancakes rather than fry them. I could pretend this is to make the pudding more compatible with modern eating habits but it would scarcely be the truth. The reason is that it is a lot simpler.

I love these with the sour cream alone, but the blueberry sauce takes this pudding to another realm. It's a doddle to make, and the fact that you can now get fresh blueberries practically all year round (or resort to frozen) makes things even easier. If using frozen blueberries, don't thaw them before cooking them. And this blueberry sauce has wider applications: it can be poured on top of ice cream, cooled and added to cream-topped meringues, eaten with a plain sponge or spooned over a milky pudding.

for the blintzes:

**2 large eggs**
**150ml milk**
**75ml water**
**pinch of salt**
**6–7 heaped tablespoons plain flour**
**100g unsalted butter**

for the filling:

**350g curd cheese**
**200g cream cheese**
**1 large egg**
**50g caster sugar**

**zest of 1/2 lemon**
**few drops vanilla extract**

for the blueberry sauce:

**200g blueberries**
**45g caster sugar**
**juice of 1 lemon**
**1 teaspoon arrowroot**

to serve:

**2 heaped teaspoons (10g) icing sugar**
**1/2 teaspoon ground cinnamon**
**1 x 284ml carton sour cream**

First make the blintzes. Beat the eggs in a blender or by hand, and beat in the milk, water and salt. Add the flour a tablespoon at a time, blending well after each addition. Stop when the batter's acquired the consistency of double cream, then pour into a jug through a sieve to get rid of any lumps. Let stand for half an hour.

Meanwhile, melt the butter, and let cool a little. When the batter's resting time is up, stir a tablespoon of the butter into it. Heat a crêpe pan or small frying pan of about

20cm diameter and add a little of the melted butter, just to provide a light film. When hot, pour in enough batter from your jug to cover the bottom of the pan. Quickly swirl it around and drain off the excess back into the jug. (This will form a slight lip on the side of the pan where the batter's been poured back. You want this, so don't worry.)

Cook on one side only until the sides curl up a little and the bottom is dry. Turn out onto a plate, cooked side up, and cover with a tea towel or cloth. Then cook the rest, stacking the pancakes up under the tea towel until you've finished. You should get 12 blintzes.

If you want you can now make the filling, stuff the blintzes and freeze them (wrapped in foil packages of 3), then cook from frozen as indicated below, only for another 10 minutes or so. Otherwise, preheat the oven to 200°C/gas mark 6. Then, using some of the melted butter, brush the bottom of the dish you'll be cooking them in; something with the proportions of a lasagne dish should be about right. Mix the filling ingredients together until they're smoothly combined. Place a blintz, cooked side down, with the tab towards you. Dollop a generously heaped tablespoon of filling onto it, fold the tab over it, then fold the side edges in. Fold or roll over to make a rectangle and place in the prepared dish. Continue until all your pancakes are used up.

Brush generously with the melted butter that remains and cook for 20–30 minutes, when the blintzes will be turning golden and puffy. While they're cooking, get on with the sauce. Put the blueberries into a saucepan with the sugar and lemon juice, and bring to the boil over medium to high heat. Let bubble away for about 3 minutes until the berries have given out copious juice and have cooked down slightly. Stir in the arrowroot and cook for about 30 seconds or so, until the sauce is thick and glossy.

Remove the blintzes from the oven, and push the icing sugar and ground cinnamon through a fine sieve or tea strainer over them, so that they are well dusted. Put on the table along with one jug of cold sour cream, and another of warm blueberry sauce. Enjoy.

Makes 12, serves 6.

# CHEESECAKES

From blintzes to cheesecakes: it's a natural progression. Now, I don't really think of cheesecakes as pudding, and of course traditionally they're not. But in practice, I recognize, pudding-time is exactly when they're eaten; and all it takes is a handful of berries scattered on a plate alongside for them to be utterly convincing in this role.

## NEW YORK CHEESECAKE

I ate a cheesecake just like this in New York once. I couldn't quite work out what gave it that airy lightness until I registered that, unlike the creamy, smooth and dense cheese-cakes I'd always known, the whites of the eggs must have been whisked.

I know the cooking instructions look odd (and if you want, you can go for the water-bath option and the more straightforward approach of the following two cheese-cakes), but for me they're part of the Jewish cheesecake tradition.

for the base:

**250g digestive biscuits crushed to fine crumbs**

**150g unsalted butter, melted**

**225g plus 3 tablespoons caster sugar**

**24cm Springform tin**

for the topping:

**2 tablespoons cornflour**

**750g cream cheese**

**6 large eggs, separated**

**2 teaspoons vanilla extract**

**150ml double cream**

**150ml sour cream**

**1/2 teaspoon salt**

**zest of 1 lemon**

**icing sugar for dusting**

**raspberries or blackberries to serve**

Mix together the crushed biscuits, melted butter and 3 tablespoons of sugar, and press into the base of the Springform tin. Put into the fridge for about half an hour to set.

Preheat the oven to 170°C/gas mark 3. In a large bowl, mix together the remaining sugar and the cornflour. Beat in the cream cheese, egg yolks and vanilla, either by hand or using an electric beater. Slowly pour in both creams, beating constantly. Add the salt and lemon zest. Whisk the egg whites to stiff peaks, then fold into the cheese mixture. Scoop onto the chilled base. Bake for 1–1½ hours without opening the oven door, until the cheesecake is golden-brown on top. Turn off the heat and let the cake stand in the oven for 2 more hours. Then open the oven door, take it out and let it stand for a further hour. Serve chilled, dusted with icing sugar.

Serves 12–14.

# LONDON CHEESECAKE

If I had a New York cheesecake, I had to have a London one, and this is surely it. My paternal grandmother instructed me in the art of adding the final layer of sour cream, sugar and vanilla: and it's true, it does complete it.

I cannot tell you how much the velvety smoothness is enhanced by cooking the cheesecake in the water bath. It's not hard, though you really must wrap the tin twice in extra-strength tin foil. Once you've tried it this way, you won't even consider cooking it any other.

for the base:
**150g digestive biscuits**
**75g unsalted butter, melted or
   very soft**
**600g cream cheese**
**150g caster sugar**
**3 large eggs**
**3 large egg yolks**
**1 1/2 tablespoons vanilla extract**

**1 1/2 tablespoons lemon juice**
**20cm Springform tin**
**extra-strength tin foil**

for the topping:
**145ml tub sour cream**
**1 tablespoon caster sugar**
**1/2 teaspoon vanilla extract**

Process the biscuits until they are like crumbs, then add the butter and pulse again. Line the bottom of the Springform tin, pressing the biscuits in with your hands or the back of a spoon. Put the tin in the fridge to set, and preheat the oven to 180°C/gas mark 4.

Beat the cream cheese gently until it's smooth, then add the sugar. Beat in the eggs and egg yolks, then finally the vanilla and lemon juice. Put the kettle on.

Line the outside of the chilled tin with strong foil so that it covers the bottom and sides in one large piece, and then do the same again and put it into a roasting dish. This will protect the cheesecake from the water as it is cooked in its water bath.

Pour the cream-cheese filling into the chilled biscuit base, and then pour hot water from the recently boiled kettle into the roasting tin around the cheesecake. It should come about halfway up; don't overfill as it will be difficult to lift up the tin. Put it into the oven and cook for 50 minutes. It should feel set, but not rigidly so: you just need to be able to pour some sour cream over it so that it will sit on the surface. Whisk together the sour cream, sugar and vanilla for the topping and pour it over the cheesecake. Put it back in the oven and let it cook for a further 10 minutes.

Take the roasting tin out of the oven, then gingerly remove the Springform, unwrap it and stand it on a rack to cool. When it's cooled down completely, put it in the fridge, removing it 20 minutes before eating to take the chill off. Unmould and when you cut into it, plunge a knife in hot water first.

Serves 8.

# PASSIONFRUIT CHEESECAKE

I am usually such a purist about cheesecake, loathing those which look as if they've got a tin of pie-filling all over them, that I don't quite know what's come over me here. I was in a passionfruit phase when I first made it, and suddenly knew that a cheesecake flavoured with the juice of this fragrant fruit, sharpened with lime maybe, would be wonderful. It was. It's up to you whether you put pips or pulp over the finished cheesecake, but the shiny jet of the pips (which you've got left over from the strained juice) looks wonderful against the thick off-white of the cheesecake; and it also makes this taste somehow more like pudding, and less like something you might be eating mid-morning with a cup of coffee.

for the base:
**150g digestive biscuits**
**50g melted or soft unsalted butter**
**20cm Springform tin**
**extra-strength tin foil**

for the topping:
**600g cream cheese**
**125g caster sugar**

**3 large eggs**
**3 large egg yolks**
**200ml double cream**
**100ml passionfruit juice (from approximately 7 passionfruit pulped in the processor and sieved)**
**4–5 passionfruit to decorate**
**juice of 1/2 lime**

Preheat the oven to 170°C/gas mark 3. Make the base and prepare the tin as before. Beat the cheese until smooth, add the sugar, then whisk in the eggs and yolks one at a time. Stir in the cream and lime and passionfruit juices, mixing everything together thoroughly. Remember, though, that beating cheesecakes too vigorously will introduce too much air, which in turn will make them rise and crack later. One of the benefits, in this respect, of a food processor is that you don't whip much air in.

Put the kettle on, then line the Springform tin with foil as before. Place it in a roasting tin, then pour the cheesecake filling over the biscuit base. Pour the hot water from the recently boiled kettle into the roasting tin so that it comes about halfway up the foil, but making sure you can still carry it safely to the oven. Cook for an hour, by which time it will have browned a little on the edges and the middle should be set, although retaining a hint of a wobble underneath.

Cool on a rack out of the foil, and then refrigerate before unmoulding. If you can be patient, leave it overnight in the fridge: it will taste better.

Before eating, you can either spread with the reserved seeds or scoop out some more passion fruit to dollop all over the top. Your call.

Serves 8.

# JOE DOLCE'S ITALIAN CHEESECAKE

I have become a bit of a bore. I can't hear anyone talk about a delicious something or other someone in their family cooks without asking for the recipe. This is the cheesecake my friend Joe Dolce told me his grandmother, Edith Guerino, always used to make. He e-mailed it to me with the message 'Eat it and weep'. You'll see.

**12 large eggs**
**1¹/₂kg ricotta**
**275g caster sugar, plus more for**
   **sprinkling**

**1 teaspoon vanilla extract or**
   **Amaretto**
**25cm Springform tin**
**kitchen towels**

Preheat the oven to 180°C/gas mark 4.

Beat the eggs until well mixed. In a separate bowl, beat the ricotta until creamy, then gradually add the sugar, eggs and vanilla or Amaretto. Pour into the Springform tin, and bake for 1¹/₄ hours. Do NOT open the oven before this time is up. It may be ready then, you may need to give it another 15 minutes. It's ready when the edges have risen into a crown of bronzed goldenness and the middle is parchment-pale and smooth but resistant, just, to the touch. At this stage, switch off the oven and leave the door open and the cheesecake inside for a further hour. Then take it out of the oven and let it sit on a rack at room temperature till cool.

Now for the difficult bit. Line two large lipless plates with kitchen towels. Gradually loosen the sides of the cheesecake with a spatula. Unclip the mould and turn the cheesecake, topside-down, onto one of the plates. Remove the tin base, now cover the cake with the other plate and turn right-side up. Remove top plate, loosely cover the cake with the kitchen towels and put into the fridge. The kitchen towels should soak up any excess moisture – and there will be plenty. At least 12 hours in the fridge is necessary to let the cheesecake dry out adequately.

An hour before you want to eat it, remove the kitchen towels from the top and again turn the cake upside-down onto a kitchen-towel-lined plate, adding yet another layer of fresh kitchen towels on top. Finally, after an hour, turn the cake right-side up onto a large, flat serving plate and leave to get to room temperature.

All this turning this way and that is tricky, but if it's any consolation, I once broke it a bit, but when it had been wodged into place on the plate you didn't notice at all.

I think this is wonderful as it is, but for a pudding in the summer, halve about 500g of strawberries, sprinkle with caster sugar and a teaspoon or so of balsamic vinegar, cover with clingfilm and leave to macerate for about an hour. When you eat, serve the cheesecake on one plate, the jewel-bright strawberries on another.

Serves 14.

CHOCOLATE

# CHOCOLATE

If you asked me, I'd say that, unlike a lot of people I know, I am not particularly keen on chocolate. So why did this chapter grow more quickly than all the other chapters in the book? Well, it turns out there really are times when only chocolate will do. But for me, chocolate has to be good, not just brown and sweet. Actually, I'd go further: chocolate, in cooking, is better the less sweet, the more subtle it is.

While I don't want to get tiresomely prescriptive, it's obvious that the chocolate you choose is crucial to the brownies or cakes you make. I have a preference for Montgomery Moore buttons – dark, milk or white (the only white chocolate I'd ever want to eat); the chocolate is extraordinarily, seductively good, and melts beautifully and quickly, but these buttons can be hard to come by. Luckily, Nestlé do chocolate buttons and lumps now too, which you may find more easily in the supermarket. Buying your chocolate already chopped saves time, but is hardly an imperative. Just stock up on the best bars of chocolate you can find, such as Valrhona, and proper, cooked-earth-coloured cocoa. Look for brands containing a minimum of 70 per cent cocoa solids. When in doubt, or in need, phone the Chocolate Society (01423 322 230).

One last thing: melting. The traditional method is to put broken-up pieces of chocolate in a bowl and that bowl on top of a pan of simmering water, making sure that the base of the bowl never comes into contact with the water (it is the steam that melts it). I am, however a complete convert to the microwave for this. I'm not quite enough of a microwave queen, though, to be confident of giving you precise instructions. What I do is give 100g of broken-up chocolate about a minute on medium, then look to see if another minute's required. Not only is it easier to melt chocolate in the microwave than in a bowl over a pan of water, but it's much harder, even in my clumsy experience, to burn it so that it seizes up and becomes expensively unusable. Though if this does happen to you, you might be able to save it by whisking in, off the heat, a knob of butter or drop of vegetable oil. But it's safer to use the microwave and proceed slowly – a hard proviso for the impatient cook, I know, but if I can do it, so can you.

# DENSE CHOCOLATE LOAF CAKE

I start with this because I think it is the essence of all that is desirable in chocolate: its dark intensity isn't toyed with, nor upstaged by any culinary elaboration. This is the plainest of plain loaf cakes – but that doesn't convey the damp, heady aromatic denseness of it. To understand that, you just have to cook it. And as you'll see, that isn't hard at all.

I also think this makes a wonderful pudding, either by itself with ice cream or, as when my in-laws were round for lunch one Sunday, with a bowl of strawberries and a jug of white-chocolate rum custard. The latter is a fussier option, but there are times when that's, perversely, what we want.

But simply sliced, with a cup of tea or coffee, it's pretty damn dreamy: as damp and sticky as gingerbread and quite as aromatic. And I will confess that I absolutely love it spread with cold cream cheese.

**225g soft unsalted butter**
**375g dark muscovado sugar**
**2 large eggs, beaten**
**1 teaspoon vanilla extract**
**100g best dark chocolate, melted**

**200g plain flour**
**1 teaspoon bicarbonate of soda**
**250ml boiling water**
23 x 13 x 7cm loaf tin

Preheat the oven to 190°C/gas mark 5, put in a baking sheet in case of sticky drips later, and grease and line the loaf tin. The lining is important as this is a very damp cake: use parchment, Bake-O-Glide or one of those loaf-tin-shaped paper cases.

Cream the butter and sugar, either with a wooden spoon or with an electric hand-held mixer, then add the eggs and vanilla, beating in well. Next, fold in the melted and now slightly cooled chocolate, taking care to blend well but being careful not to overbeat. You want the ingredients combined: you don't want a light airy mass. Then gently add the flour, to which you've added the bicarb, alternately spoon by spoon, with the boiling water until you have a smooth and fairly liquid batter. Pour into the lined loaf tin, and bake for 30 minutes. Turn the oven down to 170°C/gas mark 3 and continue to cook for another 15 minutes. The cake will still be a bit squidgy inside, so an inserted cake-tester or skewer won't come out completely clean.

Place the loaf tin on a rack, and leave to get completely cold before turning it out. (I often leave it for a day or so: like gingerbread, it improves.) Don't worry if it sinks in the middle: indeed, it will do so because it's such a dense and damp cake.

Makes 8–10 slices.

## WHITE-CHOCOLATE RUM CUSTARD

And here's one way of transforming your cake into the perfect Sunday-lunch pudding. Simply follow the instructions for the custard on p134, omitting the vanilla, using only a scant tablespoonful of sugar and adding 1–2 tablespoons of dark rum. Then, when the custard's thick, beat in 100g of melted white chocolate off the heat. Leave to cool in a jug or bowl, but remember to cover the top with a piece of damp baking parchment to prevent it forming a skin. Throw some halved, lightly sugared strawberries into a bowl to serve alongside if the idea appeals.

## VARIATION

I sometimes make these aromatic chocolate cupcakes to take as a present if we're going away for the weekend: they look so wonderful studded with gold Smarties, though actually a plain, shiny-brown Minstrel would have a certain chic allure.

for the cakes:

**110g unsalted butter**

**200g dark muscovado sugar**

**1 large egg, beaten**

**1/2 teaspoon vanilla extract**

**50g dark chocolate, melted and cooled a little**

**100g plain flour**

**1/2 teaspoon bicarbonate soda**

**125ml boiling water**

**12-bun muffin tin with paper cases**

for the icing:

**175g dark chocolate**

**75g milk chocolate**

**200ml double cream**

**1/2 teaspoon vanilla extract**

**12 gold Smarties, gold leaf or other decorations of your choice**

Preheat the oven to 180°C/gas mark 4.

Using the method above, make the batter and fill the 12 muffin paper cases in the muffin tin. Bake for 30 minutes, remove from the tin and cool on a rack.

To make the icing, break all the chocolate into pieces (if no children are eating these you may prefer to use all dark chocolate) and heat with the cream and vanilla in a saucepan until it has melted. Whisk until it's a good consistency for icing, and spoon some onto each thoroughly cooled cake. Spread with the back of the spoon and stud each one with a gold Smartie or decorate as you wish. Leave to set somewhere cool, though preferably not in the fridge.

# SOUR-CREAM CHOCOLATE CAKE WITH SOUR-CREAM ICING

For some reason, this is the only chocolate cake my daughter likes. Obviously, she has more sophisticated tastes than her mother.

It comes by way of, but not entirely from, the great American cake-maker Rose Levy Beranbaum, and the sour cream provides a wonderful mouth-filling smoothness.

for the cake:

**200g plain flour**
**200g caster sugar**
**3/4 teaspoon baking powder**
**1/4 teaspoon bicarbonate of soda**
**1/2 teaspoon salt**
**200g soft unsalted butter**
**40g best cocoa**
**150ml sour cream**
**2 large eggs**
**1 1/2 teaspoons vanilla extract**

2 x 20cm sandwich tins, buttered and
    lined

for the icing:

**80g milk chocolate**
**80g dark chocolate**
**75g unsalted butter**
**125ml sour cream**
**1 teaspoon vanilla extract**
**1 tablespoon golden syrup**
**300g golden icing sugar, sieved (plus**
    **more if needed)**
**1/2 teaspoon hot water**

Preheat the oven to 180°C/gas mark 4.

Combine the flour, sugar, baking powder, bicarb and salt in a large bowl. Then, using an electric mixer, add the butter. In a wide-mouthed measuring jug, whisk together the cocoa, sour cream, eggs and vanilla, then slowly add this cocoa mixture to the ingredients in the bowl, beating until thoroughly mixed.

Pour the batter into the prepared tins and bake for 30 minutes; when they're ready the cakes should be starting to shrink back from the edges of the tins. Leave for 10 minutes in their tins on racks, then turn out to cool.

To make the icing, melt the chocolate and butter in a microwave, or in a bowl over hot water. Let cool a little, then stir in the sour cream, vanilla and syrup. Add the sieved icing sugar and a little hot water, blending until smooth. When you've got the texture right – thick enough to cover but supple enough to spread, adding more icing sugar or water as required – you can ice the cakes.

Cut four strips of baking parchment and make an outline of a square with them on a flat plate. Sit one cake on top of the paper pieces, spread with icing, sit the second cake on top and use the rest of the icing to cover the top and sides. Leave spatula-smooth or swirl with a knife as you wish.

Serves 6–8.

# STORE-CUPBOARD CHOCOLATE-ORANGE CAKE

This is a different sort of chocolate cake: the sort you can make in a few minutes once you get home from work. Hardly any trouble, and you've got a gorgeously aromatic cake either for pudding or just to eat, as supper in its entirety, in front of the television. I think of it as a larder-standby because I tend to have all the ingredients in the house at any given time and if I don't the local corner shop stocks them all.

Even if you don't like marmalade, you should try this: all you taste is orange. Lisa Grillo, who is one of my chief guinea pigs, Italian, and thinks marmalade is a peculiar British perversion, loves it.

**125g unsalted butter**

**100g dark chocolate, broken into pieces**

**300g good, thin-cut marmalade**

**150g caster sugar**

**pinch of salt**

**2 large eggs, beaten**

**150g self-raising flour**

**20cm Springform tin, buttered and floured**

Preheat the oven to 180°C/gas mark 4.

Put the butter in a heavy-bottomed saucepan and put over a low heat to melt. When it's nearly completely melted, stir in the chocolate. Leave for a moment to begin softening, then take the pan off the heat and stir with a wooden spoon until the butter and chocolate are smooth and melted. Now add the marmalade, sugar, salt and eggs. Stir with your wooden spoon and when all is pretty well amalgamated, beat in the flour bit by bit. Put into your prepared tin and bake for about 50 minutes or until a cake-tester or skewer comes out clean. Cool in the pan on a rack for 10 minutes before turning out.

You can eat this still slightly warm (with crème fraîche, perhaps) or cold. For what it's worth, I haven't yet cooked it without someone asking for the recipe. It is, however, a plain-looking cake, and although I have no objection to that, if you want something slightly more elaborate, you could just dust it with icing sugar pushed through a tea strainer (and obviously this goes for all cakes); and if you wanted to go one further, get a cake stencil (which you can you buy in packets containing a few designs, decorative or seasonal), stick on masking tape handles (imperative if you're to lift the stencil off the cake without blurring your design), place on the cake and dust the icing sugar on top. I am particularly partial to the star and leaf designs – and I don't care who knows it.

Serves 6.

## VARIATIONS

As I've already said, you can substitute the jam of your choice, and I'd suggest, first off, raspberry or apricot; but you should also consider making this with the marmalade's weight in dark, aromatic and velvety prune purée, which supermarkets tend to sell now, either in their upmarket-larder bits or in the baking aisle. If you're going for this prune-thick chocolate cake, serve with crème fraîche to which you've added a few crucial drops of Armagnac; indeed, you could add a slug to the cake too, or just pour a little over as soon as you unmould it.

## CHOCOLATE-CHESTNUT CAKE

This is a seriously compelling piece of cake-bakery: definitely pudding – and an elegant one at that – rather than afternoon tea, though I think I might be able to force a slice down with a cup of coffee at unscheduled moments in the day. Really, you need serve nothing with it: apart from anything else, it's not so sweet as to need the masking properties of cream.

| | |
|---|---|
| **435g tin unsweetened chestnut purée** | **pinch of salt** |
| **125g soft unsalted butter** | **50g caster sugar** |
| **1 teaspoon vanilla extract** | **25g light muscovado sugar** |
| **1 tablespoon dark rum** | **22cm Springform tin, greased** |
| **6 large eggs, separated** | **and lined** |
| **250g melted chocolate** | |

Preheat the oven to 180°C/gas mark 4.

Beat the chestnut purée with the butter, then add the vanilla, rum, egg yolks and melted chocolate, blending well. I use my KitchenAid here, but an ordinary electric hand-held mixer would be fine – or even a bowl and wooden spoon. In another large bowl, whip the egg whites with the salt until they are foamy. Add the caster sugar gradually to form stiffer, glossy peaks, and then sprinkle the muscovado sugar over and either fold in or whisk in slowly. Fold the whites, gently but confidently, into the chestnut mixture, a third at a time.

Pour into the tin and cook for 45 minutes, until the cake has risen and is firm on top; it will look dry and cracked, but don't panic: it won't taste dry, and the cracks don't matter a damn.

Cool in the tin for 20 minutes, and then turn out on a rack.

When you want to eat it, dust with icing sugar and serve with modest pride.

Serves 8–10.

# TORTA ALLA GIANDUIA

Or, less fancily, Nutella Cake. This is a fabulously easy cake, another that I draw into service for birthdays: the hazelnuts on top somehow give it a burnished, ceremonial look.

Please don't feel obliged to rush out and buy a bottle of Frangelico, the most divinely déclassé hazelnut liqueur, its monkish derivation signalled by the rope that is hung from the holy-brother-shaped bottle.

I use hazelnuts bought ready-ground, but ones you grind yourself in the processor will provide more nutty moistness.

for the cake:

**6 large eggs, separated**
**pinch of salt**
**125g soft unsalted butter**
**400g Nutella (1 large jar)**
**1 tablespoon Frangelico, rum or water**
**100g ground hazelnuts**
**100g dark chocolate, melted**

**23cm Springform tin, greased and**
   **lined**

for the icing:

**100g hazelnuts (peeled weight)**
**125ml double cream**
**1 tablespoon Frangelico, rum or water**
**125g dark chocolate**

Preheat the oven to 180°C/gas mark 4.

In a large bowl, whisk the egg whites and salt until stiff but not dry. In a separate bowl, beat the butter and Nutella together, and then add the Frangelico (or whatever you're using), egg yolks and ground hazelnuts. Fold in the cooled, melted chocolate, then lighten the mixture with a large dollop of egg white, which you can beat in as roughly as you want, before gently folding the rest of them in a third at a time. Pour into the prepared tin and cook for 40 minutes or until the cake's beginning to come away at the sides, then let cool on a rack.

Toast the hazelnuts in a dry frying pan until the aroma wafts upwards and the nuts are golden-brown in parts: keep shaking the pan so that they don't burn on one side and stay too pallid on others. Transfer to a plate and let cool. This is imperative: if they go on the ganache while hot, it'll turn oily. (Believe me, I speak from experience.)

In a heavy-bottomed saucepan, add the cream, liqueur or water and chopped chocolate, and heat gently. Once the chocolate's melted, take the pan off the heat and whisk until it reaches the right consistency to ice the top of the cake. Unmould the cooled cake carefully, leaving it on the base as it will be too difficult to get such a damp cake off in one piece. Ice the top with the chocolate icing, and dot thickly with the whole, toasted hazelnuts.

If you have used Frangelico, put shot glasses on the table and serve it with the cake.
Serves 8.

# CHOCOLATE-PISTACHIO CAKE

This is a straightforward cake to make, though an expensive one. While I know that pistachios cost more than other nuts, I can't help but prefer them, especially here. There's no need to ice it, but if you do, it looks spectacular in a rewardingly subtle way. It's a very useful cake to make for an elegant birthday dinner. I adore raspberries with it: the dark glow of the chocolate and the waxy jade of the nuts, perfect partners as they are, come newly alive with the matt-ruby of those beaded berries.

for the cake:
**150g dark chocolate**
**150g caster sugar**
**150g pistachios**
**150g soft unsalted butter**
**6 large eggs, separated**
**¹/₂ lemon**
**pinch of salt**
23cm Springform tin, lined and
   buttered

for the icing:
**150g dark chocolate**
**150ml double cream**
**drop of orange-flower water,**
   **optional**
**2–4 tablespoons coarsely chopped**
   **or slivered pistachios**

Preheat oven to 190°C/gas mark 5.

Melt the chocolate in the microwave or double boiler. Process 50g of the sugar with the pistachios until they are like dust. Add the butter and another 50g of the sugar and process until smooth. Add the egg yolks one at a time, pulsing after each, then, with the motor running, slowly pour in the cooled, melted chocolate.

Wipe the inside of a bowl with the lemon half, and in it whisk the egg whites with the salt. When peaks begin to form, slowly add the remaining 50g sugar until gleaming, glossy and firm. Add a big dollop to the cake batter in the processor and pulse a couple of times to lighten the mixture. Now, a third at a time, dollop the cake batter over the whites and fold in gently but firmly.

Pour into the prepared tin, and bake for 20 minutes, then turn down to 180°C/gas mark 4 for a further 20–25 minutes, or until cooked. When the cake's ready it should be starting to come away from the sides of the tin. Leave to cool in its tin for 15 minutes on a wire rack before unmoulding. Don't ice until it's completely cold.

The icing is once again a simple ganache; though the orange-flower water, if you've got it, does add a rather *Thousand and One Nights* note, which goes well with the exotic fragrance of the nuts themselves. Break the chocolate into pieces and put them in a heavy-based saucepan with the cream and orange-flower water, if using. When the chocolate's melted, start whisking and when your mixture's thick enough to coat, but no more, pour it over the cake on its plate. I like a few drips, so just pour over and let it run down the sides of the cake; however, if you want a hatbox affair, let the icing get a little thicker by whisking some more and spread the sides with a spatula dipped in oil. And the less you touch this, the glossier it will dry. Sprinkle over the pistachios: as few or as many as you like, although here I feel less is more.

Serve with crème fraîche, plain or with a drop of orange-flower water whisked in. Serves 10–12.

## CHOCOLATE CHEESECAKE

If you'd ever told me that I'd write a recipe for chocolate cheesecake, I'd have denied it in horror. In theory, the cheesecake purist within me shudders at the idea of something so unorthodox, but for some reason I made one and I found that I shivered only with delight.

125g digestive biscuits
50g very, very soft or melted
  unsalted butter
500g cream cheese
150g golden caster sugar
3 large eggs

3 large egg yolks
175ml sour cream
1/2–1 teaspoon lime juice (to taste)
150g plain chocolate, melted
20cm Springform tin

Preheat the oven to 180°C/gas mark 4 and put the kettle on to boil.

Process the biscuits and butter together and press into the bottom of the tin, then stick the tin in the fridge until the filling is ready.

Beat the cream cheese until smooth, then mix in the sugar. Add the eggs and yolks, one by one, beating in after each addition. Now pour in the sour cream and the lime juice and beat until smooth and creamy. Taste to see if you want a sourer base-note than this and, if so, add more lime juice. Gently fold in the melted chocolate; you want a cheesecake marbled with dark chocolate, so don't combine fully.

Line the Springform with foil on the outside, and then tear off another square and repeat the exercise. Stand the tin in a roasting dish and fill it with the mixture. Pour hot water from the recently boiled kettle into the roasting tray to come 2–3 centimetres up the side of the cake tin and place in the oven to cook for about 1 hour.

When the cheesecake's ready it should have browned a little on the edges and the centre should be just set on top, with a hint of wobble underneath. Remove the cake tin and tear away the foil. Sit on a rack to cool, then refrigerate before unmoulding and leaving it to get back to room temperature.

Serves 8.

# CHOCOLATE MOUSSE CAKE

This is exactly what it says it is – as you can see from the picture. So if you feel like pure mousse, no cake, then chill it in a bowl rather than baking it in a tin.

For some reason people are put off by the words 'water bath', but if you think about it, it isn't so very hard to wrap a cake tin in foil, plonk it in a roasting tin and then, when the cake mixture's in, pour hot water into that tin. And that little bit of extra effort makes a cake of such a dreamy, light texture.

| | |
|---|---|
| **300g best dark chocolate** | **100g caster sugar** |
| **50g best milk chocolate** | **1 tablespoon vanilla extract** |
| **175g unsalted butter** | **pinch of salt** |
| **8 large eggs, separated** | **23cm Springform tin** |
| **100g light muscovado sugar** | **extra-strong tin foil** |

Preheat the oven to 180°C/gas mark 4 and put the kettle on to boil.

Line the inside of the Springform with foil, making sure you press the foil well into the sides and bottom of the tin so that it forms a smooth surface. This will prevent water getting into the cake when it is cooked in its water bath.

Melt the chocolate and butter in a microwave or double boiler, and let it cool. In another bowl, beat the eggs and sugars until very thick and pale, as creamy as mayonnaise: the mixture should form and fall in ribbons when you lift up the whisk. Stir in the vanilla and salt, and then the cooled chocolate mixture. Whisk the egg whites in a large bowl, until soft peaks form, then lighten the chocolate mixture with a briskly beaten-in dollop of whites before gently folding the rest of them into it.

Pour the cake batter into the foil-lined Springform, which you have placed in a large roasting tin. Add hot water from the recently boiled kettle to come about 2½cm up the sides of the cake tin and carefully put the roasting tin with its cargo into the oven.

Cook for 50 minutes–1 hour. The inside of the cake will be damp and moussy, but the top should look cooked and dry. Let it cool completely on a cooling rack before releasing it from the tin. This calls for a little bit of patience, because you will need to peel the foil gently away from the sides. Just go slowly and remember that this is a very damp cake, and you won't be able to prise it away from its foil-lined base – though it's easy enough to tear off excess foil once you've set the cake on its plate. Dust with icing sugar if you want, and serve with crème fraîche and maybe some raspberries.

Serves 6–8.

# MOLTEN CHOCOLATE BABYCAKES

These are the acceptable face of culinary cute: their intensity guarantees the triumph of chic over prettiness. And, what's more, they're easy to make. You can make the mixture up a few hours in advance and put it ready and waiting in the prepared tins in the fridge until you want to cook them, which must be at the moment you're ready to eat them. You might think that preparing the tins sounds fiddly, but in fact the job is just demanding enough to make one feel uncharacteristically competent in a *Blue Peter* kind of a way, but not so much that any actual dexterity is required.

This recipe comes by way of the great James McNair, America's gastro-compendium made flesh.

**50g soft unsalted butter, plus more for greasing**
**350g best dark chocolate**
**150g caster sugar**
**4 large eggs, beaten with a pinch of salt**

**1 teaspoon vanilla extract**
**50g plain or Italian 00 flour**
**6 individual pudding moulds, buttered baking parchment**

Unless you are making these up in advance, preheat the oven to 200°C/gas mark 6, putting in a baking sheet at the same time. Lay 3 of the moulds on a sheet of doubled baking parchment. Draw round them, remove, and then cut out the discs as marked. Press them all into the base of the tins.

Melt the chocolate and let it cool slightly. Cream together the butter and sugar, and gradually beat in the eggs and salt, then the vanilla. Now add the flour, and when all is smoothly combined scrape in the cooled chocolate, blending it to a smooth batter.

Divide the batter between the 6 moulds, quickly whip the baking sheet out of the oven, arrange the little tins on it and replace in the oven. Cook for 10–12 minutes (the extra 2 minutes will be needed if the puddings are fridge-cold when you start) and as soon as you take them out of the oven, tip out these luscious babycakes onto small plates or shallow bowls. Serve these with whipped double cream, the same unwhipped in a jug, crème fraîche, crème anglaise or ice cream.

Serves 6.

# CHOCOLATE-COFFEE VOLCANO

Despite a move towards chic simplification, sometimes we need a touch of vulgarity in our lives. This pudding certainly provides that. The idea came from a pudding I had at Spago, the LA restaurant, comprising chocolate Bundt cake stuffed with raspberries and topped with crème brulée. This is my version: a light chocolate cake baked in a Bundt mould – that's to say, a turban-shaped one with a hole in the middle – its hole, once the cake's turned out and dampened with liqueur, filled with chopped walnuts with a creamy coffee custard poured over; finally, imagine sugar sprinkled over and that sugar set alight so that you've got a hard, crackle-glazed top. And funnily enough, although it is very much in composition and appearance a swaggering *pièce de résistance*, it's easy to make. Just isolate the three separate tasks: the making of the cake, which is infant-school easy; the making of the custard, which is so eggy it scarcely takes 5 minutes; and the final torching to turn the coffee custard into café crème brulée. Then – pa-dah!

for the cake:

**300g caster sugar**

**140g plain flour, preferably Italian 00**

**80g cocoa powder**

**2 teaspoons baking powder**

**1 teaspoon bicarbonate of soda**

**¼ teaspoon salt**

**4 large eggs, separated, plus 2 more egg whites (from the yolks you need for the café crème)**

**125ml vegetable oil**

**125ml water**

**1 teaspoon vanilla extract**

25cm Bundt tin, oiled

for the café crème:

**225ml double cream**

**6 large egg yolks**

**3 tablespoons light muscovado sugar**

**1 tablespoon instant espresso powder**

for the topping:

**approximately 12 teaspoons (i.e., 4 tablespoons) Tia Maria or rum**

**125g chopped walnuts**

**4 tablespoons demerara sugar**

chef's kitchen blowtorch

It makes sense to get on with the custard first. So, warm the double cream gently in a saucepan. Mix the yolks, sugar and espresso powder together in a bowl, and pour the warm cream over this mixture, whisking to combine. Pour the mixture back into the rinsed-out saucepan and cook over a medium heat, stirring constantly, until it thickens; with this ratio of yolks to liquid, it won't take any time at all. Pour into a bowl, cover with wet baking parchment and leave to cool.

Get on with the cake as soon as you've made the custard. It, too, must cool before assembly. (Indeed, you may well find it easier to make both cake and custard a day in advance.) Preheat the oven to 180°C/gas mark 4, putting in a baking sheet as you do so. In a large bowl, mix together 200g of the caster sugar, the flour, cocoa, baking powder, bicarb and salt. I don't bother to sift if I'm using 00 flour; otherwise, you should. In a measuring jug, whisk together the yolks, oil, water and vanilla. Pour over the dry ingredients gradually, beating to combine.

In another bowl, whisk the 6 egg whites until they are foamy and forming soft peaks. Add the remaining 100g of sugar, a spoonful at a time, still whisking, till the whites are thick and shiny and hold their shape. Briskly beat a large dollop of whites into the cake mixture to lighten it, then, a third at a time, fold in the remaining whites.

Pour the mixture into the oiled tin and place on the baking sheet in the pre-heated oven. Bake for 40 minutes, by which time the cake should be springy and coming away from the sides of the tin. Let the cake cool in its tin on a rack for 25 minutes before turning it out.

Pour or sprinkle the Tia Maria – or rum – onto the top of the cake, letting the liqueur soak in after each teaspoon. Of course, you could use tablespoons or just pour from the bottle, but you do want to make sure the cake's moistened rather than drenched.

When you are ready to serve, place the cake on a plate with a lip – or an almost-flat wide bowl – and fill the centre with the walnuts. Pour the cold custard into the remaining space in the centre, letting it overflow a little over the shoulders, so to speak, and the sides. Sprinkle the demerara sugar, a little at a time, so that it doesn't soak in, on top of the cake, and use the blowtorch to caramelize the top.

Serves 8.

# CHOCOLATE-MARSALA CAKE

Since *How to Eat* was awash with Marsala, I have tried to limit its inclusion here. Nevertheless, the one true thing about ourselves is our palate, and so you will see it included here and there to add resiny depth to whipped creams or a mascarpone filling, in the same way I often reach for the smoky intensity of a slug of muscat. This cake could, on reflection, use either – and if you were making it for a pudding, it might make sense to use muscat and serve the rest of the bottle to drink with it. If that's the case, reduce the sugar in the cake to 150g, though leave the icing as is.

for the cake:

**100g unsalted butter**

**100g dark chocolate, broken up**

**4 large eggs**

**175g caster sugar**

**50g self-raising flour, sifted 3 times**

**3 tablespoons Marsala**

**22cm Springform tin, greased and lined**

for the icing:

**100g dark chocolate**

**1 tablespoon Marsala**

**100ml double cream**

Preheat the oven to 180°C/gas mark 4.

Melt the butter and chocolate together in the microwave or a double boiler, and then set aside to cool slightly. Beat the eggs and sugar together until thick, pale and moussy, and greatly increased in volume; it should double, triple even. Gently fold the sifted flour into the egg mixture, trying not to lose all of the air. Now fold the butter and chocolate very carefully into the cake mixture. (I should say at this point that of all the uncooked cake mixtures in this book this is without doubt my favourite: leave yourself a decent amount in the bowl for scraping-out purposes.) Pour into the tin and cook for 35 minutes, by which time the top should be firm and the cake underneath dense and desirably damp.

Cool on a rack for 5 minutes, and then pour over the Marsala. I find it easier to do this by the teaspoonful so that the liquid is evenly distributed. Leave the cake to cool completely before releasing it from its tin.

So, the icing: melt the chocolate, Marsala and cream in a heavy-bottomed saucepan over a gentle heat. Take it off the heat, and whisk until it reaches a good icing consistency: smooth, thick, but not solid. I like to spread this just on the very top of the cake, which anyway sinks on cooling so that you should have a roughly circular sunken pond to fill, leaving an outline of cooked-cake rim. When set, you're left, beautifully, with a Sacher-shiny disc of ganache suspended on top of this dusty-brown, matt cake.

Serves 8–10.

# GOOEY CHOCOLATE STACK

This is for those days or evenings when you want to usher a little something out of the kitchen that makes you thrill at the sheer pleasure you've conjured up. It isn't about showing off, it's about intensity: meringue that's marshmallow-gungy within and chewily crisp without, cocoa-flecked and feathery light; together with a slick, glossy crème patissière into which you've stirred the darkest of dark chocolates. I didn't think I believed in such things, but this is it: chocolate heaven.

Don't panic at the idea of crème patissière. It could hardly be easier: remember that the flour stabilizes it, so you don't have the knife-edge worry of its splitting; plus it's made in advance, as are the pavlova layers, so that it's just a simple stacking operation at the end.

You don't need to use the chopped pistachios I've suggested to scatter over the top: hazelnuts, almonds, indeed any nuts, would be fine; or you could go divinely retro with crystallized violets.

for the meringue discs:
**6 large egg whites**
**300g golden caster sugar**
**3 tablespoons cocoa powder**
**1 teaspoon red wine vinegar**
3 baking sheets

for the crème patissière:
**6 large egg yolks**

**100g golden caster sugar**
**2 tablespoons cocoa powder**
**2 tablespoons plain flour**
**300ml full-fat milk**
**300ml double cream**
**100g the best dark chocolate, melted**
**1 teaspoon vanilla extract**
**20g pistachios, chopped**

Preheat the oven to 140°C/gas mark 1.

Line the baking sheets with parchment and draw a 20cm circle on each one. The simplest way to do this is simply to find a bowl or cake tin with the desired dimensions, plonk it on and draw round it.

Whisk the egg whites until stiff, then add the sugar a spoonful at a time, beating in well after each addition. Believe me – and I speak as someone often criminally impatient – it does make life easier to go slowly here. Sprinkle over the cocoa and vinegar and then fold in gently but firmly.

Divide the dusky meringue between the 3 circles, spreading evenly. You don't need to worry too much about beating the air out of them as you smooth; I find they withstand a modicum of brutality.

Cook for 1 hour, then turn off the oven, leaving the meringues in until cool. Often, I just make them before I go to bed and leave them in the switched-off oven overnight. It makes for less hanging about. And as long as you keep them airtight, with sheets of baking parchment in between, you can do these a good week or so in advance.

Now for the crème patissière: beat the egg yolks and sugar together, then add the cocoa and flour, whisking well. Warm the milk and cream in a saucepan, then, whisking, pour this onto the eggs and sugar before pouring everything back into the saucepan on the heat and, stirring constantly, bring it to the boil. When the mixture has thickened, take it off the heat and stir in the melted chocolate and vanilla.

Let it cool now, but avoid putting it into the fridge as it will become too solid. You can stop it forming a skin either by covering with buttered baking parchment or greaseproof paper or by sieving a layer of icing sugar over. What I often prefer to do, however, and which cuts out more waiting around, is to plunge the saucepan into a sinkful of iced water and just keep stirring: it doesn't take long to get cold.

To assemble the cake, place one of the meringue discs on a flat plate (I rather like those tea-shop cake-stands, though preferably in glass), spread with a third of the chocolate cream, then carry on layering. Scatter over the chopped pistachios, which will gleam out, a tender grass-green against the dark chocolate. Then just cut in: and you'll find that it gives the illusion of a fine layering of multi-stacked, custard-bellied wafers; this is because each meringue, with its soft innards and crisp carapace, looks and tastes like three layers, not one.

This easily feeds 10 or 12 people, but I wouldn't let the fact that you've got fewer stop you from making it.

## CHOCOLATE MACAROONS

Look at the picture of the pistachio macaroons on p52, imagine them in chocolate and that's what we're talking about here. I suppose you could also describe them as fat little versions of the gooey chocolate stack above. Though description is irrelevant: the utter gorgeousness of just one mouthful of these chocolate macaroons – for which I have Kate Mellor's sister Lucy to thank – reveals the rank inadequacy of language. Eat them: that's enough.

for the macaroons:
**250g icing sugar**
**125g ground almonds**
**25g cocoa powder**
**4 large egg whites**
**25g caster sugar**
**2 baking sheets**

**1cm plain icing nozzle and bag**

for the ganache filling:
**90ml (6 tablespoons) double cream**
**150g plain chocolate, chopped**
**45g (3 tablespoons) unsalted butter**

Preheat the oven to 180°C/gas mark 4 and line the baking sheets with parchment or Bake-O-Glide.

Sift together the icing sugar, ground almonds and cocoa powder. Whisk the egg whites until half-stiff, sprinkle over the caster sugar and continue whisking until very stiff, but not dry. Gradually fold in the sifted ingredients.

Fit the icing nozzle into the bag, sit it in a tall glass, turn the bag back to form a cuff and fill with the macaroon mixture. Pipe out 5cm rounds on the lined baking sheets, then leave to stand for 15 minutes to form a skin.

Bake for 12–15 minutes: you want them dry on top, but still chewy underneath. Remove to cool on a wire rack, and when they are cool, sandwich with the ganache, which you make by heating all the ingredients in a saucepan until the chocolate's just melted. Off the heat, whisk until thick, and when cool spread with a knife on the underside of one macaroon, then stick another macaroon to it. Continue till you've used all of them up.

Makes 36 rounds, i.e., 18 macaroons.


## CHOCOLATE-RASPBERRY TARTS


With their dark chocolate cases and their white-chocolate mascarpone filling, these look fancy enough, but when you eat them what strikes you is their cleanly balanced simplicity. The almost dry bitterness of the cocoa-darkened pastry balances the rich, fat creaminess of the filling, which in turn is perfectly offset by the tart, neatly-beaded berries.

I won't pretend that the chocolate pastry is that easy to work with. Yes, it does tear easily, but that doesn't matter, because it patches up perfectly too. Maybe the first time you make these you should try to get just 4 little tarts out of the dough; later on, when you're more confident, you should be able to make 6 without trouble.

Like anything which relies in great part on assembly, these are much easier to make than you might think.

for the tarts:
**175g plain flour, preferably Italian 00**
**30g cocoa powder**
**50g caster sugar**
**1/4 teaspoon salt**
**125g unsalted butter**
**1 large egg yolk**
**1 tablespoon iced water**

for the filling:
**50g white chocolate**
**250g mascarpone**
**100ml double cream**
**approximately 500g raspberries**
**6 x 12cm tartlet tins with loose**
    **bottoms**

Your best bet is to make the pastry in a food processor, so put the flour, cocoa, sugar and salt into the bowl and pulse to blend. Cut the butter into small pieces and pulse with the flour mixture until it looks crumbly. Beat the yolk and iced water together and add, down the funnel, to bind the pastry. When it starts to clump together, turn it out of the processor and work it together with your hands into two discs. Wrap them in clingfilm and rest the pastry in the fridge for at least 30 minutes.

Roll out one of the dough discs; it will be quite a dry pastry because of the cocoa, so don't be too heavy-handed with the flour on your rolling surface. Then, using a tart case as a guide, cut at least 3 rough squares or circles slightly bigger than the tin. Ease the pastry squares into the tins – don't worry if they break, just patch them as best you can – and cut off the excess pastry. Do this with all 6 tins, and then freeze them for about 30 minutes or until they feel frozen. While the pastry's in the freezer, turn on the oven to 180°C/gas mark 4, and slip in a baking sheet to heat up at the same time.

Put the tartlets straight into the oven on the baking sheet, and cook for 10–15 minutes or until the pastry feels cooked and dry. The freezing plus the fact that the individual area is small means that they shouldn't puff up, which in turn means we're doing without the beans and all that blind-baking palaver. While the pastry's cooking, you might melt the chocolate for the filling, either in the microwave or in a double boiler.

When the pastry cases are cool, slip them out of their tins and finish the filling. This is simple: you just beat the mascarpone and double cream together and fold in the melted, slightly cooled, white chocolate. Go gently with your whisking: you don't want this too thick; however, a little extra unwhipped double cream stirred in at the end will thin it down if necessary. Fill the pastry cases with the cream, and then top with raspberries.

Makes 6.

# PAIN-AU-CHOCOLAT PUDDING

Of course you can make a thoroughly chocolate bread-and-butter pudding, either by adding melted chocolate or cocoa to the eggy custard, or simply by using a sliced-up chocolate loaf. But if you ask me, you're better off with this gentler, subtler take on what a chocolate bread-and-butter pudding might be: all I've done is slice up some stale pains au chocolat. It looks beautiful and tastes divine.

If you want to, by all means replace the 500ml each of double cream and milk with 1 litre of single cream.

**3–4 stale pains au chocolat**
**500ml milk**
**500ml double cream**
**3 tablespoons caster sugar**
**1 large egg**

**4 large egg yolks**
**1/2 teaspoon vanilla extract**
ovenproof dish with a capacity of
    approximately 1 1/2 litres

Preheat the oven to 160°C/gas mark 3.

Butter your ovenproof dish (I always use one of those old-fashioned oval creamware dishes), cut up the pains au chocolat – I cut rough slices of about a centimetre – and arrange them in the dish. Put the milk and cream into a pan and bring near to boiling point. Whisk the egg, the yolks and the sugar in a large wide-mouthed measuring jug. When the milk and cream are nearly boiling, pour over the eggs and sugar, whisking continuously. Add the vanilla and then pour over the slices of pain au chocolat and leave to soak for 10 minutes.

Transfer to the preheated oven and cook for about 45 minutes, or until the pudding is softly set. I can't tell you how comforting this is.

Serves 6.

# BROWNIES

I don't understand why people don't make brownies all the time – they're so easy and so wonderful. My friend Justine Picardie gave me the idea for setting the brownies so gloriously alight when she asked me to make them for her husband's birthday. Ever since then, I've copied the idea: brownies are much quicker to make than a cake, and they look so wonderful piled up in a rough-and-tumble pyramid spiked with birthday candles. And I'd much rather eat a brownie than a piece of birthday cake any day; I think most people would.

**375g soft unsalted butter**
**375g best-quality dark chocolate**
**6 large eggs**
**1 tablespoon vanilla extract**
**500g caster sugar**
**225g plain flour**

**1 teaspoon salt**
**300g chopped walnuts**
**tin measuring approximately 33 x**
 **23 x 5 1/2cm**
**birthday candles and holders, if**
 **appropriate**

Preheat the oven to 180°C/gas mark 4. Line your brownie pan – I think it's worth lining the sides as well as the base – with foil, parchment or Bake-O-Glide.

Melt the butter and chocolate together in a large heavy-based pan. In a bowl or large wide-mouthed measuring jug, beat the eggs with the sugar and vanilla. Measure the flour into another bowl and add the salt.

When the chocolate mixture has melted, let it cool a bit before beating in the eggs and sugar, and then the nuts and flour. Beat to combine smoothly and then scrape out of the saucepan into the lined pan.

Bake for about 25 minutes. When it's ready, the top should be dried to a paler brown speckle, but the middle still dark and dense and gooey. And even with such a big batch you do need to keep alert, keep checking: the difference between gungy brownies and dry brownies is only a few minutes; remember that they will continue to cook as they cool.

Makes a maximum of 48.

## VARIATIONS
You can really vary brownies as you wish: get rid of the walnuts, or halve them and make up their full weight with dried cherries; or replace them with other nuts – peanuts, brazils, hazelnuts – add shredded coconut or white chocolate chips or buttons; try stirring in some Jordan's Original Crunchy cereal. I had high hopes for chic, after-dinner pistachio-studded brownies, but found the nuts get too soft and waxy, when what you need is a little crunchy contrast.

# CREAM-CHEESE BROWNIES

This version adds cream cheese, fridge-cold and sliced, to give an inner layer of almost salty sourness. Just think of cheesecake: rich, sweet, sharp, palate-cleaving. What's not to like?

| | |
|---|---|
| **125g dark chocolate** | **75g plain flour** |
| **125g unsalted butter** | **pinch of salt** |
| **2 large eggs** | **200g cold Philadelphia or similar** |
| **200g caster sugar** | **23cm square tin, 4cm deep, greased** |
| **1 teaspoon vanilla extract** | **and lined** |

Preheat the oven to 180°C/gas mark 4.

Melt the chocolate and butter over medium-to-low heat in a heavy-based saucepan. While you're waiting for it to melt, idly beat the eggs in a bowl with the sugar and vanilla. Measure the flour into another bowl and add the salt. When the chocolate mixture has all but completely melted, take the pan off the heat. The bits of unmelted chocolate or butter will continue to deliquesce if left. Leave for a bit longer to cool slightly before beating in the eggs and sugar. Finally, add the flour and beat until smooth. Pour half the mixture into the tin, slice the cream cheese as thinly as you can and top the brownie mixture in the tin with these thin slices. Pour over the remaining half of brownie-gunge, using a rubber spatula or whatever to make sure each bit of cheese is covered. Then put in the oven and bake for about 20 minutes: the top should be slightly paled and dry, but a cake-tester poked within should reveal a still-sticky centre. Cool for about 10 minutes before cutting into little squares, and eat warm or cold, though the cooler they are the easier they'll be to lift out. Reckon on a first, botched slice: cook's treat.

Makes 8–10.

# WHITE-CHOCOLATE AND MACADAMIA BROWNIES

Blonde brownies can never have the depth or intensity of their darker sisters (I'm not implying anything . . .) but that doesn't mean they haven't got anything going for them. The important thing is to maximize squodge, to try and create a buttery caramel flavour, but one that doesn't hit you about the head with migraine-provoking sugariness. This should fit the bill.

125g unsalted butter

250g white chocolate, cut into chunks, or buttons

4 large eggs

1 teaspoon salt

350g caster sugar

2 teaspoons vanilla extract

300g plain flour

250g macadamia nuts, roughly chopped

25 x 20 x 5cm brownie tin, buttered

Preheat the oven to 170°C/gas mark 3.

Melt the butter and chocolate either in a microwave or a double boiler. In a large bowl, beat the eggs with the salt until light and beginning to whoosh up in volume, then add the sugar and the vanilla, and continue beating until really thick and creamy.

Beat in the slightly cooled chocolate mixture and then add the flour and nuts, folding in gently. Pour into your prepared tin and cook for 35 minutes or until set on top and gooey in the middle. Leave for 3–5 minutes before cutting into small squares. Bear these in mind for giving to people to eat with coffee when dinner's ended with cheese. Not that you need to add anything sweet, but again it's that idea of supplementing shrewd and pleasurable shopping with the satisfactions of a little light home-baking.

Makes 16.

## ALL-PURPOSE CHOCOLATE ICING

The chocolate icing I use most, as you will have noticed, is a ganache (see p22), which has the virtue of being as easy and quick to make as it is good to eat. But then, good chocolate mixed with good cream should taste like that. I think it's useful, though, to have another recipe, less elegant maybe, but helpful to turn a plain sponge into a chocolate-iced layer cake. It's also a good way of making a chocolate cake which otherwise may be too darkly adult into one fit for inter-generational eating.

It's only a blueprint, so fiddle about as you please: add orange oil or almond essence in place of the vanilla; use brandy instead of rum.

125g dark chocolate

75g unsalted butter

2 large eggs, beaten

500g icing sugar, sieved

1 teaspoon vanilla extract

1 tablespoon dark rum

Melt the chocolate and butter in the microwave. Beat in the eggs, then the sugar. Add the extract and rum, then leave to cool a little before using. This amount makes enough icing to cover the top, middle and sides of a 20cm layer cake.

# CHOCOLATE-CHERRY CUPCAKES

These are very easy, very good – somehow light and dense at the same time – and I love their dark, glossy elegance. When I made them for the cake stall at my daughter's school fair, they sold, even at a pound a piece, quicker than anything else. I'd have included them in the school fête section (see p235), except that they're perhaps too expensive to make a habit of. Still, if the cost considerations include time, then this probably counts as a cheap undertaking.

The jam I use for these is the morello cherry preserve from Sainsbury's special selection; if you're using a less elegant, and probably sweeter confection, reduce the sugar in the cakes a little. And if you have any Kirsch about the place, then add a splash to the batter and icing.

for the cupcakes:
**125g soft unsalted butter**
**100g dark chocolate, broken**
 **into pieces**
**300g morello cherry jam**
**150g caster sugar**
**pinch of salt**
**2 large eggs, beaten**

**150g self-raising flour**
**12-bun muffin tin and papers**

for the icing:
**100g dark chocolate**
**100ml double cream**
**12 natural-coloured glacé cherries**

Preheat the oven to 180°C/gas mark 4.

Put the butter in a heavy-bottomed pan on the heat to melt. When nearly completely melted, stir in the chocolate. Leave for a moment to begin softening, then take the pan off the heat and stir with a wooden spoon until the butter and chocolate are smooth and melted. Now add the cherry jam, sugar, salt and eggs. Stir with a wooden spoon and when all is pretty well amalgamated stir in the flour.

Scrape and pour into the muffin papers in their tin and bake for 25 minutes. Cool in the pan on a rack for 10 minutes before turning out.

When the cupcakes are cool, break the chocolate for the icing into little pieces and add them to the cream in a saucepan. Bring to the boil, remove from the heat and then whisk – by hand or electrically – till thick and smooth. Ice the cupcakes, smoothing the tops with the back of a spoon, and stand a cherry in the centre of each.

Makes 12.

# ESPRESSO CUPCAKES

You don't need to make the cappuccino cupcakes, opposite, to have with these, but they do look, and taste, wonderful together. They are on the edge of what my paternal grandfather, and my mother after him, used to condemn as landscape cookery, but I just couldn't help myself.

for the cupcakes:
**125g soft unsalted butter**
**125g dark muscovado sugar**
**2 large eggs**
**125g self-raising flour**
**1 tablespoon cocoa powder**
**1 tablespoon espresso coffee powder**
**50g dark chocolate, melted**

**1–2 tablespoons milk**

for the icing:
**300g dark chocolate**
**50g unsalted butter**
**2 teaspoons instant espresso coffee powder**
**12-bun muffin tin with paper cases**

Preheat the oven to 200°C/gas mark 6.

Pulse the butter and sugar in a food processor, then add the eggs, pulsing again. Tip in the flour, cocoa and coffee powder, and process until you have a smooth batter. Finally, add the chocolate, and thin the batter with the milk. Pour into the muffin papers in their tin and cook for 15–20 minutes. A quick poke with a cake-tester (or uncooked stick of spaghetti) should let you know if they're sufficiently cooked. Let the cakes cool out of the oven in the tin for a few minutes, then take them out to cool completely on a rack.

While they're cooling, get on with the icing. Just put the chocolate, butter and instant espresso powder in a large bowl and put it in the microwave till the chocolate's melted. (I find 2 minutes on medium does it, but I can't pretend to understand all manner of microwaves.) Whisk together to combine, then lop off a slice from the top of each cupcake so that you've got a perfectly flat surface. Spread the icing over this surface, until you've got 12 dark chocolate cupcakes doing their best to look like espressi. If you want, stud the centre of each with a chocolate-covered coffee bean.

Makes 12.

# CAPPUCCINO CUPCAKES

The only thing chocolatey about these is the white chocolate in the icing: underneath is just golden coffee sponge; I think of this combination as blonde mocha.

for the cupcakes:
**125g self-raising flour**
**125g soft unsalted butter**
**125g golden caster sugar**
**2 large eggs**
**1 teaspoon vanilla extract**
**1 teaspoon baking powder**
**1 heaped tablespoon instant espresso**
**2–3 tablespoons milk**

for the icing:
**160g white chocolate**
**60g butter**
**120g sour cream**
**260g icing sugar, sieved**
**scant teaspoon cocoa powder**
**12-bun muffin tin with paper cases**

Preheat the oven to 200°C/gas mark 6.

Put all the cupcake ingredients except for the milk into the food processor and blitz to combine. Pulse again, adding milk down the funnel to form a batter with a soft, dropping consistency. Spoon into the papers in their tin and put in the oven to cook for about 20 minutes. When ready, remove from the oven and leave in the tin to cool for 5 minutes before turning out onto a wire rack.

When they're completely cold, get on with the icing. Melt the chocolate and butter in the microwave or in a double boiler, and after it's cooled a little, stir in the sour cream. Gradually beat in the sieved icing sugar. And if the consistency isn't right for icing, add either hot water to thin or more sieved icing sugar to thicken. Spread roughly and generously over the top of each cupcake, and then dust sparingly with cocoa, by pressing a little through a tea strainer, so that they look like little cups of chocolate-dusted cappuccino.

Makes 12.

# BANANA, CHERRY AND WHITE-CHOCOLATE CUPCAKES

Isn't the name enough? If not, then note that these are risibly easy to make. The recipe comes from a much-loved American book of mine, *One-Pot Cakes* by Andrew Schloss – who's also the inspiration behind the chocolate-cherry cupcakes and the store-cupboard chocolate-orange cake above – and it's true, you do need just one pot, and the least energetic stirring with any old fork, to make this. Perfect for lunch box or picnic basket. What am I saying? Perfect for anything.

125g unsalted butter
200g caster sugar
1 teaspoon vanilla extract
3 ripe bananas
60ml (4 tablespoons) sour cream
2 large eggs
1 teaspoon bicarbonate of soda

1/2 teaspoon baking powder
300g plain flour
40g dried cherries, chopped
50g white chocolate, chopped, or
 buttons
12–bun muffin tin with paper cases

Preheat the oven to 180°C/gas mark 4.

Melt the butter in a saucepan, then, off the heat, add the sugar, vanilla and soft bananas, mashing them with a fork in the pan. Stir in the sour cream and the eggs and – still using your fork or a wooden spoon if you prefer – beat to mix. Add the bicarb and the baking powder, and stir in as well, then finally stir in the flour, cherries and chocolate.

When the mixture's just blended, divide between the 12 muffin cases and cook for 20 minutes or until golden and springy on top. Remove the cupcakes in their papers to a wire rack and leave till cool.

Makes 12.

# NIGHT-AND-DAY CUPCAKES

This, like the cream-cheese brownies, uses my favourite combination of densely sweet and smoothly sharp. I love the way chocolate-coated coffee beans look like buttons or studs on top of the creamy whiteness of the icing, but use dark chocolate coarsely shaved through a grater if you prefer.

for the cupcakes:

**2 scant tablespoons cocoa powder**

**2 tablespoons boiling water**

**75g golden caster sugar**

**50g dark muscovado sugar**

**125g self-raising flour**

**2 large eggs**

**125g very soft unsalted butter**

**1 teaspoon vanilla extract**

**1 tablespoon milk**

**12-bun muffin tin with paper cases**

for the frosting:

**200g icing sugar, sieved**

**100g cream cheese**

**juice of 1/2 a lime (or 1 tablespoon lemon juice)**

**12 chocolate-coated coffee beans or dark chocolate**

Preheat the oven to 200°C/gas mark 6. Mix the cocoa to a paste with the boiling water and set aside while you make the cupcake mixture.

This couldn't be easier: just put the sugars, flour, eggs and butter in the processor and blitz to combine smoothly. Scrape the mixture from the sides, and then pulse while you add the cocoa paste and milk down the funnel. You should have a batter with a soft dropping consistency: if not, add a little more milk. Dollop into the cases in the tin and bake for about 20 minutes, until an inserted cake-tester comes out clean.

Leave in the tin for 5 minutes, then remove, in the paper cases, to a wire rack. When cool, make the frosting by beating together the sieved icing sugar and cream cheese till soft; add lime or lemon juice to taste and then spread roughly over the waiting cupcakes. Stud each one with a chocolate-coated coffee bean or shave over some dark, bitter chocolate.

Makes 12.

# FLORENTINES

This is the one recipe using glacé cherries in which I won't beseech you to use the dark natural-coloured ones; we want that garish, chemical red here. I won't claim this isn't a fiddly recipe, but you need patience rather than dexterity or expertise, and they are so good it would be a pity if you never found the calmness from which to produce them. Hettie, who's worked with me on this book, customarily calls me Frank, as in Spencer, and if I can make these, so can you. These taste so much better than any florentines you've ever bought.

100g whole, blanched almonds

90g mixed candied peel, in whole
   chunks, not ready chopped

40g glacé cherries

25g unsalted butter

90g caster sugar

15g plain flour

150ml double cream

100g dark chocolate

100g white chocolate

2 baking sheets, greased

Preheat the oven to 190°C/gas mark 5.

Chop the almonds so that you have some fine pieces and some chunks of nut. Chop the candied peel and cherries into fairly small, even pieces. In a heavy-based saucepan, melt the butter and sugar without letting it catch. Add the flour rather as if you were making a roux for a white sauce; it should form a ball of paste. Take off the heat and whisk in the cream. The mixture should be smooth, so put it back on the heat briefly to beat out any lumps. Stir in the fruit and almonds.

Drop heaped teaspoonfuls of this florentine mixture onto the greased or non-stick baking sheets. It will look quite liquid and will spread, so leave generous space between the blobs. Place the sheets in the oven and cook for 10–12 minutes. They're ready when they've spread into larger circles and the edges are golden-brown. Take them out of the oven and leave for 2–3 minutes to firm up; at this point you can ease them back into shape if you need to, as they will be very malleable. When you feel they can be lifted, slip a metal spatula or palette knife underneath them and transfer to a wire rack to cool, ensuring you leave them flat.

Melt the dark and white chocolate in separate bowls in the microwave, and paint the flat side of each florentine; I use a pastry brush for this. Be prepared to paint over and over to get a good thick coating, although it's more of an issue with the white chocolate.

Using a fork, make wavy lines on the chocolate on each florentine, and leave to dry.

Makes approximately 30.

# GRANNY BOYD'S BISCUITS

The recipe for these biscuits was given to me, at my insistent request, by my editor, Eugenie Boyd. I don't think there is a more chic accompaniment to a tub of good vanilla ice cream: they're sturdy – in shape and form like Bendick's Bittermints – dark, smoky and melting.

**300g self-raising flour**
**30g cocoa powder**
**250g soft unsalted butter**

**125g caster sugar**
**2 baking sheets, greased**

Preheat the oven to 170°C/gas mark 3.

Sieve together the flour and cocoa, and set aside for a moment. Cream the butter and sugar until pale and soft, then work in the flour and cocoa. It might look like it needs liquid, but keep working the ingredients in and it will form a dough. Roll into walnut-sized balls and arrange these with a decent space between them (as they'll spread) on the baking sheets, then press down on them with the back of a fork: you can see the marks the tines make on them in the picture opposite p61.

Put the sheets in the oven and cook for 5 minutes, then turn the oven down to 150°C/gas mark 2 and bake for a further 10–15 minutes. It's hard to tell by looking when the biscuits are ready since the dough starts off so dark, but they should feel firm on top, although not hard; they will continue to cook and harden as they cool. Remove from the oven and transfer immediately to a wire rack to cool.

Makes about 35.

# WHITE-CHOCOLATE AND PISTACHIO BISCUITS

The pale gold of these buttery biscuits together with the waxy green of the nuts and rich whiteness of the chocolate is the perfect combination: elegance and comfort.

**100g soft unsalted butter**
**125g caster sugar**
**100g soft brown sugar**
**1 teaspoon vanilla extract**
**1 large egg**
**150g plain flour**

**1 teaspoon bicarbonate of soda**
**100g ground pistachios**
**125g whole pistachios**
**125g white chocolate, chopped**
**2 baking sheets, lined**

Preheat the oven to 180°C/gas mark 4.

Cream together the butter and sugars until soft and almost moussy. Add the vanilla and the egg, then the flour and bicarb. Don't worry if the mixture looks almost curdled after you've beaten in the egg. When you've got a smooth, thick dough, add the nuts and chocolate and mix to combine.

Pinch off pieces of dough and roll them into walnut sized balls in your hands. Place these, generously spaced, onto the baking sheets, and put in the oven for 10–12 minutes, by which time the biscuits should be a pale gold, with a darker gold around the edges.

Leave to set for a couple of minutes on the baking sheets before transferring to a wire rack to cool.

Makes about 36.

CHILDREN

# CHILDREN

Although in cooking I resist strongly the idea that there is such a thing as children's food, as distinct from 'real' food, in baking I have, I suppose, to lighten up. Not that I think that peanut-butter squares are therefore unfit for adult consumption – sadly, that doesn't appear to be the case – or that dolly-mixture cupcakes cannot lie happily with a child-free life, but they are both the sort of thing I have in mind when I talk about baking for children. Indeed, many of the recipes here can be made by children, too, although it would be hard to make a useful distinction throughout the chapter between cooking for and cooking with children – that would inevitably depend on their age. And actually, so much of children's baking isn't about what they can be left alone to get on with, but about what you do together. I love hanging around the kitchen with the children, stirring mixtures, licking out bowls, baking fairy cakes or cutting out and icing biscuits. But it's also incredibly important to me that that doesn't usurp everyday cooking; I like them with me in the kitchen helping – or not, as the case may be – with ordinary lunch or tea, not just on-side for kiddie cuisine. In fact, even though I'm lucky enough to work at home, I'm hopelessly negligent and never actually do much with my children other than cook.

# BUTTERMILK BIRTHDAY CAKE

Of course, you can make birthday cake simply enough by following the Victoria sponge recipe on p15, and I often do just that. But this is one of my most ecstatic discoveries: a cake that holds its shape whatever mould you want to cook it in, that can bear the weight of as much icing as you want to drape it with and is, after all that, the best-tasting birthday cake you will ever come across. Not, of course, that is has to be a birthday cake. My children like it on non-ceremonial occasions baked in two sandwich tins and then filled and iced with the chocolate frosting on p195.

The following quantities are enough to make a cake in one 23cm square pan, 4cm deep. So, for a birthday I would make two of these and sandwich them together with the butter icing. The quantities below will make a lot of icing, but if you're going to use various shades of food colouring – and is there a birthday cake that doesn't require it in some quantity? – then you'll need more than if you were using just one colour.

It would be impossible for me to give exact quantities for all the sorts of moulds you might want to fill (and you can hire moulds at most specialist cake-decoration shops), but let me succumb to guilt-free stereotyping and give guidelines for one boy-cake and one girl-cake. If you're using a train-shaped mould or one of those conical affairs that when unmoulded reveal themselves to be Barbie's lower half (all you have to do is plunge a bare-naked Barbie doll into the cake and cover her pert plastic torso and all in icing), double the quantities. You may end up with a bit left over, but not enough to make it worth cutting down on quantities. I should reckon on 45 minutes at 180°C/gas mark 4 for the train and probably 1 hour for Barbie.

for the cake:
**250g plain flour**
**1 1/2 teaspoons baking powder**
**1/2 teaspoon bicarbonate of soda**
**1/4 teaspoon salt**
**200ml buttermilk (or 75g yoghurt mixed with 125ml semi-skimmed milk)**
**1 1/2 teaspoons vanilla extract**
**125g soft unsalted butter**

**200g caster sugar**
**3 large eggs**
**1 x 23cm square cake tin or 2 x sandwich tins, lined and greased**

for the icing:
**300g butter**
**700g icing sugar, sieved**
**1 teaspoon vanilla extract**
**2 tablespoons milk**

Preheat oven to 180°C/gas mark 4.

Sift flour, baking powder, bicarb and salt together into a bowl and set aside. Pour the buttermilk (or yoghurt and milk) into a measuring jug and stir in the vanilla. Cream the butter and sugar in a large bowl with an electric mixer at medium speed (or by hand, of course) until light and fluffy. Reduce the speed if using the mixer and add the eggs one at a time, beating for 30 seconds between additions. Add alternating increments of the flour mixture and the vanilla-buttermilk, blending well after each addition; this should take 3–5 minutes.

Pour into the prepared tin or tins, and bake for about 40 minutes (30 if using the sandwich tins) until the cake is beginning to shrink away from the sides and a cake-tester comes out clean. Cool in the tin on a wire rack for 10 minutes before unmoulding to let cool completely. If I'm using a mould with a lot of patterning – the train, for example – I leave it for 20 minutes in the tin before unmoulding.


## NOTES ON ICING

I find butter icing easiest to use to conjure up the train in all its Thomas-the-Tank-Engine glory. Black is difficult to get right, but as with all food-colouring activities, I urge you towards the pastes rather than the liquid dyes. The black paste, called 'Liquorice', is still not emphatic enough for train-black. Either go with fashionable charcoal, or add some melted plain chocolate to add intensity.

For these complicated shapes, squeezing a nozzle is easier than laying out fondant, but for Barbie I tend to change tack. I buy great wodges of made-up ready-to-roll icing in pink, pink, pink. There is something faintly disturbing about plunging a naked doll into a cone of sponge and then painting her pointy plastic bosoms with apricot glaze so that the sugar-icing bustier you're about to cut out for her will adhere. I mean, there are grown men who'd pay to do this. Tie up her hair with freezer-bag wire, then just brush the Barbie-skirt cake and the doll herself with warmed-up apricot jam before wrapping and sticking the cut-out pieces onto her.

Buy all manner of sparkles and sweets, dip them briefly in cold water and stick on to create a sumptuously jewelled gown. At Selfridges you can buy jellybeans by weight in their separate colours; they have about 6 different pinks which come into their own here – and at girls' birthday parties generally.

# BUTTER CUT-OUT BISCUITS

It's not hard to make biscuits that hold their shape well while cooking; it's not hard to make biscuits that taste good and have a melting, buttery texture: what's hard is to find a biscuit that does all of these things together. This one, by way of a wonderful American book, *The Family Baker*, does: so any time you want to play supermummy in the kitchen, here is where you start.

Like all doughs, it freezes well, so it makes sense – in a smug, domestic kind of a way – to wrap half of this in clingfilm and stash it in the deep freeze until next needed. It's hard to specify exactly how much icing you'll need, but you might end up using more than specified below if you're using a lot of different colours. I always cut out the newly acquired age of the child on his or her birthday. My children couldn't contemplate a birthday party without them.

175g soft unsalted butter

200g caster sugar

2 large eggs

1 teaspoon vanilla extract

400g plain flour, preferably Italian 00, plus more if needed

1 teaspoon baking powder

1 teaspoon salt

300g icing sugar, sieved, and food colouring

biscuit cutters

2 baking sheets, greased or lined

Preheat the oven to 180°C/gas mark 4.

Cream the butter and sugar together until pale and moving towards moussiness, then beat in the eggs and vanilla. In another bowl, combine the flour, baking powder and salt. Add the dry ingredients to the butter and eggs, and mix gently but surely. If you think the finished mixture is too sticky to be rolled out, add more flour, but do so sparingly as too much will make the dough tough. Halve the dough, form into fat discs, wrap each half in clingfilm and rest in the fridge for at least 1 hour. Sprinkle a suitable surface with flour, place a disc of dough on it (not taking out the other half until you've finished with the first) and sprinkle a little more flour on top of that. Then roll it out to a thickness of about ½ cm. Cut into shapes, dipping the cutter into flour as you go, and place the biscuits a little apart on the baking sheets.

Bake for 8–12 minutes, by which time they will be lightly golden around the edges. Cool on a rack and continue with the rest of the dough. When they're all fully cooled, you can get on with the icing. Put a couple of tablespoons of just-not-boiling water into a large bowl, add the sieved icing sugar and mix together, adding more water as you need to form a thick paste. Colour as desired: let the artistic spirit within you speak, remembering with gratitude that children have very bad taste.

Makes 50–60.

# BIRTHDAY-PARTY AND CHILD-FRIENDLY FAIRY CAKES

Fairy cakes that you make for a child are no different from the cupcakes with which you adorn your dinner-party table (pp39–42); that's partly the point. I would say one thing, though: you should always keep some Stork, or similar, in the fridge so that you can make up a quick batch whenever necessary. (OK, I'm not mad on margarine, either, but I promise you this is an accommodation that makes sense.) Butter just won't soften quickly; the Stork you can bung straight from fridge to processor, and thus you are never more than about 20 minutes away from a tray of fairy cakes.

## TRADITIONAL FAIRY CAKES

To make 12 fairy cakes, use the recipe on p40 and ice with pink icing, using 200g icing sugar (or instant royal icing), a tablespoonful or so of water, pink food colouring and 12 natural coloured or shriekingly artificial glacé cherries.

## DOLLY-MIXTURE FAIRY CAKES

All children love these and I find them curiously therapeutic to make. Choosing the patterns and sticking down the sugary cubes is entirely absorbing without being in any way demanding. Two packs of sweets make for leftovers but artistic freedom. So important.

for the cakes:
**as on p40**

for the icing:
**250g instant royal (and you may need
   more if you're using lots of colours)
colouring of your choice
2 x 125g packets dolly mixtures**

Use the regular recipe for cakes, cutting any risen bit of cake off so you've got a flat surface to adorn. Make up the icing, following packet instructions. Dollop a tablespoonful or so into a bowl, add the colouring of your choice (I enjoy a bit of mix-and-match artistry here) and blend. Ice the cake in question, smooth with the back of an ordinary dessert spoon, and leave a few minutes before studding with dolly mixtures. If you decorate before the icing is beginning to dry, the dolly mixtures will slide off.
     Makes 12.

# HALLOWEEN CUPCAKES

for the cakes:
**as on p40**

for the icing:
**200g instant royal icing**
**100g dark chocolate**
**black and red food colouring**

This is more a guide to the icing than anything else, since the cake beneath is, again, the ordinary fairy cake.

For the cobwebs, you need to make up a batch of white icing using the instant royal icing, and another of black, which you make by melting the chocolate in the microwave (on a medium heat for a minute or two) or in a bain-marie (i.e., a bowl sitting over a pan of hot water, with the sides of the bowl not touching the water), and, when it's liquid, stirring in the black food colouring.

Cut any peaks off the cupcakes so you've got a flat surface to work on, and ice them in white. Now, just drizzling with a coffee spoon, make a dark spiral on top. Then, using either a knife or (this is what I prefer) a bamboo skewer, draw lines from the centre to the edge as though you were doing the rays of the sun or the spokes of a wheel. Don't worry too much about perfection. In the first place, you can always get your children to do them, and in the second, they look just as good when they're not perfect.

Another easy, spooky cupcake can be made by topping with white icing, then adding splodges of red icing to make a cartoon blood-stained effect.

Makes 12.

## VARIATION

Obviously, too, you can use the technique to make Halloween biscuits; just follow the recipe for butter cut-outs and use a spider's web cutter. You may want to make up some other thematically linked ones too – the cutters tend to come in packs of ghost, spider's web, witch, cat and pumpkin. The latter just need orange icing, but if you get some angelica and cut out stalks for them, it will greatly enhance the finished effect. For the cats, make up some glacé icing, say 100g, of sieved sugar and a few drops of boiling water, then stir in melted dark chocolate, as above, adding some black food-colouring paste once the chocolate and icing are combined. Place two silver balls on each cat's face for eyes.

# BUTTERFLY CAKES

for the cakes:

**as p40, plus 1 heaped teaspoon baking powder added to the flour**

for the icing:

**100g very soft unsalted butter**
**100g icing sugar, sieved**
**food colouring if wanted**

Follow the instructions and quantities for normal fairy cakes, only add a heaped teaspoon of baking powder on top of the self-raising flour so that you end up with appropriately peaked cakelets.

Cut the tops off with a small sharp knife and set aside, leaving the fairy cakes perfectly level. While they're cooling on a wire rack, make up the butter icing. Beat the butter in a bowl and add the icing sugar gradually, until you have incorporated all of it into the butter. This is not an exact science; your icing might be the right consistency before you have added all the sugar or you might want more butter at the end. Put a splodge of butter icing onto the middle of each cake, and then cut the top in half vertically before placing it back on top of the cake upside-down. With a little adjustment they should now resemble a butterfly's wings.

Makes 12.

# CORNFLAKE CRISPIES

Do you really want to have a child's birthday tea without these?

**100g milk chocolate**
**25g unsalted butter**
**1 teaspoon golden syrup**

**50g cornflakes**
**28 petit-four cases**

Melt the chocolate and butter – and see my introduction to the chocolate chapter for various methods – and add the golden syrup. Coat the cornflakes well with the chocolate mixture – the easiest way is just to fold them into the semi-liquid mix – and fill the petit-four cases. Put the paper cases on baking sheets and leave them to set in the fridge.

Makes 28.

## SNICKERS AND PEANUT-BUTTER MUFFINS

These muffins have a special charm: I think the ingredients speak for themselves. But what I should perhaps add is that they taste seriously good to adults too.

**250g plain flour**
**6 tablespoons golden caster sugar**
  **(85g)**
**1 1/2 tablespoons baking powder**
**pinch of salt**
**6 tablespoons crunchy peanut butter**
  **(160g)**

**60g unsalted butter, melted**
**1 large egg, beaten**
**175ml milk**
**3 x 65g Snickers bars, chopped**
**12-bun muffin tin with paper cases**

Preheat the oven to 200°C/gas mark 6.

Stir together the flour, sugar, baking powder and salt. Add the peanut butter and mix until you have a bowl of coarse crumbs. Add the melted butter and egg to the milk, and then stir this gently into the bowl. Mix in the Snickers pieces and dollop into the muffin cases.

Cook for 20–25 minutes, when the tops should be risen, golden and firm to the (light) touch. Sit the tin on a wire rack for 5–10 minutes before taking out each muffin in its case and leaving them on the wire rack to cool. If you can.

Makes 12.

## BANANA MUFFINS

Any sort of muffin is easy and quick for a child to make: the whole point is that the mixture must not be too vehemently or smoothly combined. The bonus here is that small children seem to have an inordinate passion for mashing bananas. In other words, an ordinarily biddable two-year-old can feel he or she is making these almost unaided. You will have to melt the butter and so on yourself, but – although I am perhaps irresponsibly insouciant about infantile involvement here – on the whole, you can take a serenely non-interventionist approach to the whole exercise.

All the ingredients can be bought at any unglamorously stocked corner shop, as can the ingredients for the recipe below. It doesn't matter whether you use mini-muffin tins or full-size ones: you will get about 24 of the former, 10 of the latter. For what it's worth, the tiny ones taste better when eaten still warm; the larger ones when cold. Just remember to buy the right-sized lining papers for whichever tins you've got.

Snickers and peanut-butter muffins

30g unsalted butter

60g (two oozingly, bulgingly heaped 15ml tablespoons) clear honey

1/2 teaspoon vanilla extract

2 large, very ripe bananas

150g plain flour

1 heaped teaspoon baking powder

1/2 teaspoon bicarbonate of soda

1/2 teaspoon cinnamon

pinch of salt

12-bun muffin tin and paper cases

Preheat the oven to 190°C/gas mark 5.

Put the butter, honey and vanilla extract in a pan on a low heat to melt, then remove and set aside for a few minutes.

Mash the bananas and, in another bowl, measure out the flour, baking powder, bicarb, cinnamon and salt. Mix the melted-butter mixture with the bananas and then mix that into the dry ingredients. Don't overmix: just stir a couple of times; you will have a not terribly attractive lumpy sludge, but don't worry about it.

Put the paper cases in the muffin trays and fill them about two-thirds full of mixture. Put in the oven and cook for about 25 minutes. Leave in the tins for five minutes, then remove the muffins in their cases to a wire rack for another 5–10 or till cool.

Makes 12.

## JAM-DOUGHNUT MUFFINS

I have to try and steer myself away from making these, as I know that every time I suggest them, simperingly pretending that I have only the pleasure of my bubs at heart, it's because I am dying to eat them, and then do. There is something about the melted butter and sugar that they're turned in while still warm that makes them irresistible. Of course, these are much easier than actual doughnuts, and the children can do most of the work themselves. All you need to do is help to eat them.

125ml milk

85ml corn or other vegetable oil, plus more for greasing

1 large egg

1/2 teaspoon vanilla extract

200g self-raising flour

100g caster sugar

12 teaspoons strawberry jam

100g unsalted butter

150g granulated sugar

1 incredibly well-greased or silicon 12-bun mini-muffin tin

Preheat the oven to 190°C/gas mark 5.

With a fork, beat together the milk, oil, egg and vanilla extract. Stir this into the flour and caster sugar to combine (just): the lumps don't matter and if you overbeat the muffins will be tough. Spoon the mixture into each muffin cup so that it's just under a third full. Then with a teaspoon add a dollop of strawberry jam – about the size of a fat broad bean – then top with more muffin mix so that the cases are just about full.

Put them in the preheated oven and cook for about 20 minutes or until the tops feel springy and resistant and the muffins have puffed up into little toadstools.

Meanwhile, melt the butter slowly in a thick-bottomed pan, and lay the sugar out in a wide, shallow bowl. As soon as the muffins are ready, remove them from their moulds, dip them in the butter and roll them in the granulated sugar. Eat warm.

Makes 12.

## PEANUT-BUTTER AND JAM JEWELS

This is really just a biscuity evocation of the American child's favourite combination, peanut butter and jelly. I am not convinced about this in a sandwich, but here, in a soft, buttery biscuit, the taste is wonderful. And they look beautiful, like the sort of jewels worn by fairy-tale princesses.

**125g soft unsalted butter**
**150g caster sugar**
**125g soft light brown sugar or light muscovado**
**200g smooth peanut butter**
**2 large eggs**
**1 teaspoon vanilla extract**

**300g plain flour**
**1/2 teaspoon baking powder**
**1/4 teaspoon salt**
**enough strawberry jam for 50 coffee-spoon-sized splodges**
**2–3 baking sheets**

Preheat the oven to 180°C/gas mark 4.

Cream together the butter and sugars, and add the peanut butter, beating to combine, then the eggs and vanilla. Mix in the flour, baking powder and salt to make a damp, sticky dough, and put it in the fridge to firm up for at least 1 hour, the bowl covered with clingfilm.

Pinch off small amounts of dough, about as much as would make a scant table-spoonful, and roll between the palms of your hands into small balls, 2–3cm in diameter and place on a baking sheet, flattening slightly with your hand. Make a thumbprint in each biscuit, being quite firm or the indent will disappear during baking.

When the trays are full, put into the oven and bake for 10–15 minutes, by which time the biscuits should be just cooked. It doesn't matter if they're a bit soft, as they'll firm up on cooling, but just check the underside of one to make sure they're no longer actually doughy.

As soon as you've taken the biscuits out of the oven, spoon a small amount of jam (about a coffee-spoonful) into each indent to make a jewel. Transfer them to a wire rack to cool, by which time the jam will have melted slightly, and will be sitting, bulging shinily, a red gem in the middle of its peanut-butter setting. The jam seems to harden slightly, not enough to make it unpleasant but enough to make it stay put, so you can pack these up, on top of each other, in tins or Tupperwares, without their coming to any harm.

Makes about 50.

## PEANUT-BUTTER SQUARES

I don't know if you've ever eaten Reese's Peanut Butter Cups, but these are a homespun version of them. And if you discount melting the chocolate (which in any case the microwave can do) there is no cooking involved. You may think that seeing how the dough is made – just peanut butter, butter and sugar – might put you off eating them. Sadly not.

for the base:
**50g dark muscovado sugar**
**200g icing sugar**
**50g unsalted butter**
**200g smooth peanut butter**

for the topping:
**200g milk chocolate**
**100g plain chocolate**
**1 tablespoon unsalted butter**
**1 x 23cm square brownie tin, lined,**
   **preferably, with Bake-O-Glide**

Stir all the ingredients for the base together until smooth. I use the paddle attachment to my mixer which my children love operating, but a bowl and a wooden spoon will do the job just as well. You will find, either way, that some of the dark muscovado sugar stays in rubbly, though very small, lumps, but don't worry about that. Press the sandy mixture into the lined brownie tin and make the surface as even as possible.

To make the topping, melt the chocolates and butter together (in a microwave for ease, for a minute or two on medium) and spread on the base. Put the tin in the fridge to set. When the chocolate has hardened, cut into small squares – because, more-ish as it undeniably is, it is also very rich.

Makes approximately 48.

# ROCKY ROAD

Ever since I read that brazil nuts are inordinately good for you, containing essential selenium, and that you should probably have three a day, I have chosen to regard these as health food. What they really are are clumps of brazil nuts and mini-marshmallows bound together by a mantle of melted chocolate. You can alter the ratio of dark to light chocolate as you wish, but, as ever, I really do think it's worth using the best chocolate that you can.

**200g milk chocolate**
**25g dark chocolate**
**75g brazil nuts**
**75g mini-marshmallows**

**1 baking sheet, lined with greaseproof, Bake-O-Glide or oiled foil**

Melt the chocolates either in the microwave or using a bowl over a pan of barely simmering water. Roughly chop the brazil nuts, and mix into the chocolate with the mini-marshmallows.

Drop heaped teaspoons onto a lined baking sheet, and leave to cool in a cold place, though not the fridge if at all possible; it will take some of the gleam from the chocolate.

Makes 24.

## VARIATION
You could chop these up and stir into slightly softened vanilla or chocolate ice cream.

# TOFFEE APPLES

However much this recipe is geared towards children it's not one you can do with them. I burnt myself twice doing this: not badly, but I wouldn't have wanted a child anywhere near.

Of course, you can use toffee-apple sticks, specifically made and sold for the purpose, but twigs straight from the tree look so wonderful. If you haven't got a garden, just take a strong pair of scissors out with you one day.

You could use this amount of toffee for several more apples, if you need them.

**10 apples, preferably organic**

**10 strong but slender twigs or sticks**

**1kg demerara sugar**

**300ml water**

**1 tablespoon vinegar**

**175g unsalted butter**

**2 tablespoons golden syrup or liquid glucose**

**1 baking sheet, lined with Bake-O-Glide or oiled foil**

If you're not using organic apples, which are unwaxed, wash your apples: the wax stops the toffee from adhering properly. Dry them, then remove the stalks and impale them, where the stalks have been, with the twigs or sticks.

Put the sugar and water into a large, heavy-based pan and heat. When the sugar's dissolved, add the vinegar, butter and golden syrup. Boil rapidly for approximately 45 minutes, though start testing after 30. To do this, fill a large bowl with iced water and drop a small amount of the toffee into the bowl: if it is ready it should harden on contact. Keep the water close because you'll need it for the apples later.

Dip each apple in the toffee, rotating on its stick. Then hold it over the pot of toffee (keeping the heat on but now turned down to low) and twirl it about 10 times so that the toffee forms a good carapace round the apple. Now plunge the toffee apple into the iced water, and twirl, submerged, another 10 times. Remove to the lined baking sheet and continue with remaining apples.

Makes 10.

# DREAM BARS

These are one of those chewy, fudgy, nutty, crisp tray-bakes that the Americans are so good at. The base is a buttery, crumbly shortbread you press into the tin and on top is a sticky mixture of nuts and coconut bound by a tender, toffee-like chewy gunge. The name suits them well.

You can use whatever chopped nuts you prefer; I just like the brazils and cashews for their rainforest-crunch qualities.

for the base:
**200g unsalted butter, very soft**
**4 tablespoons light muscovado sugar**
**4 tablespoons caster sugar**
**1 ¹/₂ teaspoons vanilla extract**
**250g plain flour**
**pinch of salt**

for the topping:
**3 large eggs**

**1 ¹/₂ teaspoons vanilla extract**
**125g muscovado sugar**
**3 tablespoons self-raising flour**
**pinch of salt**
**¹/₂ teaspoon baking powder**
**100g shredded coconut**
**75g brazil nuts, roughly chopped**
**75g raw, unsalted cashews**

**1 x 23cm square brownie tin, greased**
    **and lined**

Preheat the oven to 180°C/gas mark 4.

Cream the butter and sugars together and, when light and soft, add the vanilla, flour and salt, mixing well to combine. Tip this into the prepared tin and press down and in with your fingers. Put in the oven and bake for 10 minutes, then remove and let cool a little before spreading the topping on it.

To make this, beat the eggs together with the vanilla and then, still beating, add the sugar. Stir the flour, salt and baking powder together, and fold into the sugar-egg mixture. Now fold in the coconut and nuts and spread this on top of the part-baked shortbread base.

Put the tin back in the oven for 30 minutes, then remove and let cool, still in the tin, on a wire rack. Cut into squares or bars as you like.

Makes 10–12.

# FUDGE

I think fudge was one of the first sweet things I made as a child (we never went in for cakes much as a family) and I still love it. I like chocolate fudge, too, but real fudge for me is this sort – buttery, vanilla-flavoured and teeth-achingly sweet.

Don't get alarmed by mention of sugar thermometers and specific temperatures. Just keep a bowl of iced water next to the cooker, periodically drop a little bit of fudge into it, and if it keeps its shape it's ready. That simple. I do occasionally faff around with a sugar thermometer, since I happen to own one, but I can't say I get a tremendous amount of joy out of it. Still, there are those who prefer to tackle these things scientifically, so I give precise desirable temperatures too.

**500g caster sugar**
**50g unsalted butter**
**100ml evaporated milk**

**1 teaspoon vanilla extract**
**20 x 16cm tin or 15 x 12½cm foil tin,**
  **buttered**

Put the sugar, butter and evaporated milk into a heavy-based saucepan and bring to the boil. Boil this mixture gently, stirring occasionally to prevent it sticking. Carry on until a thermometer reaches 115°C, or the mixture's holding its shape in the water. This will take between 5 and 10 minutes.

Take the pan off the heat, beat in the vanilla, and continue beating until the fudge becomes thick and creamy – grainy almost – and then pour the mixture into your buttered tin and allow to cool.

Cut the fudge into little squares, or however you like.

Makes 25–30 squares.

# CINDER TOFFEE

This is just a more poetic and old-fashioned name for honeycomb – 'cinder' presumably referring to the splintered texture made by the whoosh of air introduced by the bicarb.

**200g caster sugar**
**4 tablespoons golden syrup**

**1 tablespoon bicarbonate of soda**
**1 x 21cm square tin, well-greased**

Grease the 21cm square tin (or 20cm if that's what you've got) generously with butter.

Off the heat, mix the sugar and golden syrup in a heavy-bottomed saucepan, then put over a medium to low flame and simmer for 3–4 minutes (this is based on using a 20cm diameter saucepan). The mixture is ready to come off the heat when it's a thick bubbling mass, the colour of rusty caramel – no darker.

Take off the heat and quickly whisk in the bicarb and watch the caramel foam up in a sudsy and opaque golden cloud like something out of a sci-fi film. Pour into the waiting tin and leave to set. This takes a few hours. Then you can try and cut it, but the best way of treating this is to bash it into splintered pieces.

## VARIATION

You can slice this the best way you can, not worrying too much about uniformity and neatness, and dip into melted chocolate before letting dry on Bake-O-Glide or oiled foil to make your own Crunchies.

Or, to make your own hokey-pokey ice cream, fold splinters of this, un-chocolated, into home-made or good shop-bought vanilla ice cream.

# EASTER NESTS

Yes, these are cute; yes, they are kitsch, but I love them all the same. Can't say I'm absolutely mad about eating them, but luckily my children are.

**200g milk chocolate**
**25g dark chocolate**
**25g unsalted butter**
**100g shredded wheat**

**about 25 multicoloured sugar-coated little chocolate eggs**
**1 baking sheet, lined with Bake-O-Glide or oiled foil**

Break up the chocolate into small pieces and put it in a glass bowl with the butter. Melt on a medium heat in the microwave for about 2 minutes – I give it a minute, then look to see how much more it might need – or over water. When it's melted, give it a stir, then leave it to one side for a moment or two. You need it to be a bit cooler or it might burn the children's hands. Crumble the shredded wheat into another bowl.

Now mix the contents of the two bowls and remove a small handful of messy mixture to the lined baking tray and form into a round nest shape, about 7cm in diameter. Don't worry if you feel it won't stick together: it will as it cools. Leave in a cool place (though not the fridge) until set, then remove to a plate or a wooden board and fill the centre with the eggs (about 5 per nest).

Makes 5.


# MERINGUES (AND MERINGUE NESTS)

I've never met a child who didn't like meringues, and they're child's play to make, too. The best way of getting meringue-making fixed into your (or your child's) head is to remember that for each egg white you need 60g caster sugar, and that this in turn will make you around ten 6cm-diameter meringues. For this reason, I give method only:

Preheat the oven to 140°C/gas mark 1.

Whisk the egg white(s) till stiff, but not dry; peaks should be firm and hold their shape. Resume whisking, adding the sugar tablespoon by sprinkled tablespoon till all's incorporated and you have a gleaming, satiny mass. You can pipe meringues onto lined (but not greased) baking trays, but I mound dessertspoonfuls onto the trays and then use the back of the spoon, wiggling it around so that I have neat-nippled, small-bosomed shapes. To make nests, simply use the back of the spoon to make a nest shape. Bake for 60–70 minutes, then leave in the switched-off oven for 20 minutes before removing to cool.

## SOOT'S FLAPJACKS

Flapjacks are such old-fashioned, comforting things, the sort of food you should make from a mother's recipe. My mother, however, didn't go in for this sort of cooking. Hettie, who has been a reassuring and calming spirit throughout our work on this book, luckily had a mother, Soot, who did. This is the recipe we took out of the handwritten book Hettie inherited from her.

It's not orthodox, but following the advice of a friend who's eaten them like that in Alderney, I add a scant tablespoonful of sesame seeds, sprinkled on them before baking.

| | |
|---|---|
| **450g rolled oats** | **50g golden syrup** |
| **75g soft brown sugar** | **sesame seeds, optional** |
| **300g unsalted butter** | **1 x 23cm square brownie tin, buttered** |

Preheat the oven to 190°C/gas mark 5. Mix the oats with the sugar, then melt the butter with the golden syrup very gently over a low heat, and stir in the oats and sugar. Press the mixture into the tin, sprinkle over sesame seeds if using and cook for 25 minutes. While they're still warm, about 10 minutes out of the oven, cut the flapjacks into 9 squares, and then cut each of the squares into triangles.

Makes 18.

## COCA-COLA CAKE

I really don't plan to become the Coca-Cola cooking queen of Europe, but I came across several versions of this cake in various American books and naturally, after the ham in Coca-Cola in *How to Eat*, had to try it. It's really just a divinely tender-crumbed chocolate cake – and there's nothing wrong with that. And however odd you might think it, everyone loves it when I make it.

| | |
|---|---|
| for the cake: | **125ml buttermilk (or 30g yoghurt** |
| **200g plain flour** | **mixed with 100ml semi-skimmed** |
| **250g golden caster sugar** | **milk)** |
| **½ teaspoon bicarbonate of soda** | **1 teaspoon vanilla extract** |
| **¼ teaspoon salt** | **125g unsalted butter** |
| **1 large egg** | **2 tablespoons cocoa powder** |

**175ml Coca-Cola**

**22–23cm Springform, lined with foil to prevent the batter leaking, then greased**

for the icing:

**225g icing sugar**

**2 tablespoons (30g) butter**

**3 tablespoons (45ml) Coca-Cola**

**1 tablespoon cocoa powder**

**1/2 teaspoon vanilla extract**

Preheat the oven to 180°C/gas mark 4 and put in a baking sheet at the same time.

In a large bowl, combine the flour, sugar, bicarb and salt. Beat the egg, buttermilk (or yoghurt and milk) and vanilla in a measuring jug. In a heavy-based saucepan, melt the butter, cocoa and Coca-Cola, heating it gently. Pour into the dry ingredients, stir well with a wooden spoon, and then add the liquid ingredients from the jug, beating until it is well blended.

Pour into the prepared tin and bake on the warm sheet for 40 minutes or until a tester comes out clean.

Leave to stand for 15 minutes in the tin before unmoulding. Then unclip, unwrap and turn out on a wire rack, making sure you've got a sheet of newspaper or something underneath the rack to catch any icing that drips through.

Sieve the icing sugar and set aside for the moment. In a heavy-based saucepan, combine the butter, Coca-Cola and cocoa and stir over a low heat until the butter has melted. Remove from the heat, add the vanilla, and spoon in the sieved icing sugar, beating as you do so, until you've got a good, spreadable, but still runny, icing.

Pour this icing over the cake, while the cake is still warm, and leave till cool before transferring to the plate on which you're serving it.

Serves 8–10.

## VARIATIONS

Fold 50g chopped walnuts into the cake batter just before pouring it into the tin, and then press a few, or as many as you want, walnut halves on top of the iced cake.

Or make Coca-Cola cupcakes by pouring this batter into a 12-bun muffin tray lined with paper cases. Pour the icing over just after you've taken them out of the oven. Instead of studding each with a walnut half, you could buy those wine-gummy sweets which look like miniature bottles of Coke and press one in on top of each cupcake once the icing's cooled a little but before it has set hard.

Makes 12.

# MINT DOMINOES

This are simply small, flat bricks of peppermint cream dipped in dark chocolate to resemble dominoes. I'm not sure I'd want to bring these out with the coffee after dinner – though you never know – but for a childish culinary conceit, they're perfect. Besides, as Mr Bendicks knows, the contrast between bitter chocolate and sinus-clearing mint is a good one. Even though these are for children, I still use the darkest, blackest, meanest chocolate I can find.

**500g icing sugar**
**2 egg whites, beaten till frothy**

**1/2 teaspoon peppermint essence**
**100g dark chocolate, melted**

Sift the icing sugar into a bowl and add enough beaten egg white to form a stiff dough. Add a few drops of peppermint essence to taste. Knead the paste lightly, and then roll out to about 5mm thickness on a work surface lightly dusted with icing sugar. Cut into domino-sized rectangles, and then leave them to dry for a day.

Paint half of each domino with the melted chocolate, drop little dots of chocolate on the white halves, using a wooden skewer, and arrange the dominoes on a piece of Bake-O-Glide or oiled foil to dry.

Makes about 22.

## VARIATION
To make traditional peppermint creams, after rolling out the kneaded paste cut into 3cm rounds using a plain cutter. Leave them to dry as before, and dip them entirely in the chocolate.

Makes about 25.

# COOKING FOR THE SCHOOL FÊTE

There comes a certain time in your life when you are suddenly required to be a provider of cakes, biscuits and assorted sweetmeats for whatever fund-raising event or fair your children's school goes in for; and there will be many. Of course, you don't need to make anything – many parents bring along bought stuff – but it's strange how one batch of home-made cupcakes can assuage a term's guilt at being late for parents' evening.

## MINI-CHEESECAKES

These are very easy to make, but I do have to say that lining the mini-muffin tins with the digestive biscuit crust can get a little tedious. This is where your darling children come in – their little fingers are made for the job.

| | |
|---|---|
| **100g unsalted butter** | **2 tablespoons (30ml) sour cream** |
| **250g digestive biscuits** | **1/2 teaspoon vanilla extract** |
| **200g cream cheese** | **2 teaspoons lemon juice** |
| **50g caster sugar** | **2 x 12-bun mini-muffin tins** |
| **1 large egg** | |

Preheat the oven to 190°C/gas mark 5.

Melt the butter in a pan. Put the digestive biscuits, broken up roughly, in the processor, and blitz. Still processing, add the melted butter down the funnel and turn this wet sand onto a plate or into a bowl. Put a heaped teaspoonful of the biscuit base into each mini-muffin tin, press it around the edges and up the sides of the tin with your fingers and let it harden in the fridge.

Beat the cream cheese until it's smooth, and then add the sugar. (You can do all this in the washed-out processor bowl.) Add the egg, beating well, and then the sour cream, vanilla and lemon juice, combining everything until it's smooth and creamy.

Put the cream-cheese mixture into a measuring jug and pour some into each mini-muffin tin, leaving the top of the biscuit still visible. Put in the oven and cook for about 10 minutes, by which time the cheese mixture should have set.

Let them cool and then put them in the fridge for at least 3 hours before gently easing them out of the tins. Or, if you're like me and lose patience, after some cautious prising with a rubber spatula turn the tins upside-down and rap firmly, and the little cheesecakes fall out unharmed.

Makes 24.

# FRESH GINGERBREAD WITH LEMON ICING

Having run the cake stall at my daughter's school last year, I can say that there are two types of optimum fête-fare: small, individual pieces that look cute and fetch high unit-prices and tray-bakes that can be made without effort or dexterity and sliced up easily. This recipe fits the latter category and has the added virtue of appealing to parents and grandparents who feel that something from the cake stall should be gratifyingly old-fashioned. The fresh ginger is a modern touch, admittedly, but I always keep some in the fridge and wanted to try it in a less contemporary, pan-Asian way one day (it worked). The lemon icing may not be conventional either, but there is another starkly practical reason for it: brown things – if they're not gooily chocolate – don't sell so well; and the lemon spruceness of the topping is perfect with the musky sweetness beneath it.

for the gingerbread:

**150g unsalted butter**

**125g dark muscovado sugar**

**200g golden syrup**

**200g black treacle**

**2 teaspoons fresh ginger, finely grated**

**1 teaspoon ground cinnamon**

**250ml milk**

**2 large eggs, beaten to mix**

**1 teaspoon bicarbonate of soda, dissolved in 2 tablespoons warm water**

**300g plain flour**

roasting tin, approximately 30 x 20 x 5cm, greased and lined with Bake-O-Glide, foil or parchment

for the icing:

**1 tablespoon lemon juice**

**175g icing sugar, sieved**

**1 tablespoon warm water**

Preheat the oven to 170°C/gas mark 3.

In a saucepan, melt the butter along with the sugar, golden syrup, treacle, ginger and cinnamon. Off the heat, add the milk, eggs and bicarbonate of soda in its water.

Measure the flour out into a bowl and pour in the liquid ingredients, beating until well mixed (it will be a very liquid batter). Pour it into the tin and bake for 3/4–1 hour until risen and firm. Be careful not to overcook it, as it is nicer a little stickier, and anyway will carry on cooking as it cools.

And when it is cool, get on with icing. Whisk the lemon juice into the icing sugar first, then gradually add the water. You want a good, thick icing, so go cautiously and be prepared not to add all the water. Spread over the cooled gingerbread with a palette knife, and leave to set before cutting.

Makes 20 squares.

# MINI-PAVLOVAS

Because of the fruit – and the cream, for that matter – these are not cheap to make, but I always have a stash of egg whites in my deep freeze so I reckon I'm halfway there before I start. And actually, you can probably sell them for quite a lot too. You need to make sure that you've got a supply of paper plates and napkins, though, as they're not small enough to eat in one neat mouthful.

What I do is take with me a large Tupperware of meringues, another airtight bowl of the whipped double cream and, in another, or still in their punnets, the berries. I also bring with me my tea-strainer, a teaspoon, a packet of icing sugar, paper plates and little plastic forks. When I arrive at my pitch, I set out the meringue bases, dollop the cream on top, arrange the fruit and dust with icing sugar, being ready to top up from time to time as the sugar dissolves into the berries. It's a palaver, but worth it: they look so pretty people can't stop themselves spending whatever extortionate price you've put on them.

| | |
|---|---|
| **8 large egg whites** | **750ml whipping cream, duly whipped** |
| **pinch of salt** | **750g blackberries** |
| **500g caster sugar** | **750g raspberries** |
| **4 teaspoons cornflour** | **icing sugar for dusting** |
| **1 scant teaspoon vanilla extract** | 3 baking sheets, lined with parchment |
| **2 teaspoons white wine vinegar** | tea-strainer |

Preheat the oven to 180°C/gas mark 4.

Whisk the egg whites with the salt until they're holding firm peaks but are not stiff. Gently add in the sugar, spoonful after spoonful, still beating, until you've got a bowl full of gleaming, satiny, snowy meringue. Sprinkle the cornflour, a few drops of vanilla and the vinegar on top and fold in to combine.

Draw 6 circles of approximately 10cm circles (using a pint glass as a guide, if this helps) on each of the parchment-lined sheets. Spoon the meringue onto the baking parchment into the delineated circles, and spread and smooth to fill. You want to make the meringue slightly higher at the rims, or just use the back of the spoon to make an indentation in the centre to hold the cream and fruit later. Put into the oven, turn it down to 150°C/gas mark 2, and bake for 30 minutes. Turn the oven off and leave them in for another 30 minutes, then take out of the oven to cool. I just transfer them, on their baking parchment, to wire racks. When you want to assemble them, dollop cream into the indentation, and smooth it with the back of a spoon, leaving the odd peak. Place, one by one, a few blackberries and a few raspberries so that they look well filled but not crammed. Dust with icing sugar.

Makes 18.

# ROXANNE'S MILLIONAIRE'S SHORTBREAD

This is the recipe, given to me by a fellow-mother at my daughter's school, that introduced me to the notion of melting chocolate in the microwave. I am now a complete convert: it is truly the best way to do it. And you make the caramel in the microwave, too, so what would normally take a good couple of hours takes only a few minutes. Another revelation. It's not that I had never used a microwave before, but I hadn't ever realized it could do things better as opposed to just faster.

You can make this a good week in advance if you like. Keep the shortbread in a cold place or in an airtight tin, and it'll be fine. Or you can even freeze it for up to 6 months. If frozen, the squares should be allowed to defrost for 3–4 hours at room temperature.

**225g plain flour**
**75g caster sugar**
**375g unsalted butter**
**397g can sweetened condensed milk**
**4 tablespoons golden syrup**

**325g plain chocolate**
**1 x 23cm square brownie tin or similar, greased and the bottom lined**

Preheat the oven to 170°C/gas mark 3.

Put the flour and sugar into a bowl and rub in 175g of the butter, clumping the dough together to form a ball. Press this sandy shortbread mixture into the tin and smooth it with either your hands or a spatula. Prick it with a fork and cook for 5 minutes, then lower the oven to 150°C/gas mark 2, and cook for a further 30–40 minutes until it is pale golden and no longer doughy. Let it cool in the tin.

Melt the remaining 200g of butter in the microwave (in a large microwavable bowl) for 2–3 minutes, then add the condensed milk and golden syrup. Whisk the mixture well until the butter is thoroughly incorporated. Heat for 6–7 minutes until it is boiling, stirring thoroughly every minute. As a microwave novice, I found this bit difficult and had to watch that I didn't burn the toffee mixture (I did once), which is why I caution you to check and stir every minute. It's ready when it's thickened and turned a light golden-brown. Pour this molten toffee evenly over the cooled shortbread and leave it to set.

Break the chocolate into pieces and melt it in a bowl in the microwave. Pour and spread it over the fudge mixture (the less you touch it, the shinier it will be) and leave it to cool. Once set, cut the caramel shortbread into pieces. The squares can be stored in the fridge to keep them firm, though if it's winter that shouldn't be necessary.

Makes about 24.

# MINI KEY-LIME PIES

The base for these is the same as for the cheesecakes, and the filling is taken from one of the lime pies from pp103–4. I have sometimes dyed these green with just a little food colouring, otherwise you can't quite tell the difference between these and the mini-cheesecakes. But, for a chic alternative (if you'd rather not use the food colouring) just grate some lime zest over the top once they're cooked and cooled.

**100g unsalted butter**
**250g digestives**
**2 large eggs, separated**
**1 x 200g can sweetened condensed milk**

**zest and juice of 2 limes**
**pinch of salt**
**2 x 12-bun mini-muffin tins**

Preheat the oven to 170°C/gas mark 3.

Make the biscuit base as for the cheesecakes, leaving the tins in the fridge as above.

Beat the egg yolks until thick – I use an electric mixer for this – then add, still beating, the condensed milk and lime juice. If you're making these the day before they're needed, keep the lime zest in an airtight bag, or just bag up the lime-halves and zest them the next day.

In a separate bowl, whisk the egg whites with the salt until soft peaks form and gently fold into the yolk mixture. Using a dessertspoon (and a teaspoon for scraping), fill the biscuit-crusted mini-muffin tins. Transfer to the oven and cook for 10 minutes. Remove, let cool in the tins, then refrigerate for a day.

Turn out the mini key-lime pies following the advice for the cheesecakes. Using a Microplane or other very fine grater, dust with the zest of the limes.

Makes 24.

# MINI LIME-SYRUP SPONGES

This is really just the miniaturization of the lemon-syrup sponge on p13. You could do them in lemon here, too, or use a mixture of ordinary orange juice and lime juice to evoke the wonderful acerbity of Seville oranges. (Or indeed use those when in season.) It doesn't matter what the citrus is: there is just something about these small-scale, perfectly formed loaves that make them particularly appealing.

125g unsalted butter, softened
175g caster sugar
2 large eggs
zest of 1 lime
175g self-raising flour
pinch of salt
4 tablespoons milk

8-bun mini-loaf tin, buttered very
    well

for the syrup:
4 tablespoons lime juice (of 1–2 limes),
    plus zest for decoration
100g icing sugar

Preheat the oven to 180°C/gas mark 4.

Cream together the butter and sugar, and add the eggs and lime zest, beating them in well. Add the flour and salt, folding in gently, and then the milk. Spoon into the mini-loaf tin, and cook for 25 minutes.

While the cakes are cooking, prepare the syrup by putting the lime juice and sugar into a small saucepan and heating gently so that the sugar dissolves.

As soon as the mini-sponges are ready, take them out of the oven and prick them with a cake-tester all over. Pour over the syrup evenly. Try to let the middle absorb the liquid as well as the sides, then leave it to soak up the rest. Don't try to take the cakes out of the tin until they have cooled slightly and the syrup looks like it has been absorbed, but be aware that if you leave these to go completely cold they might be very difficult to get out of the tin.

So, after an hour or two, turn them out onto a rack and grate some lime zest over them before serving (or selling).

Makes 8.

CHRISTMAS

# CHRISTMAS

I think it is probably the case that even people who never, ever bake might consider doing so at Christmas. This doesn't mean I'm going to load you down with homework, presenting this chapter as a kind of holiday-season project; the real point is that at Christmas you might feel you've got more time to play around with some of these recipes (or indeed any of the recipes in this book).

I must emphasize that, having never been someone to bake her own Christmas cake, make her own Christmas pudding, it is deeply satisfying when you do. This doesn't mean it has to become a yearly obligation, a source of pressure rather than pleasure. One of the best things about being adult is that you can decide which rituals and ceremonies you want to adopt to give shape to your life and which you want to lose because they just constrain you. True, I think it takes more determination to shuck off the habits that you've inherited but don't actually want at Christmas time; it's hard not to feel that the way you always did it when you were a child is the way it should be done. So, I've consciously enjoyed setting my own pattern here, choosing what I want to be part of my family's Christmas.

You surely know by now that, as ever, what follows is suggestion, not instruction.

# CHRISTMAS CAKE

I think you do need to have a blueprint for a basic fruit cake that you can make up in whatever size you need. I've already given you recipes from Hettie Potter, who's worked with me on this book; she gave me this, too, from her brother-in-law's mother, Hazel, in New Zealand. The only change I make is to ignore the suggestion of brandy or sherry in favour of Marsala. You do entirely as you wish.

As with all rich fruit cakes, this should be made at least 3–4 weeks before you plan to eat it. And the actual preparation does have its *Blue Peter* moments – you'll need brown paper, as well as baking parchment, to line the tin and stop the cake from scorching.

Place all of the fruit in a large bowl, and add the brandy or sherry. Cover and let the fruit soak overnight.

Preheat your oven to 150°C/gas mark 2. Line your tin with a double thickness of brown paper, then line again with baking parchment, both to come up a good 10cm above the rim of the tin.

Cream the butter and sugar, then beat in the orange and lemon zest. Add the eggs one at a time, beating well after each addition, and then the marmalade. Sift the dry ingredients together, then mix the fruit alternately with the dry ingredients into the creamed mixture, combining thoroughly.

Put the cake mix into the prepared tin and bake following the table above, or until a cake-tester comes out clean.

When the cake is cooked, brush with a couple of tablespoons of extra liqueur. Wrap immediately in its tin – using a double-thickness of tin foil – as this will trap the heat and form steam, which in turn will keep the cake soft on top. When it's completely cold, remove the cake from the tin and rewrap in foil, storing, preferably in an airtight tin or Tupperware, for at least 3 weeks.

For icing, see my comments in the recipe for black cake below (p250).

|  | 110g (¹/₄lb) | 225g (¹/₂lb) | 350g (³/₄lb) |
|---|---|---|---|
| sultanas | 350g | 700g | 1kg |
| raisins | 110g | 225g | 350g |
| currants | 50g | 110g | 175g |
| glacé cherries | 50g | 110g | 175g |
| mixed peel | 50g | 110g | 175g |
| brandy or sherry | 60ml | 120ml | 180ml |
| butter | 110g | 225g | 350g |
| brown sugar | 90g | 195g | 300g |
| orange zest, grated | ¹/₃ teaspoon | 1 teaspoon | 1¹/₂ teaspoon |
| lemon zest, grated | ¹/₂ teaspoon | 1 teaspoon | 1¹/₂ teaspoon |
| large eggs | 2 | 4 | 6 |
| marmalade | 1 tablespoon | 2 tablespoons | 3 tablespoons |
| plain flour | 250g | 350g | 525g |
| mixed spice | ¹/₂ teaspoon | 1 teaspoon | 1¹/₂ teaspoons |
| cinnamon | pinch | ¹/₄ teaspoon | ¹/₄ teaspoon |
| nutmeg | pinch | ¹/₄ teaspoon | ¹/₄ teaspoon |
| almond essence | ¹/₂ teaspoon | 1 teaspoon | 1 teaspoon |
| salt | pinch | pinch | ¹/₄ teaspoon |
| tin: round | 18cm | 23cm | 25¹/₂cm |
| or square | 15cm | 20cm | 23cm |
| temperature | 150°C/gas mark 2 | 150°C/gas mark 2 | 150°C/gas mark 2, reduce to 140°C/ gas mark 1 after 1 hour |
| cooking time | 2–2¹/₂ hours | 3–3¹/₂ hours | 4–4¹/₂ hours |

# BLACK CAKE

This recipe comes from one of my favourite books, Laurie Colwin's *Home Cooking*. There are few food books that have such genuineness of tone, such love of food and of life. Laurie Colwin died young, and I often think of her family, her daughter, whom she writes about with such passion and interest. It's an extraordinarily powerful legacy that she's left her.

This cake was introduced to Laurie Colwin by her daughter's West Indian babysitter: 'Its closest relatives are plum pudding and black bun, but it leaves both in the dust. Black cake, like truffles and vintage Burgundy, is deep, complicated and intense. It has taste and aftertaste. It demands to be eaten in a slow, meditative way. The texture is complicated, too – dense and light at the same time.' Here is the recipe, altered only slightly by me.

for the fruit:

**250g raisins**

**250g prunes**

**250g currants**

**250g natural-coloured glacé cherries**

**165g mixed peel (the real thing, not the chopped stuff in tubs)**

**1/2 bottle Madeira**

**1/2 bottle darkest rum you can find**

Chop all the fruit very finely in the food processor. I advise you to go slowly, one fruit at a time, or else you'll find you've got purée.

Put the chopped fruit into a huge Tupperware and mix pleasurably and stickily with your hands to combine and then pour over the Madeira and rum. I should perhaps say that Laurie Colwin suggested Passover wine, but unless you're doing this around Easter/Passover you'll never find it; and Madeira is, I'm told, the best substitute for it.

Cover the fruits and leave to steep for at least two weeks, but up to six months. I say up to six months – which is what Colwin writes in *Home Cooking* – but I must tell you that I steeped all the fruits one year in November only to find in December that I was just too exhausted to make the cake. So I used it up the following year, after 13 months' marinating. It was strong, but it was good.

for the cake:

**250g soft unsalted butter**
**250g dark muscovado sugar**
**1/2 the marinated fruit mixture**
**1/2 tablespoon vanilla extract**
**1/4 teaspoon freshly ground nutmeg**
**1/4 teaspoon ground cinnamon**

**6 large eggs**
**275g plain flour, preferably Italian 00**
**1 1/2 teaspoons baking powder**
**125g black treacle**
deep, 23cm cake tin, lined as for
    Christmas cake, above

Preheat the oven to 180°C/gas mark 4.

Cream the butter and sugar, and beat in the fruit, rum and wine mixture. I use my KitchenAid free-standing mixer for this: it wouldn't be impossible to do by hand, but it takes a lot of muscle. Add the vanilla, nutmeg and cinnamon, and then beat in the eggs. Stir in the flour and baking powder, and finally the black treacle. The batter should be dark brown.

Pour this dark batter into the prepared tin and cook for 1 hour, then turn the oven down to 170°/gas mark 3 and cook for a further 2½–3 hours. Remove to a wire rack but do not unmould till the cake's completely cold, at which stage, wrap it in a double-thickness of foil and put it back in a Tupperware until you want to ice it.

for the icing:

**1/2 jar marmalade (about 200g)**
**icing sugar for sprinkling**

**500g marzipan**
**1kg ready-to-roll icing**
**1 pair of holly-leaf cutters**

I was teased mercilessly last year for proposing my white-on-white holly-decorated Christmas cake, but as precious as it sounds, it is simply beautiful. And I promise you those who at first mocked, ate their words and my cake.

I don't think there is anything better than an all-white cake – especially with an interior as dense and dark as this one's – but you could easily cut holly leaves out of dark green icing if you wanted. Holly-leaf cutters tend to come in pairs – a smaller and a larger leaf – complete with vein-stamping *truc*. The berries you have to roll yourself, but for this I suggest in any case you buy the icing ready to roll. Of course you can whisk sieved icing sugar with egg whites until it's the right consistency to roll out and ice, but the bought stuff, especially if it comes from a cake-decoration shop, is fine.

Heat the marmalade in a saucepan and when hot and runny strain into a bowl to remove rind. With a pastry brush, paint all over the cake to make a tacky surface. Dust a work surface with icing sugar, roll out the marzipan and drape over the cake. Then press against the cake and cut off the excess with a sharp knife. If you need to do this twice (with two lots of 250g marzipan), that's fine, but make sure to smooth over any joins, so that the icing on top lies smoothly. Dust the work surface again with icing sugar and plonk down your block of icing. Beat it a few times with the rolling pin, then dust the top with icing sugar and roll out. Cover the cake with it, again cutting off the excess and sticking bits together to patch up as you need, sprinkling with cold water first. Transfer the cake to a cake stand or board: once you've added the leaves you really don't want to move it again.

Re-roll the remaining icing and start stamping out the larger holly leaves (dipping the cutter into icing sugar first) and pressing down on them with the vein-stamper. Wet the underneath of each with a little cold water and stick onto the cake to form a circle about 3cm in from the cake's edge. Don't make all the holly leaves face the same way: you want this to look a bit like a holly wreath, which means that although most leaves should be placed aslant, they shouldn't be in a uniform ring. Now do the same with the smaller leaves, sticking them to make a circle around the base of the cake, in other words, blurring the line between cake board and cake. Make tiny balls, to resemble the berries, out of some of the icing that remains. Again, don't be uniform about the way you stick them on: put one berry between some leaves, a bunch of three between others, and so on.

# SNOW-TOPPED SPICE CAKE

This cake – fruitless, light but aromatic – is the perfect replacement for the standard Christmas cake for those who hate it or just haven't got time to make it. The dripping blanket of royal icing certainly lends a seasonal touch, but the dark gingerbread spiciness is enough on its own if you'd prefer to keep it very simple.

I know the list of ingredients is long, but check out the method before deciding this is too labour-intensive: as you'll see, it's about the easiest cake you could make. And if you want to see what it looks like, give or take, turn to the picture of the chocolate-coffee volcano (p180); I use the same cake mould for both.

for the cake:

**4 large eggs, separated, plus 2 extra large egg whites**

**125ml vegetable oil**

**125ml water**

**2 tablespoons runny honey**

**200g dark muscovado sugar**

**75g ground almonds**

**150g plain flour**

**2 teaspoons baking powder**

**1 teaspoon bicarbonate of soda**

**pinch of salt**

**1 teaspoon ground ginger**

**1 teaspoon cinnamon**

**1/2 teaspoon all-spice**

**1/4 teaspoon ground cloves**

**zest of 1/2 an orange**

**100g caster sugar**

**25cm Bundt tin, well buttered**

for the icing:

**250g instant royal icing**

Preheat the oven to 180°C/gas mark 4.

Whisk together the yolks and oil, then add the water, honey and dark muscovado sugar. Add the almonds, flour, baking powder, bicarb, salt, spices and zest, folding in gently. In another bowl, beat the egg whites until soft peaks form and then gradually add the caster sugar. Fold the whites into the cake mixture, and pour into the Bundt tin. Cook for 45 minutes, or until the cake is springy on top and beginning to shrink away from the edges. Let the cake cool in its tin on a rack for 25 minutes before turning it out.

When it's completely cold, you can make up the icing. Put the icing sugar in a bowl with as much water as specified on the packet and whisk till thick. And you do need this to be thick, or else it will just melt into the damp stickiness of the cake. Use more icing if you want a thicker coating, but leave to dry before slicing.

# CERTOSINO

This is the most fabulous Italian spicy fruit cake, decorated glossily with candied fruits and nuts, and best eaten in the tiniest slices with a glass of vin santo or, crossing continents for a moment, Australian black or orange muscat. I'm afraid I've taken terrible liberties with the recipe given to me by Anna del Conte; this is an anglicized version insofar as I've greatly augmented the apples to give a much wetter cake. I do think Italians appreciate a dry cake in the way that we don't. I've also, for purely personal reasons, got rid of the candied peel. As for the decorative topping: I've been vague about quantities because it depends completely on what you want to use and how.

75g seedless raisins

30ml Marsala

350g plain flour

2 teaspoons bicarbonate of soda

150g clear honey

150g caster sugar

40g unsalted butter

3 tablespoons water

1 tablespoon anise or fennel seeds

1 teaspoon ground cinnamon

375g Coxes apples (2 medium), roughly grated

200g blanched almonds, coarsely chopped

50g pine nuts

75g bitter chocolate, chopped

75g walnuts, chopped

25cm Springform cake tin, buttered and lined

suggestions for decorating:

4 tablespoons apricot jam to glaze

pecan halves

natural-coloured glacé cherries

blanched whole almonds

marrons glacés

glacé fruits

Soak the raisins in the Marsala for 20 minutes, and while they're steeping, preheat the oven to 180°C/gas mark 4. Measure the flour and bicarb out into a large bowl. Heat the honey, sugar, butter and water in a saucepan until the sugar dissolves. Add the anise or fennel seeds and cinnamon, pour this mixture over the bowl of flour and bicarb, and stir to combine.

Mix in all the other ingredients, not forgetting the soaked raisins and their liquid, then spoon into the tin and cook for ³/₄–1 hour; and should you find the cake needs that final 15 minutes, you may need to cover it with foil to stop it catching. When the cake has cooled, heat the apricot jam in a small pan and, using a pastry brush, paint most but not all of it over the top of the cake to glaze and give a sticky surface to which the fruits and so forth will adhere. Decorate with glacé fruits and nuts of your choice, leaving no gaps of cake visible on top. Brush with scant remaining glaze so all looks burnished and shiny.

# CHRISTMAS PUDDING

'Stir-up Sunday', the day on which we're all supposed to make our puddings before they're left to mature for Christmas Day itself, falls towards the end of November, on the Sunday after Trinity. Of course, the real stirring-up – as in, 'Stir up, we beseech thee, O Lord, the wills of thy faithful people' – was a religious injunction rather than a culinary one, but it's still a good time, faith or no, to mix up the pudding. Traditionally, as well, everyone in the house is meant to give one stir, wishing for luck as they do so; thus superstitious paganism gets a look-in too, and everyone's happy.

Don't worry too much over every detail in the list of ingredients. Use it rather as a guide towards general bulk rather than specific, must-have items.

If you can't buy candied peel in whole strips, which you then cut up yourself, don't bother with it at all. Just augment quantities of other fruits.

100g currants
100g mixed raisins and sultanas
50g natural-coloured glacé cherries, chopped into quarters
50g dried blueberries
50g prunes, roughly chopped
50g marron glacé pieces, chopped
60g candied peel, finely chopped
150ml rum
£1 coins, cleaned (see below)
90g self-raising flour
125g white breadcrumbs

150g shredded suet
1 quince or 1 medium cooking apple, to provide 120g, roughly grated
150g dark brown sugar
1/2 teaspoon mixed spice
pinch of salt
3 large eggs
zest of 1 orange
125ml vodka for flambéing
sprig of holly for decoration
1 1/2–litre plastic pudding basin with fitted lid

Soak the fruit in the rum overnight.

Mix all the ingredients together in a large bowl and then add the soaked fruit. At the same time, add the cleaned £1 coins. I know a pound a go sounds extravagant but the heaviness of these coins, and their glinting goldness, makes them most appropriate; soak in Coca-Cola overnight to clean. Butter the pudding basin and put the mixture into it. Cover with a piece of greaseproof in which you have folded a pleat, and put on the lid. Boil or steam the pudding for 3½ hours. Rewrap the pudding and store somewhere cool until Christmas. Reheat in the same way, that's to say, steam or boil for another 3½ hours. Now, the flambéing. I know brandy's traditional, but ever since I read that Fanny Cradock advised vodka (because it burns for longer), I have, of course, followed suit. Put the vodka in a small pan and heat on the hob. Light it, pour it over the pudding and bring ceremoniously to the table.

# THREE SAUCES

I hate to recycle recipes from *How to Eat*, but Christmas puts me into something of a quandary because it's not about innovation but tradition, and you can't have Christmas pudding or mince pies without brandy butter. And so evangelical have I become about the Sauternes custard and iced rum sauce, I really couldn't bear to leave them out.

## BRANDY BUTTER

This is what was always traditionally called hard sauce, but somehow it looks affected and twee to call it that now. We all know it as brandy butter these days. I add ground almonds because my mother did, and so it's the taste I know, and because they give it a glorious marzipanny depth and velvetiness.

You need the butter to be as soft as possible before you start but not at all oily. Obviously it makes life a lot easier if you can do this in a machine, either a mixer or processor; I prefer the former. There is one new modification to this: I now use golden unrefined icing sugar, which gives a gorgeous fudginess to it all.

**150g softened unsalted butter**
**225g unrefined golden icing sugar**

**50g ground almonds**
**3 tablespoons brandy, or to taste**

Cream the butter until soft and then add the sifted icing sugar and beat them together till pale and creamy. Mix in the ground almonds and when all is smooth add the brandy. Add a tablespoon at first, then taste, then another and see if you want more. You may find that the suggested 3 is far from enough: it is a question of taste and what is lethally strong for one person seems insipid to another; you must please yourself since you can't please everyone.

# ICED RUM SAUCE

This is a rum-sodden and syrupy egg-nog with cream that's put in the fridge for a few hours before eating. You put it on the searing hot pudding and it melts on impact. A taste sensation.

**300ml double cream**
**2 large egg yolks**

**2 tablespoons golden syrup**
**2 tablespoons dark rum**

Beat the cream until stiff. In another bowl beat the yolks until extremely frothy. Add the golden syrup and the rum to the frothy eggs, still beating. Then fold this mixture into the thick cream, transfer to an airtight container and stash in the deep freeze (though it's pretty good as it is, unfrozen).

Leave in the deep freeze to set hard, and then remove to the fridge to ripen for about 40 minutes before eating, so that it isn't absolutely rock hard.

# SAUTERNES CUSTARD

You don't actually need to use Sauternes for this; any desirably ambrosial and honeyed dessert wine will do. To tell the truth, I hadn't thought of making this to go with the Christmas pudding until *You* magazine did. Now I always do.

**500ml single cream**
**200ml Sauternes**

**7 large egg yolks**
**60g caster sugar**

Half-fill the sink with cold water. Put the cream and wine into separate saucepans and heat both to just under boiling point. Whisk together the egg yolks and sugar and, still whisking, add first the hot wine and then the warm cream. Pour into one of the saucepans and cook over a low to medium heat, stirring constantly, until the custard thickens. If at any time it looks as if it's about to curdle, plunge the saucepan into the cold water in the sink and beat like mad – preferably with a Magiwhisk.

# MINCE PIES

I always think I don't like mince pies: in my memory, they're too sweet, too dense, too cloying. And then I eat one. I think the trick is, if you're using bought mincemeat, to grate over a little sharp apple and squeeze in some lemon juice. But you'll see from the recipes below that making your own mincemeat is not a strenuous activity.

I've given three recipes here, and I should say that I've copied the small, star-topped ones, in idea if not actual recipe, from the mince pies I used to buy from Waitrose. They are the perfect size: one small mouthful.

## MANGER MINCE PIES

Originally, I learnt fairly recently, mince pies were cooked in barquette (little boat) moulds because they were meant to represent the manger. Since this tin is routinely used by French pâtissiers to make small fruit tarts, it's not hard to find the wherewithal to make them now. I've added a shredded filo topping, in part to make them different from the usual, but also in a clumsy attempt to carry on the symbolism: think of it as the straw bedding. If you can get hold of konafa (a sort of shredded-wheat version of filo) so much the better.

And, even if you're using home-made mincemeat, add the extra seasonings here; this version should be even more aromatic than usual.

for the pastry:
**300g plain flour, preferably Italian 00**
**75g Trex or other vegetable fat**
**75g cold unsalted butter**
**juice of 1 orange**
**1 teaspoon orange-flower water**
**pinch of salt**

for the filling:
**approximately 400g mincemeat**
**1/4 teaspoon ground cloves**
**finely grated zest of the orange**
**1/2 teaspoon orange-flower water**
**6 sheets filo or 90g konafa**
**50g unsalted butter, melted**
**icing sugar for dusting**
**12-mould barquette tray**

Measure the flour out into a shallow bowl or dish and, using a teaspoon, dollop in little mounds of Trex, add the butter, diced small, combine with your hands and put in the deep freeze for 20 minutes. Mix the orange juice, the orange-flower water and the salt in a small jug and put this in the fridge.

Empty out the flour and fat into the bowl of the food processor and blitz until you've got a pale pile of porridge-like crumbs. Add the salted juice down the funnel, pulsing till it looks as if the dough is about to cohere; you want to stop just before it does (even if some orange juice is left). If all your juice is used up and you need more liquid, add some iced water. Turn out of the processor and, in your hands, combine to a dough. Then form into two discs. Roll out one of the discs to make a rectangle approximately 40 x 32cm. Lay this on top of the tray, gently pushing the pastry down into the moulds with your fingertips. Give yourself a lot of slack. When you feel all the moulds are lined with pastry, take your rolling pin and roll over the top of the pastry to cut off the excess. When you take that away you should be left with 12 lined barquette moulds. Put this tray in the fridge for 20 minutes, preheating the oven to 200°C/gas mark 6 as you do so.

Empty the mincemeat into a bowl and stir in the ground cloves, orange zest and orange-flower water, then drop 2 scant teaspoons into each barquette mould, spreading it gently to fill. Add more if you want, but remember that the pastry sides will slip down as they bake. Either snip the filo into shreds with scissors or pinch off bits of the konafa and crumble over the mincemeat in the moulds. Drizzle the filo or konafa with the melted butter, transfer to the oven and bake for about 15 minutes, or until the pastry cases and filo topping are cooked and golden.

Remove from the oven and, using a palette knife, help the pies out of the tray and onto a wire rack to cool. When the barquette moulds are cold, start again with the second disc of pastry.

Dust with icing sugar pushed through a tea-strainer before serving.
Makes 24.

## STAR-TOPPED MINCE PIES

Please don't think these will be better if you make the pastry out of butter rather than the butter and Trex mixed; it's the vegetable shortening which makes the pies so celestially light (though by all means use lard if you object to 'fake' fats). And it's the acid in the orange juice that makes the pastry especially tender.

**240g plain flour, preferably Italian 00**
**60g Trex or other vegetable fat**
**60g cold unsalted butter**
**juice of 1 orange**
**pinch of salt**
**approximately 200g mincemeat**
**1 large egg, mixed with a tablespoon**
 **water, to glaze (optional)**

**icing sugar for dusting**
**tray of miniature tart tins, each indent**
 **4¹/₂cm in diameter**
**5¹/₂cm fluted round biscuit cutter**
**4cm star cutter**

Make the pastry following the method for manger mince pies, but form it into three discs (since you're going to have to make these in three batches, unless you've got enough tart tins to make all 36 pies at once). Wrap each in clingfilm and put in the fridge to rest for 20 minutes. Preheat the oven to 220°C/gas mark 7.

Roll out the discs one at a time as thinly as you can without exaggerating; in other words, you want a light pastry case, but one sturdy enough to support the dense mincemeat. Out of each rolled-out disc cut out circles a little wider than the indentations in the trays. Press these circles gently into the moulds and dollop in a scant teaspoon of mincemeat. Then cut out your stars – re-rolling the pastry as necessary – and place them lightly on top of the mincemeat.

If you want to glaze the mince pies, then brush the stars with a pastry brush dipped into the egg and water mix (actually, the pies in the picture on p261 haven't been glazed). Sometimes I do, sometimes I don't: the difference really is one of appearance and only you can decide whether you want them pale and matt or gold and shiny.

Put in the oven and bake for 10–15 minutes: keep an eye on them, they really don't take long. Remove from the oven, prising out the little pies straight away and letting the empty tin cool down before you start putting in the pastry for the next batch. Carry on until they're all done. Dust over some icing sugar by pushing it through a tea-strainer before serving them.

Makes 36.

# FRANGIPANE MINCE PIES

If you try making these in little moulds, you'll drive yourself mad. But if you've already got a batch of tiny pies and another of manger-shaped ones, it's a good idea to make a third that are the size of real, grown-up mince pies. These are no light, airy mouthfuls, but dense, almondy, buttery mounds – rather like a Christmas version of Bakewell tart, now I come to think of it. And indeed there's nothing stopping you from making this in a 26cm quiche mould to make one sliceable Bakewellian pudding.

for the pastry:
**175g plain flour, preferably Italian 00**
**30g ground almonds**
**65g icing sugar**
**pinch of salt**
**125g cold unsalted butter, diced**
**2 large egg yolks, beaten with a**
  **tablespoon of iced water**

for the topping:
**approximately 200g mincemeat**
**2 large eggs**
**90g caster sugar**
**90g unsalted butter, melted**
**90g ground almonds**
**4 tablespoons flaked almonds**
**2 x 12-bun tartlet trays**
**7cm fluted biscuit cutter**

Make the pastry by putting the flour, ground almonds, sugar and salt into the bowl of the food processor and pulse to combine. Add the diced butter and process till you've got a flaky, crumbly mix. Now start adding, tablespoon by tablespoon, the egg and water mix down the funnel, pulsing as you do so, until the pastry looks like it's about to form a ball around the blade. Turn it out onto a surface, press to form a cohesive dough, shape into 2 discs, cover with clingfilm and put into the fridge to rest for 30 minutes. Roll out one of the discs and stamp out 12 circles slightly larger than the tart indentations. Press these in gently, patting base and sides and put back in the fridge for 15 minutes. Preheat the oven to 200°C/gas mark 6.

Put a scant teaspoon of mincemeat into each pastry-lined cavity. In a bowl, beat together the eggs and sugar, then pour in, still beating, the melted butter. Stir in the ground almonds and then dollop a tablespoon of this mixture on top. Sprinkle with flaked almonds and then put in the oven to cook for 15 minutes, or until the pastry is cooked through and the frangipane gold and brown-flecked.

Take out of the oven and leave to cool in the tins for 5 minutes before transferring to a wire rack to cool. When the tin's cold, repeat with the second disc, remaining mincemeat and frangipane.

Makes 24.

# HETTIE POTTER'S SUET-FREE MINCEMEAT

I know it looks illogical to give the recipe for mincemeat after the mince pies, but I thought I'd make you *want* to have it. And once you've decided to make your own mince pies, why compromise, undermining your satisfaction, by missing out what is the easiest part of the exercise?

So many people object to suet that it seemed sensible to begin with Hettie's recipe for a suet-less mincemeat. The extra apples make up for the fat by keeping everything tender and moist.

250g soft, dark sugar
250ml medium-dry cider
1kg cooking apples, peeled, halved
  and quartered
1/2 teaspoon mixed spice
1/2 teaspoon ground cinnamon
250g currants
250g raisins

75g natural-coloured glacé cherries,
  roughly chopped
75g blanched almonds, fairly finely
  chopped
rind and juice of 1/2 a lemon
90ml (6 tablespoons) brandy or rum
4 x 500g preserving (or old jam) jars

In a large saucepan, dissolve the sugar in the cider over a gentle heat. Roughly chop the apples, and add them to the saucepan. Then add all the other ingredients except the brandy or rum, and simmer for 30 minutes or until everything looks pulpy. Take off the heat and when it has cooled a little, stir in the brandy or rum. Spoon into sterilized jars.

This should make around 2kg.

# QUINCEMEAT

I came across this recipe of Frances Bissell's in *The Times* when I was in the first flush of my love affair with the quince, and of course I had to make it straight away. This 'quince-meat', as we call it at home, is a model of seasonal exploitation.

You don't need to go out and buy a bottle of eau de vie de coings – you can use brandy instead – but I did, and have since found it strangely useful in prinking up all manner of other things. (Or, really making the most of the short season, follow the recipe for home-made quince brandy on p340.)

Since I've already given a recipe for a suet-free mincemeat, I should clarify my own position on suet: I love it. Ideally, you want fresh suet from the butcher, which you then grate yourself. Failing that – since it's virtually disappeared from sale now – buy boxed, shredded vegetable suet.

1kg quinces
2 tablespoons unsalted butter, melted
250g sultanas, chopped
250g raisins, chopped
250g dried apricots, chopped
250g light muscovado sugar
250g shredded vegetable suet
1 teaspoon ground cardomom
1 teaspoon ground cloves

1 teaspoon ground cinnamon
1/2 teaspoon ground mace
100g real crystallized peel, chopped
100ml eau de vie de coings, Poire William or my quince brandy, see p340
shallow roasting tray
4 x 500g jars or equivalent

Preheat the oven to 150°C/gas mark 2.

Peel and quarter the quinces and cut into wedges (this is the hardest part of the whole operation). Toss them in the melted butter and put them in the tray and into the oven to roast gently, for 40 minutes or so, until tender.

Remove and leave to cool, then chop or grate or process the fruit (but do not pulp it) and put in a large bowl along with any cooking juices. When completely cold, stir in all the remaining ingredients and put in your clean jars. Now, was that so hard?

Makes 2kg.

# CHRISTMAS CUPCAKES

These beauties also make a very good alternative to mince pies. I buy the icing ready-made and dyed (which is why it isn't a very convincing colour for holly, let's be frank) and use cranberries as the holly berries. The cake underneath is somewhere between chocolate and gingerbread. If you're thinking of taking anything to friends' houses, may I suggest these?

**150g plain flour**
**1 teaspoon baking powder**
**1/2 teaspoon bicarbonate of soda**
**1 teaspoon ground mixed spice**
**pinch of salt**
**100g soft unsalted butter**
**160g dark brown sugar**
**2 large eggs**
**3 tablespoons sour cream**

**125ml boiling water**
**75g dark chocolate, broken into pieces**
**1 teaspoon instant coffee**
**250g instant royal icing**
**1 packet green ready-to-roll icing**
**about 30 cranberries for decoration**
**small holly-leaf cutter with veining stamp**
**12-bun muffin tin and papers**

Preheat the oven to 200°C/gas mark 6.

In a large bowl, mix together the flour, baking powder, bicarb, mixed spice and salt. In another bowl, cream the butter and sugar with an electric mixer. Add the eggs one at a time, mixing well after each addition, and then beat in a third of the flour mixture followed by a tablespoon of the sour cream, repeating till all is used up.

Put the water, chocolate and instant coffee in a pan and heat gently, just until the chocolate's melted. Fold this into the cake batter, but don't overbeat. The mixture will be very thin, but don't worry about that: just pour carefully into the waiting muffin cases and put in the oven for about 20 minutes, until each little cake is cooked through but still dense and damp. Let cool in the tin for 5 minutes, then slip out the cakes in their papers and sit on a wire rack until completely cold.

To ice them, make up the royal icing according to the packet instructions and cover the tops of the cupcakes thickly. Cut out holly leaves and sit two on each cake, and then press on your berries, perhaps putting two on some, three on others.

Makes 12.

# MAIDS OF HONOUR

Some people really cannot stomach mincemeat, so it's useful to have some little pie to serve as a substitute for mince pies. The recipe from the Maids of Honour tea rooms in Richmond, Surrey, is what is commonly called a 'closely guarded secret', but unofficial recipes abound for these tarts, with their filling somewhere between cheesecake and custard. This one is the result of a collaboration between me and one of my oldest friends, Tracey Scoffield.

I like a shortcrust pastry case, but if you prefer puff pastry – which many, including my collaborator, do – you should find 250g ready-made enough for the job in hand.

for the pastry:
**300g plain flour, preferably Italian 00**
**75g cold unsalted butter, diced**
**75g vegetable fat such as Trex, in scant teaspooned lumps**
**2 large eggs**
**2 teaspoons lemon juice**
**pinch of salt**
**1 x 12-bun tartlet tray**
**7cm plain round cutter**

for the filling:
**1 vanilla pod**
**150ml double cream**
**50g unsalted butter**
**50g caster sugar**
**50g ground almonds**
**1 large egg, beaten**
**zest of 1 small lemon and juice of 1/2**
**fresh nutmeg**

Preheat the oven to 220°C/gas mark 7, and prepare the pastry following the method on p83. Cut lengthways down the vanilla pod with the tip of sharp knife, put it in a saucepan, over a medium heat, with the cream, and heat till just below boiling point. Take out the pod, scraping some of the seeds into the milk, then add the butter, sugar, ground almonds, egg and lemon rind and juice. Stir, take off the heat and leave to stand for about 5 minutes.

Roll out half the pastry, cut out 12 rounds and place these into the tart moulds, pressing down with your fingers so they're well lined. Spoon in the filling (remembering you'll have a second batch to do). Leave a good centimetre below the rim, as the custard will rise up as it bakes. Grate over some fresh nutmeg and transfer carefully to the oven and bake for 15–20 minutes until the custard's golden and puffy.

Let the tarts sit in the tin for a few minutes before standing, unmoulded, on a wire rack to cool. When the tin's cold, repeat with the remaining ingredients. Leave the tarts to cool a little before serving, but they are best eaten still slightly warm. And unlike mince pies, they don't keep at all.

Makes 24.

# MULLED WINE

With mince pies, goes mulled wine. Don't fight it.

**1 bottle red wine**
**60ml (4 tablespoons) dark rum**
**125ml Earl Grey tea**
**1 orange, quartered, each quarter**
    **stuck with 1 clove**

**2 cinnamon sticks**
**1 star anise**
**1 tablespoon dark muscovado sugar**
**1 tablespoon honey**

Put all the ingredients in a saucepan, bring almost to the boil, but before the aromatic wine actually boils, turn down to the lowest possible heat and keep it warm as you ladle it into any nearby glass.

## VARIATION

If you need to make mulled wine that isn't really mulled wine because you have to provide drink that's non alcoholic (as I had to do for the Christmas fair at my daughter's school last year) then you can substitute a bottle of red grape juice for the wine, half a bottle of rum flavouring (I'm sorry) for the rum.

# SWEDISH GLÖGG

I was sent this recipe during a culinary crusade on the part of some Swedish trade mission, and I'm sure the interested party will be only too pleased that I've now passed it on to you.

**1 bottle red wine**
**150ml Swedish vodka**
**2 cinnamon sticks**
**8 cloves**

**12 cardamom seeds**
**25g caster sugar**
**25g blanched almonds**
**25g raisins**

Combine all ingredients except for the raisins and almonds in a large pan and let steep, preferably overnight.

To serve, put a sprinkling of raisins and almonds in the bottom of everyone's mug, put the pan on the heat and slowly bring almost to the boil. Strain into a jug and pour over the raisins and almonds in the waiting mugs.

# CHRISTMAS DECORATIONS

I like these as spiced and peppery as German *Lebkuchen* and decorated only in white and silver or gold. I tend, also, to limit myself to bells, angels and stars, but if you want to go bolder and brighter, you should. And if you want these to be milder and therefore more likely to please young children, use the smaller amount of pepper. But keeping them peppery is also a good way of keeping them hanging on the tree . . .

Of all Christmas rituals up for adoption, making these is probably the most satisfying one.

for the biscuits:

**300g plain flour**

**pinch of salt**

**1 teaspoon baking powder**

**1 teaspoon mixed ground spice**

**1–2 teaspoons freshly ground pepper**

**100g unsalted butter**

**100g dark muscovado sugar**

**2 large eggs beaten with**
   **4 tablespoons runny honey**

**set of Christmas cutters**

**2 baking sheets, lined or non-stick**

for the icing and trimmings:

**300g icing sugar, sieved**

**3 tablespoons boiling water**

**gold or silver balls or sprinkles**

**florists' ribbon for hanging**

Combine the flour, salt, baking powder, mixed spice and pepper in the processor. With the motor on, add the butter and sugar, then, slowly, the eggs and honey, though don't use all of this liquid if the pastry has come together before it's used up. Form two discs and put one, covered in clingfilm or in a freezer bag, into the fridge while you get started on the other. Preheat oven to 170°C/gas mark 3.

Dust a surface with flour, roll out the disc, also floured, to about 5mm and cut out your Christmas decorations. Re-roll and cut out some more, setting aside the residue from this first disc, well covered, while you get on with rolling out the second. When you've got both sets of leftover clumps of dough, roll out and cut out again and keep doing so till all the dough's used up. Now take a small icing nozzle and use the pointy end to cut out a hole just below the top of each biscuit (through which ribbon can later be threaded to hang them).

Arrange on the baking sheets and cook for about 20 minutes: it's hard to see when they're cooked, but you can feel; if the underside is no longer doughy, they're ready.

Transfer them to cool on a wire rack. Make up ordinary glacé icing by mixing approximately 3 tablespoons of boiling water with the sieved icing sugar and stir till you've got a thin, glossy glaze. Ice the cold decorations using a teaspoon (the tip for dripping, the back for smoothing) and scatter sparkles or sprinkles as you like.

# BAKLAVA

Of course, I don't really think this is a part of the traditional Yuletide feast, but there is something about the intense sweetness and aromatic succulence that makes it appropriate. It is so temple-achingly sweet that one small marked-out diamond, or maybe two, is enough. But even so, I love its perfumed sugariness – as much as I love the tender, rose-shot green of its equally fragrant nubbly interior. It's also a very good present to take to people over Christmas, which is why I've indicated one of those foil baking trays below.

for the syrup:

**300ml water**

**500g caster sugar**

**juice of ¹/₂ a lemon**

**1 tablespoon rosewater**

**1 tablespoon orange-flower water**

for the pastry:

**325g pistachios, chopped in a processor until medium–fine**

**125g unsalted butter, melted**

**400g (2 packets) filo pastry**

square foil tin, 23 x 23 x 4cm from a supermarket or kitchen shop

To make the syrup: bring the water, sugar and lemon juice to the boil, and keep it at boiling point for 5 minutes. Add the rosewater and flower water, and then remove it from the heat. Pour it into a jug, let it cool and then chill it in the fridge.

Preheat the oven to 180°C/gas mark 4.

Brush the tin with butter, and then each of the filo pastry sheets as you line the tin with them. Use one packet for the bottom layer, placing them in the tin evenly so that the pastry goes up the sides with a little overhang. As the tin is square and the filo pastry is often a rectangular shape, you should try to arrange the sheets so that each side is covered in turn. When you have used one packet, spread the pistachios evenly over the filo sheets. Then carry on with the rest of the pastry in the same way. The last sheet on top should also be buttered well, and then with a sharp knife trim around the top edge of the tin to give a neat finish. Cut parallel lines 4–5cm apart to form diamond shapes, making sure you cut the baklava right through to the bottom of the tin.

Put in the oven and cook for 30 minutes, by which time the filo will have puffed up and become golden-brown. As soon as it comes out of the oven, pour over half the cold syrup. Leave it a few minutes to soak in and then pour over the rest.

Makes approximately 16 pieces.

# LATKES AND LOUKAMADES

I came across loukamades in a wonderful book called *The Food of the Jews of Greece* (and yes, I do know this is the Christmas chapter) when I was writing a piece about food and Hanukkah, the Jewish Festival of Lights, about which until that time I knew absolutely nothing. For the record, Hanukkah is an eight-day affair which tends to fall in December and has thus been appropriated as a kind of Yiddisher Christmas by Jewish-Americans who want their own party to go to as well. It is, in fact, a significant but small commemoration of the victory of the Maccabees in 165BC, and is called the Festival of Lights because – the story goes – when the Jews returned to Jerusalem after the Maccabean victory, they found that the pagans had desecrated the temple, polluting the oil and stopping all but one lamp from burning. There was only enough oil to let it burn for one more day, but when the Jews poured it into the lamp it burned for eight, allowing them to clean the temple and replenish their supplies of holy oil. The miracle of the oil is celebrated culinarily by using it in great vats into which are dunked, splutteringly, latkes, doughnuts, batter-wrapped pieces of chicken, fritters – the Jewish genius is that this festival provides divine ordinance to eat fried food.

Eating latkes – desirably stodgy little potato cakes – is the commonest British way of marking Hanukkah. I like them with cold meats but they are perhaps at their best palate-skinningly hot with cold, cinnamon-infused apple purée dolloped on top. I did give a recipe for them in *How to Eat*, but briefly reprise it here.

650g–700g potatoes, peeled
½ medium onion, peeled and
   coarsely chopped
1 large egg
good pinch of salt

good grind of fresh pepper
1–2 tablespoons self-raising flour
   or matzo meal
vegetable oil for frying
heavy-based frying pan

Push the potatoes through the grater disc of the food processor. Remove and drain in a sieve, pushing well to remove all excess liquid. Then fit the double-bladed knife and put the onion, eggs, salt, pepper and the self-raising flour (or the matzo meal, which is better according to my mother-in-law) in the bowl and process briefly. Then add the grated potatoes and give a quick pulse till the mixture is pulpy but not totally puréed. This should be a thick sticky mess; if it is at all runny add more flour.

Fry the latkes in lumps of about a tablespoonful in the frying pan with hot oil bubbling away in it to a depth of about 1¼cm. About 5 minutes a side should do it, maybe even less.

Makes 20.

*

Edda Servi Machlin, in her resonant, elegiac book, *The Classic Cuisine of the Italian Jews*, writes of her aunt's *frittelle di chanukà*, yeasty, diamond-shaped doughnuts fried till golden and then drenched in a lemon and honey syrup. It's the Greek version, loukamades (eaten all over Greece all the year round, in fact, regardless of ethnicity), which I have adopted as part of our family ritual. They have the virtue, too, of not being yeast-leavened and therefore requiring less time to make. They're not really doughnuts, but spoonfuls of choux pastry, deep-fried and then rolled, straight out of the fiercely hot oil, in a chilled aromatic syrup. Make them and hand out to waiting children (and inevitably their parents), to be eaten straight away with fingers.

for the syrup:
**400g sugar**
**500ml water**
**1 stick cinnamon**
**1 teaspoon orange-flower water**

for the loukamades:
**100g plain flour**

**175ml water**
**75g unsalted butter, diced**
**pinch of salt**
**2 large eggs, beaten**
**approximately 1 litre olive (or vegetable) oil for frying**
**heavy-based frying pan**

You can make the syrup in advance if you like. Put the sugar, water and cinnamon stick in a saucepan, slowly bring to the boil (you want the sugar to dissolve before it boils), then turn up the heat and let bubble ferociously for about 7 minutes. Add the orange-flower water and give it another minute or 3. What you want is a syrup that isn't exactly runny, but isn't honey-thick either, for it will thicken as it cools. Pour the syrup into a jug or bowl to cool and remove the cinnamon stick. Now, you will have a lot of syrup, but that's because I like lots: I want these doughnuts swimming in it. If your tastes are more austere, make less.

Now for the loukamades. Pour the oil for frying into a wide pan to come up to about 4cm. I specify, first, olive oil, because it is, in this context, the holy oil. Of course, substitute vegetable oil if you want, but it isn't *echt*. If you're using olive oil it shouldn't be extra virgin: just the ordinary, pale golden, faster flowing (and cheaper) stuff. In my pan (which is 23cm in diameter and 7cm deep), the oil takes a good 20 minutes to get hot enough for deep-frying, so there's no rush. Just make sure you've got everything for the choux weighed out and to hand before you start.

Sieve the flour. Put the water, butter and salt in a medium-sized saucepan on the hob and heat until the butter's melted and the water's begun to boil. Take the pan immediately off the heat (you don't want the water to evaporate at all) and beat in the flour. Use a wooden spoon for this and don't worry about how lumpy it is or how unyielding, just keep beating until it comes smoothly together – a minute or so should do it. Put the pan back on the heat and keep beating until the dough begins to come away from the sides of the pan to form a smooth ball.

Now beat in the eggs, either by hand (but you'll need muscle power) or by machine. So, either turn the dough into a mixing bowl and add spoonfuls of egg as you continue to beat with your wooden spoon, or turn it into the bowl of the food processor fitted with the double blade and pour, gradually, the egg through the funnel while blitzing. You may not need all of the egg, so go carefully, until you have a smooth, gleaming dough, soft but still stiff enough to hold its shape.

When the oil for frying is haze-waftingly hot, dip a teaspoon into it (so the dough doesn't stick) and then into the mixture. Push the dough off the spoon, spoonful by spoonful, into the hot oil and watch the lumps of choux paste swell up and grow golden as they cook. I find 4 minutes does them (and I cook 4–5 at a time). But just taste as you go along (make that sacrifice) to check the insides are soft but cooked, rather than still doughy. As you remove the spiky little doughnut balls from the pan – with one of those fine-meshed stock de-scummers for preference – put them immediately on a waiting plate, spoon the syrup over and continue to roll them in it. In fact, this is best done by a pair of you: the one to cook the loukamades; the other to ladle over the syrup and then roll them assiduously in it.

Makes about 30. Enjoy.

# CHRISTMAS-MORNING MUFFINS

I do think that part of creating a family life is establishing those shared rituals, as important as getting out the same old familiar box of decorations for the tree each year. Now, it's true that children are too excited about their presents to take a lively interest in breakfast on Christmas Day, but consider making these all the same: there's something so warmly reassuring in knowing that soon this cinnamon-sweet smell of baking and oranges will come to signify Christmas morning to them.

You may find it easier to measure out the cranberries, flour, baking powder, bicarb and sugar the night before, so that all you've got to do is mix together the orange juice, milk and eggs, melt the butter and combine all the ingredients on Christmas morning itself.

for the muffins:
**200g plain flour**
**3 teaspoons baking powder**
**1/2 teaspoon bicarbonate of soda**
**75g demerara sugar**
**good grating fresh nutmeg**
**1 clementine or small orange**
**approximately 50ml milk**

**60g unsalted butter, melted**
**1 large egg**
**150g dried cranberries**
**12-bun muffin tin with papers**

for the topping:
**2 teaspoons demerara sugar**
**1/2 teaspoon cinnamon**

Preheat the oven to 200°C/gas mark 6.

In a large bowl, combine the flour, baking powder, bicarb and sugar, and grate over a generous amount of fresh nutmeg. Squeeze the orange or clementine juice into a measuring jug, then pour in milk on top till it comes up to the 150ml mark. Add the melted butter and the egg, and beat to combine. Pour the jug of liquid ingredients into the bowl of dry ingredients and stir till the ingredients are more or less combined, remembering that a lumpy batter makes light muffins. (Bearing this in mind, you could easily get the children to make up the mixture.) Last of all, lightly fold in the cranberries and fill the muffin cases or cups. The amount of cranberries specified here makes for heavily fruited muffins; if you want them sparser, use half the amount.

Mix together the demerara sugar and ground cinnamon and sprinkle over the tops of the muffins. Stick them in the oven and bake for 20 minutes, by which time the air should be thick with the promise of good things and the good things themselves golden-brown and ready to be eaten – as they are, or broken open and spread heapingly, mouthful by mouthful, with unsalted butter and marmalade.

Makes 12.

# BOXING DAY EGG-AND-BACON PIE

This recipe comes from Beryl Scoffield, the mother of one of my oldest friends, and a woman with a reputation for her pies. This one is my ideal Boxing Day supper, to be eaten on a tray with some cornichons and a glass of beer or cider, as I slump, perfectly contented and guiltless, in front of the television.

for the pastry:

**240g plain flour**
**60g Trex or other vegetable shortening**
**60g butter**
**3–5 tablespoons salted iced water – or enough to bind**

for the filling:

**500g pancetta or bacon, chopped into small batons**
**1 medium onion, finely chopped**
**1 spring onion, finely chopped**
**approximately 2 tablespoons chopped parsley**
**2 large eggs**
**20cm pie plate**

Make the pastry by freezing the fats and flour together for 10 minutes, then tip out into the processor and blitz to a flaky rubble. Add enough iced water to bind, then form into 2 discs, cover them with clingfilm and rest in the fridge for 20 minutes.

Preheat the oven to 200°C/gas mark 6.

Cook the pancetta or bacon in a frying pan with the onion, peppering well. Beat the spring onion, parsley and eggs together, and set aside while you roll out the pastry.

Using one of the discs, line the dish, leaving an overhang. Roll out the other half to make a lid, and set aside for one moment. Transfer the pancetta and onion mixture to the pastry-lined pie plate and pour over the spring onion, parsley and eggs. With a little cold water, dampen the edges of the pastry case and cover with the rolled-out lid. Cut off excess pastry, and seal and pinch all around the rim. Make a hole in the lid to let out steam, put in the oven and bake for 30 minutes.

Sit on a wire rack until slightly above room temperature, or eat cold.

Serves 6.

# GAME PIE

The idea of making a raised-crust pie is a daunting one, I know, but I should tell you that a 15-year-old boy, Nick Blake, came to spend a day with us during the photo-shoot for this book, and ended up making the one that you see opposite, without any earlier preparation or experience. These things, you see, are worth attempting. And the beautiful, designed-for-the-purpose tins that you can buy from most kitchen shops take a lot of the uncertainty out of it.

I love grouse so much that it's the only game I want in my pie, but venison, pheasant, wild rabbit, anything you want to use, is fine. I buy fresh veal stock, made by Joubère and available from some butchers, delicatessens and supermarkets.

for the filling:
**200g pork belly**
**150g lean pork**
**150g lean veal**
**125g thin rashers of streaky bacon**
**3 tablespoons Marsala**
**1 teaspoon English mustard powder**
**1 teaspoon all-spice**
**breasts from a brace of grouse or
    200g of whatever game you're
    using**

for the pastry:
**200ml water**

**175g lard**
**500g plain flour**
**1/2 teaspoon salt**
**1 large egg, beaten with 1/2 teaspoon
    salt, to glaze**
1 game-pie mould, 22cm long

for the jellied stock:
**2 leaves gelatine**
**225ml veal stock**
**75ml Marsala**
**squeeze of lemon**
**1 teaspoon salt**
**fresh-ground pepper**

Put the pork, veal, bacon, Marsala, a teaspoon of salt, a fair bit of pepper, mustard and the all-spice into the food processor and blitz to a coarse purée, then transfer to a bowl and sit, covered, in the fridge. Chop whatever game you're using into rough chunks and set these aside, too, while you make the pastry.

In a saucepan, bring the water and lard to a boil. Then turn into a bowl containing the flour and salt. Mix everything well, creating a smooth dough. Cover the dough and leave it until it's no longer too hot to handle, but don't let it get cold. Now preheat the oven to 200°C/gas mark 6.

Cut off a quarter of the pastry for the lid, and set it aside, covered, for a while. Using the rest of the pastry, line your beautiful, hinged game-pie mould. Push the pastry up the sides of the tin – gently, though, and making sure there are no cracks. Pack the processed filling into the pastry, adding the rough chunks of game as you go, filling right to the top. Roll out the pastry you've put aside for the lid, arrange it on top and pinch to seal. Make a central hole, with the point of a sharp knife or skewer, put in an icing nozzle or similar (for ease of stock-pouring later), and decorate the pastry lid around it. I'm afraid I had no entirely appropriate cutters when I made this one here and am not talented enough to do it freehand, but I did find, to most other people's consternation, a rather fetching duck (and elephant, but I wasn't allowed to use it) in my collection. Brush the underside of your decorations with the beaten egg and stick them on the lid. Now brush all over the top with the beaten egg (and don't throw away what's left), put it in the oven for 30 minutes, and then turn the oven down to 170°C/gas mark 3 and cook for a further 1½ hours so that you can be confident that the meat is cooked through thoroughly.

Now make the jellied stock: put the gelatine leaves to soak in a dish of cold water and put the veal stock and Marsala in a measuring jug and heat in the microwave for a couple of minutes until very hot. Squeeze in some lemon and add the salt and a vicious grating of black pepper. Taste: you do need this much more highly seasoned than you might think. Squeeze out the gelatine leaves and drop them into the jug of hot stock, stirring to dissolve them.

When the pie's had its time, remove it from the oven and sit it for 20 minutes before unclipping the mould. If the pastry looks pallid up the sides, brush with beaten egg and put back in the oven for 10 minutes. Otherwise, sit it on a tray (to catch spills) and pour the jellied stock through the nozzle-cum-funnel, going very slowly as you may well not need all of it and you don't want excess to make the crust soggy.

Leave for about 24 hours before eating.

Serves 6–8.

# CHRISTMAS PAVLOVA

For me, pomegranates are more essentially Christmassy than cranberries, but it's not just for seasonality that I include this here: I love the contrast between the crunchy, edible jewels on top and the soft, yielding cream and marshmallowy base beneath.

**8 large egg whites**
**pinch of salt**
**500g caster sugar**
**1 tablespoon cornflour**
**2 teaspoons vinegar**

**1 teaspoon rosewater**
**2 pomegranates**
**juice of 1/2 a lemon**
**500ml double cream**
**1 baking tray and baking paper**

Preheat the oven to 180°C/gas mark 4. Line your baking tray with the baking paper and draw a 20cm circle on the paper.

Beat the egg whites and salt until satiny peaks form. Beat in the sugar, a scattered spoonful at a time, until the meringue is stiff and shiny. Sprinkle over the cornflour, vinegar and rosewater, and fold in lightly. Mound onto the baking tray within the circle, flatten the top and smooth the sides. Put in the oven and immediately reduce heat to 150°C/gas mark 2. Cook for 1¼ hours. Turn off the oven and leave the pavlova in it to cool completely. If you've got an electric oven, however, open the oven door. When cool, you can keep it in an airtight container for a week or so.

Cut 1 of the pomegranates in half and juice it – is easy to do if you've got an electric juicer, but manageable without. Decant the juice into a small saucepan along with the lemon juice. Bring to the boil and let bubble for a few minutes or until syrupy, then take off the heat and let cool.

Whip the double cream until thick but not stiff; an airy floppiness is what you're after. Invert the pavlova meringue onto a big flat-bottomed plate, peel off the baking parchment and on top of the marshmallowy whiteness pile on the cream with not too much regard for neatness or regularity. Now halve the second pomegranate and hold one half, cut side down, over the cream-peaked meringue and start bashing it with a wooden spoon, being careful not to hit the hand that's holding the pomegranate in so doing. After a while, pomegranate seeds will start slowly falling out, then faster, until the cream is beaded with pink. You might not need all of the other half, but be generous with it all the same, letting seeds fall on the rim of the plate as they will. Finally, drizzle over the puce syrup that's been waiting for this moment, and take to the table.

Serves 10–12.

# CRANBERRY UPSIDE-DOWN CAKE

It's very useful around this time of year to have one or two seasonal puddings to boost a lunch or dinner otherwise made up of leftovers. Not that I wish to imply that leftovers constitute inadequate eating; indeed, it's my favourite sort of food.

I love the Christmasiness of this, all that glowing, berried redness.

**50g plus 125g unsalted butter**
**150g plus 125g caster sugar**
**175g cranberries**
**125g self-raising flour**
**pinch of salt**

**1 teaspoon cinnamon**
**2 large eggs**
**1–1½ tablespoons full-fat milk**
tarte-tatin dish, cast-iron straight-sided
20cm frying pan or similar

Preheat the oven to 180°C/gas mark 4, and put in a baking sheet to heat up at the same time.

Put the cast-iron frying pan – or tarte-tatin dish if you've got one – on the hob over a medium heat and melt the 50g of butter. Add the 150g of sugar, stir, then empty in the cranberries and turn to coat in the syrupy liquid. Set aside while you get on with the cake.

Put the flour, salt, cinnamon, 125g of sugar, 125g of butter and the eggs in the processor and blitz to combine. Pulse while you add enough milk down the funnel to make a batter of a soft, dropping consistency. Pour it over the berries in the pan and transfer immediately to the heated baking sheet in the oven. Cook for 30 minutes or until the cake is bouncy, gold and risen, and beginning to shrink back from the edges.

Take out of the oven and place a plate on top of the pan. Turn upside-down and lift the pan off. Be careful here – it's easy to burn yourself, as I prove time and time again.

Serve warm with crème fraîche or ice cream.

Serves 6.

# CHRISTMAS CRÈME BRÛLÉE

I don't need to tell you how beautiful this is: you can see. It's extravagant, certainly, but it's meant to be. And it feels like a treat, breaking through that gilt-tortoiseshell crust to the voluptuous depths of egg-nog-scented cream beneath.

The tip of freezing the bowl before pouring in the smooth cream-custard I culled from Simon Hopkinson, for which and for whom I am always grateful.

**600ml double cream**
**1 teaspoon orange-flower water**
**good grating fresh nutmeg**
**8 large egg yolks**
**3 tablespoons caster sugar**

**6 tablespoons demerara sugar**
**3–4 sheets edible gold leaf, optional**
**pie dish approximately 20cm in**
**  diameter**
**chef's blowtorch**

Put the pie dish in the freezer for at least 20 minutes and half-fill the sink with cold water. Put the cream, orange-flower water and a brave grating of fresh nutmeg into a saucepan, and bring to boiling point, but do not let boil. Beat the egg yolks and caster sugar together in a bowl, and pour the flavoured cream over, still beating. Rinse and dry the pan and pour the custard mix back in. Cook over a medium heat (or low, if you're worried) until the custard thickens: about 10 minutes should do it. You do want this to be a good, voluptuous crème, so don't err on the side of runny caution. Remember you've got your sinkful of cold water to plunge the pan into should it really look as if it's about to split.

When the cream's thick enough, grate over a little more nutmeg and pour into the severely chilled pie dish. Leave to cool, then put in the fridge till truly cold. Sprinkle with demerara sugar, spoonful by spoonful, and burn with a blowtorch till you have a blistered, tortoiseshell carapace on top. Dab edible gold leaf onto the hard but sticky burnt-sugar crust, using a fat pastry brush or, easier still, your fingertips. Press it gently onto the surface in a random but decorative way, smoothing it down.

Serves 8.

# MONT BLANC

I think this may be my favourite pudding of all time. The chestnuts have a dizzying intensity which is a perfect foil for the fat, smooth blandness of the cream. This version is very much easier than the traditional way, which involves cooking then peeling all the chestnuts before you can get started; I know purists insist on it, but it does seem to me to be the fast route to a nervous breakdown, especially at Christmas.

This time of year demands a certain amount of vulgarity, which is why I go for the snowstorm effect with the meringue at the end. Bought meringues are fine, since you pulverize them in your hands to end up with white dust, but by all means make your own if you prefer.

**750g vacuum-packed peeled chestnuts**
**375ml milk**
**scant teaspoon vanilla extract**
**4 tablespoons dark rum**
**225g caster sugar**
**100g best dark chocolate**

**600ml double cream**
**2–3 meringue nests or meringues**
**made with 1 large egg white and**
**60g caster sugar (p231)**
potato ricer

Put the chestnuts in a saucepan with the milk, vanilla and 3 tablespoons of the rum. Bring to a simmer, and cook until the milk has pretty well been absorbed and the chestnuts are good and tender. This will take about 20 minutes and I find that I have to mash some of the chestnuts with a wooden spoon towards the end of the cooking time to aid the process.

Remove the chestnut mixture to a food mill (the middle/medium disc) or push it through a sieve back into the saucepan. Stir in the sugar and the final tablespoon of rum and cook over a low to medium heat, stirring all the while for about 10 minutes or until the mixture comes together in a cohesive lump. Remove to a bowl and let cool. I sometimes do this a good couple of days in advance.

Just before you sit down for lunch, get out a huge flat round plate and put an upended cereal bowl in the centre. This is to make it easier to make the mountain shape. Now push the cold chestnut purée through the potato ricer – or the food mill – to make a snakey mound over the bowl and plate. Grate the chocolate either by hand or, easier, in the food processor and sprinkle it over the chestnuts, making sure a lot of the dark dust hits the outside rim of the plate. Then beat the cream till thick and dollop over the chestnuts to make the crowning snowy mound. Just before presenting it, smash the meringues to dust in your hands and sprinkle over. That's it.

Serves 10–12.

# GALETTE DES ROIS

I should come clean about my interest in the traditions of the Epiphany: it also happens to be my birthday, and I find following French tradition by eating this cheers me more than taking down the Christmas decorations. The galette itself is simple: puff pastry covering a disc of damp frangipane, hidden within which is a china bean or charm; the person who gets this charm becomes king for the day and is crowned with the gold-paper crown which comes automatically with the cake as sold in French pâtisseries.

You can use bought puff pastry or my easy-puff recipe on p83. If you're not making your own, you'll need to get the square wodges of puff in 500g packets, since the ready-to-roll kind isn't big enough to line or cover the tin. Read through the recipe calmly first, to see how easy in fact it is.

2x 500g packets puff pastry
400g ground almonds
250g unsalted butter, very soft indeed
250g caster sugar
50g plain flour, preferably Italian 00
1 teaspoon baking powder

1/2 teaspoon almond extract
2 teaspoons orange-flower water
a dried broad bean or charm, such as
  a little china figure
gold-paper crown
26cm Springform tin

Preheat the oven to 200C°/gas mark 6, putting a baking sheet in to heat up at the same time.

Roll out one of the packets of puff pastry till you can cut out a big enough circle to line the bottom and sides of your tin, with a generous overhang. Put in the fridge while you make the frangipane: put all the remaining ingredients (i.e., from ground almonds down to orange-flower water) in the processor and whizz until all's amalgamated.

Open the other packet of puff pastry and roll it out till you've got enough to cut out a circle about 5cm more than the diameter of the tin. Get the tin out of the fridge, dollop in the frangipane, hide the charm somewhere, level with a spatula, then place the top round to cover. Using scissors (it's easiest) snip off the overhang so that both top and bottom layers of pastry have only about 2–3cm excess around the edge. Curl the edges over inwards, so that you've got a tightly-furled sealed rim, and then press all round with the tines of a fork. Now decorate the top of the galette: make a small hole (with the point of a small, sharp knife) in the centre, and then, using the same knifepoint, draw swirly lines, like elongated S's, coming out from the centre towards the cake's rim.

Place on the hot baking sheet in the oven and bake for 30–40 minutes until the pastry is golden and well risen. Remove to a wire rack and leave for at least 20 minutes before unclipping. Adorn with crown (or not, as you wish) and present it to the person who gets the charm.

Serves 10–12.

# BREAD AND YEAST

## BREAD AND YEAST

Baking with yeast is the most addictive of pastimes. Once you start, you realize, first, how easy it is, and second, how almost ridiculously satisfying. Partly, this is to do with the feel, the way you sense the dough coming alive under your hands. But perhaps that's what seems spooky to some people – the thought of live yeast. That's why I am such a champion of those little sachets of easy-blend yeast: real, live, fresh yeast isn't hard to use (see below) but the sachet stuff seems more approachable at first.

The point is to get stuck in, and then you can move on to fresh yeast if it's available – and now that most supermarkets have in-store bakeries it tends to be. But if I'm entirely honest, I'm not sure I could detect the difference between bread that's been risen with fresh yeast and bread that's been made with the easy-blend sachets.

The one sort of yeast I cannot, however, get on with is active dried yeast, which manufacturers of bread machines seem so keen on. To me, it tastes too intensely yeasty. And while we're here, I should say that the bread machine leaves me cold, also. Why make bread – when anyway you can buy such wonderful loaves now – if it involves no collaboration on your part? There's none of that crucial satisfaction, that warm feeling of homespun achievement. I don't want to suggest that bread-baking is the province of the terminally smug – the rewards are real, and stem from real activity – but it's very hard not to feel better after kneading dough. As Margaret Costa wrote in her seminal *Four Seasons Cookbook*, it does make 'the baker see herself in an almost biblical light as a valiant woman whose children shall rise up and call her blessed'.

It's also the case that although the bread machine does a good job of kneading the dough it does a pretty hopeless one of baking the loaf. You may disagree, but this has been my experience, and I did once spend some weeks trying one out. And when my experimental time was up, I was very, very glad to send it back.

The baking of the loaf can be a problem: domestic ovens just aren't good at producing that perfect crackly crustiness. You can try all those tricks that are meant to turn your oven into a professional baker's one – spraying the oven with water from a spritzer as you put the loaf in and regularly thereafter, slipping in underneath it a baking tray filled with ice cubes, and so on – but I have never found they work; or not enough to make the faffing about worthwhile.

But still I bake bread, and urge you to. And you can bake good bread, or I wouldn't be telling you about it. For one thing, you can concentrate on loaves which don't rely on a crackly crust; I love white bread baked with just a dusting of flour. The Finnish loaf, too, has a chewy crust, made by glazing it with melted butter the minute it comes out of the oven. True, my sourdough bread may not be quite as the San Franciscans would make it, but it's still tangy, chewy and distinctive. I don't believe even an extremely well-appointed steam-injected oven could improve on them.

I've mentioned the kneading process earlier, and I want to return to it, just in case I've given the impression that I'm entirely of the no-pain-no-gain school: I'm not. There is a very good case for letting a mixer fitted with a dough hook do a lot of the hard work for you. But all I'd say is allow yourself just to finish it off, to do a couple of minutes' therapeutic kneading after the machine's done its efficient business. I think, probably wrongly, that the bread's better for it; certainly I feel better.

My way of baking bread is designed to make it fit more easily into the sort of lives we lead. It can be very hard to find time to leave the dough to rise for a couple of hours, and then another hour, and then bake it. What I do – and it does happen to develop and enrich the taste at the same time – is let the bread rise overnight in a cold place, even the fridge. This means that you can ease yourself out of the day with a little bit of bedtime kneading, and then the next morning all you need to do is let the chilly dough get to room temperature, form it into a loaf or fit it into a tin and then leave it to get puffy and oven-ready while you get dressed or read the papers or whatever. It still means that this is more likely to be undertaken as a weekend or holiday activity, but not exclusively so.

In the recipes that follow, I specify an amount of instant yeast – i.e., yeast that doesn't need to be reconstituted: I do not, ever, mean the extra-fast-acting one – and give as an alternative double the amount of fresh yeast, and then proceed to give, unfamiliarly, exactly the same methods for using both. This is because – as I learnt from a professional baker – you do not need to mix fresh yeast with liquid and then wait for it to foam; you just add it to the flour and so on as if it were the instant sort. I find cutting out this step really does erode any psychological barrier to bread-making.

The quality of flour you use makes a difference. I tend to use organic bread flours from reputable mills, but not exclusively. Don't let lack of time for right-on sourcing be the excuse to stop you from immersing yourself pleasurably – if tentatively at first – in this chapter.

# THE ESSENTIAL WHITE LOAF

I love home-made white bread, springy and tender-crumbed, with a crust dusted with oven-caramelized flour. The best tip I can give you for making good white bread with a light crumb that lasts longer before going stale – which is ever the problem with home-made bread – is to plead with you to use old potato water as the liquid. By this, I just mean the water in which peeled potatoes have cooked. Remember, though, to check the saltiness of the water before throwing in the full amount of salt specified below. I am eccentric enough to keep the water when I drain potatoes, and then bag it up in 300ml quantities and stash them in the deep freeze to use when the bread-making urge is next upon me. Otherwise – and this works remarkably well – you can add a scant tablespoonful of instant mash to ordinary warm water. I think it's worth doing this, and not hard to make sure you've got a packet of Smash or whatever in the house, however offensive it might be to your culinary self-image.

Perhaps here is the place to try and impress upon you that all bread recipes are approximate guides; the amount of liquid that flour absorbs changes according to the flour and the weather.

500g strong white bread flour, plus
   more for kneading
7g (1 sachet) easy-blend yeast or
   15g fresh yeast
1 tablespoon salt

approximately 300ml warm tap or
   potato water
1 tablespoon unsalted butter, softened
1 baking sheet or 500g loaf tin

Put the flour, yeast and salt in a bowl and pour in 200ml of the water, mixing as you do so with a wooden spoon or your hands. Be prepared to add more water, but bear in mind that you want to end up with a shaggy mess (and this of course is the technical term). Add the butter, and mix that in. Now, either start kneading, or if you've got a free-standing mixer, put in the dough hook and let it do the work. Kneading is easy to do but hard to describe. Basically, what you do is press the heel of your hand into the dough, push the dough away, and bring it back and down against the worksurface, for at least 10 minutes. You may need to add more flour as you do so; if the dough seems stickily wet, it means you do want a little more and often a lot more. When you've kneaded enough you will be able to tell the difference – it suddenly feels smoother and less sticky. It's a wonderful moment.

Form the dough into a ball and put into a large oiled or buttered bowl, turning once so the top of the dough is greased. (Most often, I wash out the bowl I've just been using, dry it up and use it again, letting its residual warmth give a starting oomph to the yeast.) Cover with clingfilm and put into a cold place or the fridge overnight, or in a warm place for an hour or two. If you're giving the bread a short warm rise, then just keep an eye on it; it's ready when it's more or less doubled in size. If you've given it a long cold rise, remove the dough from its cold storage – the next morning, later on that day, whenever – and, if it's doubled in size, punch it down, which means doing exactly what that sounds like: punch it until it deflates; I love doing this. If it doesn't look risen much, leave the bowl out at room temperature for a while (obviously, it's easiest to make bread over the weekend so you have a longer morning) and then proceed as above.

Preheat the oven to 220°C/gas mark 7 and then, after kneading the dough for a scant minute, form it into a round loaf shape (or however you want) and sit it on the baking sheet (or in the loaf tin) covered loosely with clingfilm or a tea towel and leave for half an hour or so until puffy and again almost doubled in size. Just before you put it in the oven, remove the towel or plastic and dust with flour; as I've already said, since you can't get a truly crusty loaf from a domestic oven you might as well go for a different effect to start off with.

Bake for 35 minutes or until cooked through; the way to check is to lift up the loaf or remove it from its tin and knock with your knuckles on the underside: if it makes a hollow noise, it's cooked; if not, put it back in the oven for a few minutes. Even if it's been in a tin, do this bit unmoulded. When ready, remove to a rack and let cool, if you can, before eating.

And look, I know that home-baked breads can look bulging and full of cracks and fissures – mine, for example, and see the photo on p295, look rather like the Venus of Willendorf – but that's fine, that's because they're home-made.

## MY BROWN BREAD

Everyone has a way of mixing different flours to make the breads they like, and this is one of my favourites for an everyday but highly flavoured brown loaf. Follow the essential white loaf recipe, only replace the 500g white flour with:

**200g rye flour**                    **200g strong white flour**
**200g wholewheat flour**

Be prepared to add slightly more water – and here use ordinary, not potato, water – and bake the bread in an oven preheated to 200°C/gas mark 6 for about 45 minutes.

# POTATO BREAD

This takes the potato-water idea one stage further: you're actually adding cold, cooked potatoes to the dough. This doesn't make a heavy bread, as you might suppose; the whole deal is that the starch in the potato seems to facilitate the yeast and lighten the loaf. But if this is light, it isn't airy: there is a certain chewiness about it, and an almost waxy softness, which makes it perfect for dunking into the wine-dark juices of a rich meat stew. And the toast it makes is incredible.

**300g cold or warm boiled potatoes**
**700–800g strong white flour**
**1 tablespoon salt**
**7g (1 sachet) easy-blend yeast or 15g**
   **fresh yeast**

**1 tablespoon Greek yoghurt**
**300ml tepid potato water**
1 baking sheet

Press the potatoes through a ricer into a large bowl – or just mash them once in it – and add 600g of the flour together with the salt and the yeast. Mix together, adding the yoghurt and then the water slowly. (Even if your potato water's salty, still add the salt to the flour earlier; on cooking, the potatoes themselves tend to neutralize salinity so you have to emphasize it – though not exaggerate it – at this stage.) When you've got something approaching a dough, tip it out onto a floured surface (or keep it in the bowl and use the mixer's dough hook) and begin kneading, adding more flour as you need it. I find I can end up using another 200g or so.

This is damper and stickier than ordinary white bread dough, so be prepared to keep kneading for a bit longer, but when you have something that looks like it's hanging together densely (I give it about 10 minutes in my KitchenAid with the dough hook fitted, then 2 minutes by hand), form a heavy ball – it won't be very neat – put it into a buttered bowl, turn to coat well, cover with clingfilm and leave in a cold place overnight or a warm place for an hour or so.

When the dough's doubled in size, punch it down, letting any repressed anger joyfully out, knead for a minute and form into a loaf of whatever shape pleases you, and preheat the oven to 220°C/gas mark 7. Sit it on the baking sheet, loosely covered with a tea towel, and after about 30 minutes, when the bread's puffy and almost doubled in size, put it in the oven for 20 minutes, before turning the temperature down to 190°C/gas mark 5 and giving it another 10 minutes or until it's cooked through. Test, as usual, by knocking on the loaf's underside: when cooked, it should give a distinctly hollow sound.

Remove from the oven and let cool on a rack.

# FINNISH RYE BREAD

This is my adaptation of a wonderful loaf which comes from the equally wonderful Beatrice Ojakangas. It's dense, dark and aromatic in an extraordinarily comforting way. I'm not Finnish, and yet I warm to this loaf as if I were brought up on it.

225g rye flour

300g strong white flour

7g (1 sachet) easy-blend yeast or
    15g fresh yeast

1 tablespoon dark muscovado sugar

2 teaspoons salt

300ml warm water

45g (3 tablespoons) unsalted butter,
    melted

1 baking sheet

Put the flours, yeast, sugar and salt into a large bowl and slowly add the water, mixing with your hands or a wooden spoon, until you've got a messy but vaguely cohesive lump of dough. Add a tablespoonful of the melted butter and mix just to incorporate it. Start kneading, either by hand or with the dough hook, until the dough comes together smoothly to form a dense ball, adding more water or flour (and I use the strong white, not the rye, mainly) as necessary.

Use some more of the melted butter to grease a bowl and turn the dough ball in it so that the top is oily (and won't therefore dry out), then cover the bowl with clingfilm and leave to rise in a cold place overnight or for an hour or so somewhere warm.

When the dough's doubled in size, punch it down. This is never quite as satisfying with dense doughs as it is with white breads, but it's pleasurable all the same. Give a good few kneads, and then form into a round loaf. Sit the loaf on the baking sheet, cover it with a tea towel and leave to get puffy for about 30 minutes, during which time preheat the oven to 190°C/gas mark 5. Bake for 45–55 minutes, or until the loaf is cooked through. It should sound hollow when you rap it on its underside with your knuckles, and an inserted skewer should come out clean.

Brush with the remaining tablespoon of melted butter and leave on a wire rack to cool.

# SOURDOUGH

The reason this isn't quite a real sourdough is that it uses a teeny-weeny bit of yeast in the starter, rather than relying only on wild yeasts picked up from the atmosphere. I am not going to give an entire history and account of what a sourdough loaf is, but it helps to think of it as a bread made in three parts, with time in between for the dough to mature and acquire the characteristic tang. I know the idea of a long-drawn-out, tripartite baking process is not necessarily a welcome one, but presumably you do this because you want to, not because you are trying to find time-saving ways in the kitchen and kind of stumbled onto this by mistake.

Anyway, first you have the starter, which is really just a mixture of flour and water, with – and this is the unorthodox, not to say improper, way I do it – the addition of a drop of milk and pinch of yeast. You leave this to get good and sour and bubbly, and then you use some of it to mix the second part – the sponge – with more flour and water. Third and finally, you make the dough, which is the sponge with, again, more flour and more water. I add yeast to this; I'm not sure I should, but the American who first showed me the way of the sourdough did, so I carry on in this vein.

It is the method which is significant with sourdough; you can decide which flours you use to make it. I tend to make rye sourdough or an ordinary white sourdough loaf. I say ordinary, but it isn't at all. It's rather like – and is indeed related to – that wonderful, dense and chewy French *pain gris*. And I've made good bread by using the rye starter in a loaf otherwise made exclusively with white flour too.

The hardest thing about sourdough is not making the bread but keeping the starter alive. I always forget to feed it, which is the term used for adding flour and water to it regularly to keep it going. It dies on me. Or rather, I should say, I kill it out of neglect. To keep it alive, every time you use a cup, stir in another $\frac{1}{2}$ cup of water and $\frac{3}{4}$ cup of flour and leave out of the fridge for 4 hours. Do this once a fortnight if you can.

for the starter:
**150g rye or strong white flour**
**pinch of yeast from an easy-blend**
    **yeast sachet (like a small pinch of**
    **salt) or a fatter pinch of fresh yeast**

**½ teaspoon of milk**
**approximately 200ml water**

Combine the flour, yeast and milk and as much water to make a mixture like a thick pancake batter, and leave, loosely covered, for 3 days.

for the sponge:

**180ml of starter**

**180ml of warm water**

**100g rye or strong white flour**

If you've got American cup measures, you can use the ¾-cup measure for this, which is roughly the equivalent of 180ml. It makes measuring out very much easier.

Mix all the ingredients together and leave tightly covered for 12–18 hours; longer is better but the shorter time is enough if that's all you've got.

for the dough:

**375g wholemeal bread flour (for the rye sourdough) or 500g strong white flour**

**the rest of the easy-blend yeast sachet or 15g fresh yeast**

**all the of the sponge from above**

**1 scant tablespoon salt**

**1 tablespoon caraway seeds (for rye sourdough only)**

**250–300ml warm water**

**vegetable oil for greasing bowl**

**1 baking sheet**

Put the flour and yeast in a large bowl, then stir in the other ingredients till you've got a shaggy mess that looks like it's on its way to becoming a dough. Knead, either by hand or by machine, adding more flour as needed, to form a dense, smooth dough.

Form into a ball and put in an oiled bowl, turning once so that the top is also greased. Cover with clingfilm and leave to double in size, either overnight in a cold place or the fridge, or for an hour or so somewhere warm.

When the dough's done its stuff, punch it down, knead it for 1–2 minutes and form it into a round loaf and sit it, covered with a tea towel, on a baking sheet. Preheat the oven to 200°C/gas mark 6, and let the oven warm up while the loaf is left, for about 30 minutes, until it's puffy.

Uncover, and score the top of the loaf. For ease, you should use a razor blade or *lame* for this, but a sharp knife will do. It must be very sharp, though, because you don't want to use any pressure or the now nicely puffy loaf will deflate. I make about 5 slashes all the way over the top diagonally one way, and then the other to make a rough chequerboard design. Transfer to the oven and bake for about 45 minutes, until the loaf is cooked and sounds hollow when you rap it firmly on its underside.

# NORWEGIAN MOUNTAIN LOAF

This was one of the recipes – along with the cinnamon buns on p322 – I greedily plundered from Trine Bell, a friend who's half Norwegian and is generous with her culinary birthright. As much as I love a good, British white loaf, I have a real weakness for those nubbly Northern European breads which are dense and virtuously substantial.

Because this is very easy to make, it can soon become part of a pretty painless routine. You can play around, as you like, with flours, seeds and grains.

250ml semi-skimmed milk

250ml water

350g wholemeal bread flour

50g rye flour

7g (1 sachet) easy-blend yeast or
　15g fresh yeast

50g porridge oats (not instant)

25g wheatgerm

3 tablespoons sunflower seeds

3 tablespoons linseeds

1 tablespoon salt

silicon loaf-shaped mould or baking
　sheet or ordinary well-buttered
loaf tin

Mix the milk and water together in a measuring jug, and combine all the other ingredients in a large bowl. Pour the liquid into the dry ingredients, stirring all the while, to make a sticky, porridge-like mixture.

Scrape into an incredibly well-buttered loaf tin – or better still, a Paton Calvert silicon loaf mould which you need not prepare in any way – and put into a cold oven. Turn it on to 110°C/gas mark $\frac{1}{4}$ and after 30 minutes turn it up to 180°C/gas mark 4. Bake for 1 hour, though in some ovens it may need 10–15 minutes more. You should be able to slip it out of its tin and check by the knocking method, but with a loaf of this heaviness that's not always a reliable gauge, so do poke in a cake-tester or fine skewer to make sure; if it comes out clean, the loaf's cooked. If not, you can just put it back into the oven without its tin and give it another few minutes.

# MAPLE-PECAN BREAD

You won't find much in the way of flavoured breads here, fashionable though they are. I don't go in for them. Bread, like a pasta, is best at conveying other flavours, not jumping about in a ra-ra skirt showing off its own. But this is an exception: it has nuts and syrup in, but the overall effect is muted. And it stays true to its proper calling: that's to say, this is a bread that comes into its own with cheese.

**500g wholemeal bread flour**
**150g strong white flour**
**1 tablespoon salt**
**7g (1 sachet) easy-blend yeast or**
    **15g fresh yeast**
**300–400ml warm water**

**4 tablespoons maple syrup**
**50–100g chopped pecans (or walnuts)**
**oil (walnut oil, if you've got some) or**
    **butter for greasing**
**1 baking sheet**

Combine the flours, salt and yeast in a large bowl. Measure out 300ml of the warm water and stir in the maple syrup. Pour the liquid into the dry ingredients and stop when you've got a rough dough; you may need an extra 100ml or so of water to reach this stage. Knead for a few minutes, then leave for 20 minutes.

Start kneading again, sprinkling in the nuts. It's entirely up to you how nutty to make this: with cheese I think the upper limit is fine; as an ordinary eating loaf, I'd go for the lighter amount. Carry on kneading until the dough feels smooth and elastic (though this amount of wholemeal means it can't feel that elastic) and then form into a ball.

Grease a bowl with oil, and turn the dough ball in the oil, so that the top is lightly slicked with it too. Cover the bowl with clingfilm and leave to rise in the kitchen for 1–2 hours or until about doubled, or follow the general method for a cold, slow rise.

Punch the dough down, knead for 1 minute and then form into a loaf. Sit this loaf on a baking sheet, cover with a tea towel, preheat the oven to 220°C/gas mark 7 and leave the dough for about 30 minutes or until puffy.

Score the loaf with a blade or sharp knife – I tend just to give three short diagonal slashes on this one – and transfer to the oven. After 15 minutes, turn the temperature down to 190°C/gas mark 5 and give a further 20 minutes or so. Check the bread's ready by rapping its bottom, then transfer to a wire rack to cool.

# BAGELS

I know that making your own bagels seems like a fairly abstruse practice. I include a recipe partly because most of the bagels for sale here are not bagels at all, but bread rolls with a hole in the middle – real bagels should be chewy, not remotely airy, with a tightly woven crumb – but also because they're a pleasure to make. They belong here, and not in the children's chapter, though children really enjoy making them, or rather forming them. I do too.

The cooking isn't hard – though it's a dough that needs muscle power – even if it is a two-staged affair: you poach them first, and then bake them. The recipe is adapted from George Greenstein's *Secrets of a Jewish Baker* – where else should you be getting a bagel recipe? – whose tip it is to add malt to the poaching liquid to help the bagels acquire that characteristic sweet and shiny crust. Malt syrup, or extract, is sold at most chemists; but failing that, just use sugar.

**1kg strong white flour, plus more as necessary for kneading**

**1 tablespoon salt**

**7g (1 sachet) easy-blend yeast or 15g fresh yeast**

**2 tablespoons sugar**

**1 tablespoon vegetable oil, plus more for greasing**

**500ml warm water, plus more as needed**

**2 tablespoons malt or sugar, for poaching the bagels**

**2–3 baking sheets, oiled or greased**

Combine the flour, salt and yeast together in a large bowl. Add the sugar and oil to the water. Make a well in the dry ingredients and add the liquid, mixing to a dough with a spatula or wooden spoon.

Knead the dough either by hand or with a dough hook, trying to add more flour if you can. Often with doughs you want them as wet as you can manage; here, dry is good.

The dough will be very stiff and hard work, I know, but knead until you've got a really smooth, elastic dough; even with the dough hook and an electric mixer, this takes about 10 minutes.

Form the dough into a ball, and put it into an oiled bowl, turning once to coat all round, then cover the bowl with clingfilm and leave it to rise for about 1 hour. It should be well risen, and, when you poke it with your finger, the impression should remain.

Now punch the dough down, really punch, and then give a good knead and divide the dough into 3 pieces. Using your hands, roll each piece into a rope, then cut each rope into 5 pieces. Roll each piece between the palms of your hands into a ball, and

then roll into another rope, curling it round to form a ring. Seal the ends by overlapping them a little and pinching them together. At about this time put on a large pan of water to boil. When it boils, add the malt or sugar.

Sit the bagels on the baking sheets, cover with tea towels and leave for about 20 minutes, by which time they should be puffy. Now preheat the oven to 240°C/gas mark 9 or your maximum oven temperature.

When the malted water's boiling and your bagels are good and puffy, start poaching them. Drop a couple of bagels at a time into the boiling water and boil for 1 minute, turning them once. I use a couple of large spatulas for this (wasn't it Portnoy who always presumed spatula was a Yiddish word?).

As you poach them, put them back onto the oiled baking sheets, well spaced, then bake for 10–15 minutes or until they're shiny and golden-brown.

Makes 15 bagels.


## GARLIC AND PARSLEY HEARTHBREADS

These are something between garlic nan and herby focaccia: dimpled, doughy and headily pungent. When lunch is cold and sparse – some sharp cheese, some sliced tomatoes, a green salad – these bring everything substantially, chin-drippingly together. (But please try making them once to eat with fried eggs and maybe some fried or grilled tomatoes.)


**500g strong white flour**
**7g (1 sachet) instant yeast or**
  **15g fresh yeast**
**1 tablespoon salt**
**300–400ml warm water**
**5 tablespoons olive oil, plus more for**
  **greasing and for pouring over the**
  **garlic**

**3 large or 4 small heads of garlic**
**extra virgin olive oil for drizzling**
**bunch of flat-leaf parsley**
**salt, preferably Maldon, for sprinkling**
**2 baking sheets**

Preheat the oven to 190°C/gas mark 5.

Combine the flour, yeast and salt in a bowl. Pour 300ml warm water into a measuring jug and stir in the olive oil. Mix the liquid with the dry ingredients to make a soft but firm dough, adding more liquid as needed, and either turn this out onto a surface and knead by hand or keep in the bowl and use a mixer fitted with the dough hook and knead until smooth, supple and full of elastic life. Form into a ball, wash out

and dry up the bowl, oil it and turn the dough in it so it's lightly oiled all over. Cover the bowl with clingfilm and leave to rise for an hour or so until doubled in size.

While the bread is rising, trim the top off the heads of garlic, making sure they remain whole, sit them in some torn-off squares of foil, dribble over some oil and wrap them loosely. That's to say, the packages should be baggy but the foil tightly sealed at the edges. Cook the garlic packages for 45 minutes; they should not be mushy by this stage but still just holding their shape. Remove from the oven, unwrap and let cool till you can handle them. Turn the oven up to 200°C/gas mark 6.

Tear the parsley from their stems and add a good handful of the leaves to the bowl of the food processor – not worrying if some stems here and there are left on – and chop. Squeeze the soft garlic cloves out of their skins and into the bowl and process again. Pour enough extra virgin olive oil to make a runny paste down the funnel, while still processing, and leave this pungent emulsion where it is while you get back to the bread.

When the dough's risen, punch it down and leave to rest for 10 minutes. Divide the dough in 2, and get out 2 sheets of baking parchment or Bake-O-Glide. Sit a ball of dough on each, and roll out to form a curved rectangle or bulky oval. Then, using your hands, press out a little more. Transfer the breads on their papers to the baking sheets, cover with tea towels and leave to prove and get puffy for about 25 minutes.

Poke your fingers all over the tops of the breads to dimple them, then go back to the processor and pulse once or twice to make sure the parsley, garlic and oil are combined and pour this green mixture all over the corrugated flatbreads.

Put the baking sheets into the oven and bake for 20 minutes or until the breads are cooked – becoming golden in parts, with the garlic flecks a darker brown, and the rims puffing up around the oily topping. Whip out of the oven and drizzle over a generous amount of good extra virgin olive oil. Sprinkle over some salt and set down on the table for people to tear greedily at with their bare hands.

Serves 4 generously.

# SCHIACCIATA WITH GORGONZOLA AND PINE NUTS

When I lived in Florence, I ate what is routinely called focaccia here but knew it as 'schiacciata'. This is another softer, doughier pizza, like the hearthbreads, but topped with Gorgonzola and a scattering of pine nuts. I love it as a first course with some salty-sweet Parma ham.

**350g strong white flour**
**150g plain flour, preferably Italian 00**
**7g (1 sachet) instant yeast or**
   **15g fresh yeast**
**2 teaspoons salt**
**300–400ml warm water**
**3 tablespoons olive oil**

**150g Gorgonzola**
**freshly ground pepper**
**grating fresh nutmeg**
**3–5 tablespoons extra virgin olive oil**
**3 tablespoons pine nuts**
**roasting tin, measuring approximately**
   **20 x 30 x 5cm**

Combine the flours, yeast and salt in a bowl. Pour 300ml of the warm water into a measuring jug and stir in the 2 tablespoons of olive oil. Pour the liquid over the dry ingredients and mix to form a soft but firm dough, adding more water as necessary.

Now start kneading, treating this dough exactly as in the hearthbread recipe, only when it's risen and doubled in size, don't divide it in two but sit it in the roasting tin and press to fit, letting it rest for a few minutes if it looks as if it's never going to stretch to all four corners (it will) and then going at it again. Cover the dough with a tea towel and preheat the oven to 220°C/gas mark 7. After 30 minutes or so, the dough should be puffy and ready for its topping.

In a bowl, with a fork, mash the cheese till soft and keep mashing while you add a generous amount of pepper and a meaner amount of nutmeg. Keep forking while you add the extra virgin olive oil; if the 3 tablespoons aren't enough to make this a spreadable, just pourable mixture, add more.

Poke your fingers all over the dough to dimple it and then pour over the Gorgonzola mixture. Sprinkle the pine nuts on top and bake for 10 minutes. Reduce the heat to 190°C/gas mark 5 and cook for a further 15–25 minutes until the rims of the schiacciata are golden-brown and the cheese is bubbling.

Remove from the oven, cut into fat, chunky slices and let people take them straight from the tin – or transfer to a board or plate if you feel happier that way.

# NIGELLAN FLATBREAD

Look, the name is meant to be a bit of joke, but what I'm talking about is a pitta-like bread, glazed golden with beaten egg and sprinkled with nigella seeds. I came across a recipe rather like it in Eric Treuille and Ursula Ferrigno's inspirational *Bread* and made it, you could say, my own. (You can get the nigella seeds, usually marked 'kalonji', from shops that sell Indian food, and many more besides.)

This is what I make when I'm in mezze-mode. It's not hard, and although I love some of the flatbreads you can buy (not particularly the pittas, but the doughier, softer, tear-shaped hearthbreads), it gives me more pleasure to make these, doubling the quantity and putting the flat oval loaves in the oven in batches so there's always a wooden board of warm, dippable bread on the table.

for the bread:

**500g strong white bread flour**

**7g (1 sachet) easy-blend yeast or
   15g fresh yeast**

**2 teaspoons salt**

**2 tablespoons yoghurt**

**2 tablespoons olive oil, plus more for
   greasing**

**approximately 300ml warm water**

for the glaze:

**1 large egg**

**1 teaspoon water**

**1 teaspoon yoghurt**

**1 tablespoon nigella seeds**

2 baking sheets

Combine the flour, yeast and salt in a large bowl and make a well. Dollop the yoghurt and oil into a measuring jug and add warm water to come up to the 350ml mark. Give a quick beat with a fork to combine, then pour this liquid into the dry ingredients, and mix with your hands or a wooden spoon, adding more liquid as needed, to form a firm but soft dough.

Turn out onto a floured surface (or set your mixer and dough hook to work) and start kneading. Add more flour as needed until you've got a smooth, supple and elastic dough. Form the dough into a ball, grease a bowl and turn the dough in it so it's lightly oiled all over. Cover the bowl with clingfilm and leave to rise for about an hour or so, until doubled in size.

Punch the dough down, then leave to rest for 10 minutes. Preheat the oven to 220°C/gas mark 7. Tear the dough into 3, and then halve each piece. Form each of these 6 little pieces into an egg-shape and, one by one, roll them out to make a flat, elongated, if irregular oval. Place on baking sheets about 3cm apart, cover with tea towels and leave to prove for 20 minutes, until puffy.

Using the blunt side of an ordinary kitchen knife, draw diagonal parallel lines across the loaves about 2 centimetres apart. Do the same now the other direction, so you've got a loose criss-cross.

Beat the egg with the water and yoghurt and, using a pastry brush, paint this over the breads. Sprinkle on the nigella seeds and bake in the hot oven for 8–10 minutes, by which time the loaves will be golden, puffed up in places and cooked through.

Remove them from the oven and drape immediately and for a few minutes with a tea towel so that these small, flat, breads don't dry up and get too crusty.

Makes 6.

## LAHMACUN

This is one of the first things I order in Turkish restaurants – though there are variants of it in all Eastern Mediterranean cuisines – and if you haven't tried it, do so now. The simplest, if not the most appetizing, way to describe it is to say that it is a sort of Turkish pizza with a topping of finely ground lamb. Imagine discs of gold-rimmed soft-crumbed flatbread, with a smear of spiced and peppery-lemony meat daubed on top. We make these for lunch, with just a green salad and maybe some sharp goat's cheese to go with.

You can find pomegranate molasses or syrup at supermarkets these days as well as at Middle Eastern stores, but lemon juice can be substituted. It hasn't got the depth or rounded bitterness of the pomegranate molasses, but the short, sharp sourness of the citrus brings its own pleasing contrast with the sweet, spiced meat. As for that, do buy it minced if you prefer, but this is one of the few times you actually want the fine pulping that the blades of the food processor bring about.

for the dough:

**150g bread flour**

**100g plain flour**

**1 teaspoon easy-blend yeast or**
**   6g fresh**

**1/2 teaspoon salt**

**125ml warm water**

**1 tablespoon olive oil**

for the topping:

**1 medium onion, finely chopped**

**1 fat garlic clove, finely grated**

**2 tablespoons olive oil**

**250g lamb, very finely chopped in the**
**   processor**

**pinch of cayenne**

**pinch of ground allspice**

**1/2 teaspoon cumin**

**2 tablespoons tomato purée**

**2 tablespoons finely chopped flat-leaf**
**   parsley, plus more for serving**

**1 tablespoon pomegranate molasses**
**   (or lemon juice)**

**4 tablespoons melted butter**

**2 baking sheets, oiled**

Combine the flours, yeast and salt in a large bowl. Add the water and oil, and mix to a dough. Knead for 5–10 minutes, depending on whether you are using your hands or a dough hook on a mixer. You can stop kneading when the dough is smooth and elastic.

Place in an oiled bowl, turn well, and cover with clingfilm. Let it rise in a warm place for about an hour or until it has doubled in size.

Preheat the oven to 220°C/gas mark 7.

Meanwhile, to make the lamb paste for the top, fry the onion and garlic in the oil until soft but not coloured. If you sprinkle in a pinch of salt it should help stop them browning. Add the minced or processor-pulped lamb, along with the cayenne, allspice and cumin, and then stir in the tomato purée. Move the lamb about to break it up well, and cook for about 10 minutes until the lamb is no longer pink. Finally, add the parsley and pomegranate molasses or lemon juice and, after tasting, season with salt and pepper to taste.

Knock the dough back to get rid of the air, and divide into 8 egg-sized pieces.

Roll these out into circles of about 12cm in diameter. Let them rest on the oiled baking sheets, with tea towels draped over them, for about 10 minutes.

Dollop about 1 tablespoon of the lamb paste onto each circle, spreading to cover the centre of each one well. Paint the pizzas with melted butter, especially the edges, and cook for 8–10 minutes. When they come out of the oven, cover with a cloth – I know it will get dirty, but *tant pis* – to prevent a hard crust forming. The point about these is that they should be soft enough for you to bend them in two or roll them up to eat.

Sprinkle over more parsley, if you want, as you put them out on the table.

Makes 8 (enough for 4 people, just).

# PIZZA CASARECCIA

This is the pizza as made in the Calabrian home of my own domestic goddess, Lisa Grillo. While we all struggle to produce that thin-crusted, charcoal-redolent pizzaiolo's pizza and fail, the Italians recognize that you need to go to the pizzeria for that and have instead devised a home-made alternative, doughier and with more topping, but very good in its own but different way.

   I've marked the anchovies for the topping as optional, but in truth all of it is. The list that follows was how Lisa made it, but I suspect it was how Lisa made it because that was what she had in the house. And as for the cheese, don't worry if you don't have parmesan or mozzarella: Italians are mad about Cheddar on pizza.

for the dough:
**250g plain flour, preferably Italian 00**
**1 heaped teaspoon (1/2 sachet)**
   **easy-blend dried yeast, or 3**
   **tablespoons fresh**
**1/2 teaspoon salt**
**approximately 150ml warm water**
**2 tablespoons extra virgin olive oil**
1 baking sheet

for the topping:
**200g tinned chopped tomatoes**
**2-3 pinches dried oregano**
**4 slices fine-cut ham**
**2-3 gherkins, chopped**
**5 anchovies, optional**
**fresh parmesan, mozzarella or cheese**
   **of your choice**

Combine the flour, yeast and salt in a large bowl, and stir in the warm water and the olive oil, adding more water as necessary to form a dough. When you've got a shaggy mess that's on its way to being a dough, tip the contents out onto a lightly floured surface and knead for about 5 minutes (or do all this with an electric mixer's dough hook) or until the dough is smooth and bouncy, though expect this still to be on the sticky side. Put into an oiled bowl and turn it to cover it lightly with the oil. Then cover the bowl with cling-film and leave somewhere warm for an hour till the dough's doubled in size.

   Preheat the oven 240°C/gas mark 9.

   Knock the air out of the dough using well-oiled hands, knead a little, and press onto the baking sheet in either a rectangular or round shape. Cover with the chopped tomatoes which have been seasoned with some salt, pepper and the oregano. Put into the very hot oven for about 20 minutes or until the dough has a hollow sound when knocked.

   Add the topping of your choice, then put the pizza back in the oven and cook for a further 5–10 minutes or until the cheese has melted and the base is crisp.

   Serves 4 generously.

# GERMAN PLUM TART

I first made this a couple of years ago now, and it was one of the recipes that drew me to yeast cookery, made me want to do more. The inspirational force is Linda Collister – you just cannot read her without wanting to put on an apron and get your hands stuck into some flour – and this comes from *Sweet Pies and Tarts*. While the two yeasted flat tarts that follow this are more suitable for long, greedy weekend breakfasts, this makes a sumptuous pudding. You could easily make the dough in the morning, sit it in the fridge for a slow rise all day and then, with relative lack of effort, get this finished once you've got back from work, even if it's quite late. And the one thing it doesn't taste like is a hastily knocked-up little something.

for the dough:

**3¹/₂g (¹/₂ sachet) easy-blend yeast**
**or 7g fresh yeast**
**about 350g strong white bread flour**
**¹/₂ teaspoon salt**
**50g golden caster sugar**
**200ml milk, lukewarm**
**1 medium egg, beaten**
**20g unsalted butter, very soft**

for the filling:
**500g plums, halved and stoned**

**3 tablespoons demerara sugar**

for the crumble topping:
**140g plain flour**
**100g light muscovado sugar**
**110g unsalted butter, diced**
**200g walnut or pecan pieces**
**1 large baking sheet – about 32 x 24cm – greased or non-stick, or a roasting tin approximately 20 x 30 x 5cm, also greased or non-stick**

To make the dough, put the flour, yeast, salt and sugar into a mixing bowl, and slowly pour in the warm milk, stirring as you do so. Add the beaten egg and the soft butter, and stir to a soft and sticky dough. Turn out onto a floured board and knead for a good 10 minutes, or for about half that time in an electric mixer fitted with a dough hook. Don't use a food processor. The dough should be soft and satiny but not stickily wet: if you think you need to add more flour, then do; different flours absorb different amounts of liquid. Cover and let rise for 1 hour at room temperature.

To prepare the filling, toss the prepared plums with the sugar (and I sometimes use half light muscovado, half caster rather than the stipulated demerara) and set aside.

Preheat the oven to 190°C/gas mark 5.

To make the crumble topping, combine the flour with the sugar in a mixing bowl, then work in the butter with your fingers to make pea-sized clumps of dough. Stir in the nuts and set aside.

Knock down the risen dough with your knuckles, and push out into a rectangle to cover the baking sheet or press it out in the roasting tin. (This is easier than rolling it and then transferring it, and you are not trying to produce a smooth, even finish.) Top with the plums, cut side up, then sprinkle with the nutty crumble topping. Bake in the preheated oven for about 30 minutes until the base is golden, the fruit tender and the topping crisp and brown.

Serve warm, with cream, crème fraîche or ice cream – vanilla or Hill Station's cinnamon if you can get it.

Serves 8.

## VARIATIONS

You can use whatever fruit you like here, with or without the topping or a version thereof. Cherries, messily stoned over the pastry sheet so that you lose none of the juices, are wonderful, especially with almonds in place of the pecans. Apples are also good, with or without blackberries. The wonderful thing about this yeasted pastry is that it absorbs and acts as a foil to any amount of fruity juiciness.

But please, don't rule out a yeasted base for savoury tarts, too. Sweat onions or leeks in butter or bacon fat and spread them out on a puffy sheet of dough made by following the recipe above, but leaving out the sugar, zest and spices. Grate over cheese if so wished, cut into rough squares and eat while still warm.

# APPLE KUCHEN

*Kuchen*, in German, just means cake. In America, it means something more specific – that yeasted, plain, but often fruit-topped, coffee cake that the German immigrants brought with them to the New World. As you might expect, it is good with coffee, and makes a fabulous breakfast if you've got people staying and you want to sit around the table eating, drinking, talking, reading the papers in an aromatic fug of apple-pie spice and buttery yeasty dough.

What I do is make the dough up before I go to bed and leave it, clingfilmed, etc., in the fridge overnight. When I get up the next morning, I turn on the oven, let the dough come back to room temperature and then I get on with the rest. It's probably ready about an hour after I've got up which, considering how spectacular this is, is not bad going. It freezes well, too, so you can always do one batch to last you over a few weekends' worth of breakfasts.

for the dough:
**350–400g strong white flour**
**¹/2 teaspoon salt**
**50g caster sugar**
**3¹/2g (¹/2 sachet) easy-blend yeast,**
  **or 7g fresh yeast**
**2 large eggs**
**¹/2 teaspoon vanilla extract**
**grated zest of ¹/2 a lemon**
**good grating fresh nutmeg**
**125ml milk, lukewarm**
**50g unsalted butter, softened**
Swiss-roll tin or ovenproof rectangular
  dish approximately 30 x 20cm

for the topping:
**1 large egg**
**1 tablespoon of cream**
**grating of fresh nutmeg**
**2 Granny Smiths**
**1 tablespoon demerara sugar**
**1 tablespoon caster sugar**
**¹/4 teaspoon allspice**
**2 tablespoons flaked almonds**

for the icing:
**75g unrefined (golden) icing sugar,**
  **sieved**
**1 tablespoon hot water**

Put 350g of the flour in a bowl with the salt, sugar and yeast. Beat the eggs and add them, with the vanilla, lemon zest and nutmeg, to the lukewarm milk. Stir the liquid ingredients into the dry ingredients, to make a medium-soft dough, being prepared to add more flour as necessary. I generally use about 400g, but advise you to start off with the smaller amount: just add more as needed. Work in the soft butter and knead by hand for about 10 minutes or half that time by machine. When the dough is ready it will appear smoother, and springier. It suddenly seems to plump up into glossy life.

Cover with a teatowel and leave till doubled (1–1¹/4 hours), or leave to rise slowly in a cold place overnight. Then punch down and press to line the tin. You may think it's never going to stretch to fill, but let it rest for 10 minutes or so mid-stretch, especially if the dough had a cold rise. When it's pressed out on the tin, leave it to prove for 15–20 minutes. Preheat the oven to 200°C/gas mark 6. Peel and core the apples and chop them finely; I use a processor but there's really no need. And you could use other apples, too, if you prefer: whatever you've got to hand; cooking apples can easily be substituted and are better if you want a pulpier covering.

When the dough's ready, beat the egg with the cream, grate over a little nutmeg and brush the top of the dough with this mixture. Cover the egg-glazed dough with the apples, then mix together the sugars and allspice and sprinkle over. Top with the flaked almonds and put in the oven for 15 minutes. Then turn down to 180°C/gas mark 4 and cook for a further 15 minutes or so, until the dough is swelling and golden at the edges and cooked within.

Remove from the oven and make a runny paste with the sieved icing sugar and the hot water. Spoon or trickle over the cake.

Leave to cool for about 15 minutes, then slice it, and eat while it's still warm and juicily, stickily fragrant.

Serves 8.

# RHUBARB-CRUMBLE KUCHEN

Well, this is the introduction of a very British taste to a very un-British confection and it works wonderfully – there is sometimes something to be said for melting-pot cooking.

This is a minor point, but I do think you need to drink tea, not coffee, with it.

for the dough:

**350–400g strong white flour**

**1/2 teaspoon salt**

**50g caster sugar**

**3 1/2g (1/2 sachet) easy-blend yeast, or 7g fresh yeast**

**2 large eggs**

**1/2 teaspoon vanilla extract**

**grated zest of 1/2 a lemon**

**good grating of fresh nutmeg**

**125ml milk, lukewarm**

**50g unsalted butter, softened**

Swiss-roll tin or ovenproof rectangular dish approximately 30 x 20cm

for the filling:

**1 large egg**

**1 tablespoon of cream**

**grating of fresh nutmeg**

**500g rhubarb (to make 350g trimmed weight)**

**75g caster sugar**

**1/4 teaspoon allspice**

for the crumble topping:

**30g unsalted butter, cold and diced**

**50g self-raising flour**

**1 tablespoon caster sugar**

**1 tablespoon demerara sugar**

For the dough, follow the recipe for the apple kuchen.

When you've pressed the dough out in the tin, leave it to prove for 15–20 minutes. Preheat the oven to 200°C/gas mark 6. When the dough is ready, beat the egg and cream together, grate over some nutmeg and brush the mixture over the dough.

To make the crumble topping, rub the cold, diced butter into the flour until it becomes like oaty sand, then stir in the sugars with a fork. Chop the rhubarb finely and stir it together with the sugar and allspice. Don't do this until the last minute, though, as the sugar will make the rhubarb leach out water as it stands. Sprinkle the rhubarb-sugar mix over the egg-washed dough, and then the crumble on top of that. Put in the oven for 15 minutes, then turn down to gas mark 180°C/gas mark 4 and cook for a further 15 minutes or so, until the dough is swelling and golden at the edges and cooked within.

Remove from the oven, and leave in the tin for about 15 minutes – if you can – then slice and eat, still warm.

Serves 8.

# NORWEGIAN CINNAMON BUNS

The Northern Europeans, and especially the Scandinavians, are wonderful bakers and eating these for breakfast or tea on a cold winter's day makes one feel ours is a climate to be grateful for. But then, I've always thought that bad weather has its compensations, most of them culinary.

for the dough:

**600g flour**

**100g sugar**

**1/2 teaspoon salt**

**21g (3 sachets – yes, really) of**
   **easy-blend yeast or 45g fresh yeast**

**100g butter**

**400ml milk**

**2 eggs**

for the filling:

**150g soft, unsalted butter**

**150g sugar**

**1 1/2 teaspoons cinnamon**

**1 egg, beaten, to glaze**

**roasting tin approximately 33cm x**
   **24cm or large brownie tin, lined**
   **with baking parchment bottom and**
   **sides**

Preheat the oven to 230°C/gas mark 8.

Combine the flour, sugar, salt and yeast in a large bowl. Melt the butter and whisk it into the milk and eggs, then stir it into the flour mixture. Mix to combine and then knead the dough either by hand or using the dough hook of a food mixer until its smooth and springy. Form into a ball, place in an oiled bowl, cover with clingfilm and leave it to rise for about 25 minutes.

Take one-third of the dough and roll it or stretch it to fit your tin; this will form the bottom of each bun when it has cooked. Roll out the rest of the dough on a lightly floured surface, aiming to get a rectangle of roughly 50 x 25cm. Mix the filling ingredients in a small bowl and then spread the rectangle with the buttery cinnamon mixture. Try to get even coverage on the whole of the dough. Roll it up from the longest side until you have a giant sausage. Cut the roll into 2cm slices which should make about 20 rounds. Sit the rounds in lines on top of the dough in the tin, swirly cut-side up. Don't worry if they don't fit snugly together as they will swell and become puffy when they prove. Brush them with egg and then let them rise again for about 15 minutes to let them get duly puffy.

Put in the hot oven and cook for 20–25 minutes, by which time the buns will have risen and will be golden-brown in colour. Don't worry if they catch in places – see mine in the picture. Remove them from the tin and leave to cool slightly on a rack – it's easy just to pick up the whole sheet of parchment and transfer them like that – before letting people tear them off, to eat warm.

Makes 20.

# SCHNECKEN

*Schnecken* means 'snails', which is what these German-American coiled buns resemble. They are like the Norwegian cinnamon buns, only more so. By which I mean they are stickier, puffier, gooier and generally more over the top. God, I love them.

I first came across them in one of my favourite books, *The Village Baker's Wife* by Gayle and Joe Ortiz, and I've relied heavily on their method and approach (as I do often). If you're at all keen on baking or even the idea of it, do look at this book, and its companion volume and precursor, *The Village Baker*.

for the dough:
**500g bread flour**
**50g caster sugar**
**1/2 teaspoon salt**
**7g (1 sachet) easy-blend yeast or**
   **15g fresh yeast**
**75g unsalted butter**
**150ml milk**
**2 large eggs**

for the syrup:
**125g unsalted butter**
**2 tablespoons demerara sugar**
**4 tablespoons maple syrup**
**3 tablespoons golden syrup**

**200g walnut or pecan pieces**

for the glaze:
**1 large egg**
**2 tablespoons milk**

for the filling:
**50g caster sugar**
**100g demerara sugar**
**1 tablespoon cinnamon**
**12-bun muffin tin, buttered**
**parchment-lined roasting tin or baking**
   **tin for turning the sticky buns out**
   **onto later – large enough to cover**
**muffin tin**

Combine the flour, sugar, salt and yeast in a large bowl. Melt the butter in the milk – use a microwave and a measuring jug for ease – beat in the eggs and stir into the dry ingredients to make a dough. Knead for 10 minutes or for 5 with a dough hook. When it's springy and satiny, form it into a ball, put into an oiled bowl, turn to coat, and cover with clingfilm. Leave in a warm place for 1 hour or until doubled in size.

Using an electric mixer, start on the syrup: beat the butter until soft and smooth and add the sugar, still beating. Beat in the syrups and then divide this mixture between the muffin cups. Top with the walnuts, about a tablespoonful in each sticky-based waiting cup.

Preheat the oven to 180°C/gas mark 4. When the dough's ready, knock it back, knead once or twice and then roll out to a large rectangle, approximately 60 x 30cm, with the long side nearest you. Beat the egg and add the milk. Glaze the dough, using a pastry brush to paint, or just your fingers.

Mix the filling ingredients in a little bowl and sprinkle onto the dough. Now, roll up from the long side and away from you, carefully and firmly (though not too tightly), keeping a firm sausage shape.

Cut into 12 even slices, and lie each slice spiral-swirly cut side up, on top of the nuts and syrup in the muffin cups.

Leave to prove for about 20 minutes and when they're risen and puffy, put into the oven and bake for 20–25 minutes, by which time they should be golden and cooked: crisp in parts, voluptuously gooey in others.

Place the roasting tin or baking sheet on top and turn the whole thing the other way up. (You will need oven gloves and a degree of caution for this.) Remove the muffin tray and dislodge any nuts that are still stuck in it, adding them, along with any residual syrup, to the upturned buns. Leave to cool, then apply to face – as if you needed my encouragement.

Makes 12.

## VARIATION

These killer sticky buns are also wonderful (and probably more authentic) made with a half-batch of processor Danish pastry – see below.

# PROCESSOR DANISH PASTRY

I've mentioned Beatrice Ojakangas already in the recipe for Finnish rye bread. I came across her joyfully easy way of making Danish pastry in Dorie Greenspan's *Baking with Julia*. I've adapted it to fit my practice and prejudices, but her idea of mixing everything in the food processor is revolutionary. Truthfully, I don't think I'd even have considered making Danish pastry otherwise. It's good to know, indeed crucial, that this still produces an authentic Danish pastry. Beatrice Ojakangas helpfully writes, 'Don't think you're cheating by taking the fast track – this is the way it's done these days all over Denmark.'

60ml warm water

125ml milk, at room temperature

1 large egg, at room temperature

350g white bread flour

7g (1 sachet) easy-blend yeast or
　15g fresh yeast

1 teaspoon salt

25g caster sugar

250g unsalted butter, cold, cut into
　1/2cm slices

Pour the water and milk into a measuring jug and add the egg, beating with a fork to mix. Put to one side for a moment. Get out a large bowl, then put the flour, yeast, salt and sugar in the processor, and give one quick whizz just to mix. Add the cold slices of butter and process briefly so that the butter is cut up a little, though you still want visible chunks of at least 1cm. Empty the contents of the food processor into the large bowl and quickly add the contents of the jug. Use your hands or a rubber spatula to fold the ingredients together, but don't overdo it: expect to have a gooey mess with some butter lumps pebbling it. Cover the bowl with clingfilm, put in the fridge and leave overnight or up to 4 days.

To turn it into pastry, take it out of the fridge, let it get to room temperature and roll it out to a 50 x 50cm square. Fold the dough square into thirds, like a business letter, turning it afterwards so that the closed fold is on your left, like the spine of a book. Roll out again to a 50cm square, repeating the steps above 3 times. Since each recipe below uses half of this, cut in half, wrap both pieces and put each in the fridge for 30 minutes (you can keep them in the fridge for up to 4 days, if you haven't already done so at the earlier stage), or refrigerate one to use now and put the other half in the deep freeze to use later.

Having made the Danish pastry, you need to know what to do with it. Obviously, the first stop is to go into making what we call Danish pastries, and they call 'Vienna bread'. There are two here: my all-time favourite, a cheese Danish, which you can rarely buy over here; and an almond Danish, exquisite and much better than even a good shop-bought one.

# ALMOND DANISH

for the pastry:

**a half quantity of processor Danish pastry dough, rolled out and ready to use, as above**

**2 baking sheets, oiled or lined**

for the filling:

**150g blanched almonds, toasted**

**80g icing sugar**

**2 tablespoons unsalted butter at room temperature**

**1/2 teaspoon almond extract**

**1 large egg white, beaten lightly**

for the egg glaze:

**1 large egg, beaten with**

**2 tablespoons milk**

for the clear glaze:

**100g caster sugar**

**60ml water**

for the sugar glaze:

**100g icing sugar**

**1–2 tablespoons warm water**

To make the almond filling, process the almonds and icing sugar together until finely ground. Add the butter, pulse again, then the almond extract and 2 tablespoons of the egg white. (This can be made in advance and kept in the fridge for a week.)

Roll out the pastry into a big square and cut into thirds horizontally. Then cut in half down the middle, giving you 6 rough squares. Take each square and put a tablespoon of the almond mixture – which you've shaped roughly into a sausage – onto the pastry at a diagonal. Bring up the opposite corners and pinch together, then flatten the pastry slightly to give you a cigar shape.

Place on the baking sheets and brush with the egg glaze. Leave them to rise until they double in size, about 1¹/₂ hours; and again they should feel like marshmallow. Meanwhile, preheat the oven to 180°C/gas mark 4.

Cook for 15 minutes or until puffy and beautifully golden-brown.

Transfer to a wire rack and let them cool slightly before brushing with the clear glaze; then later, when they are a lot cooler, drizzle over the sugar glaze.

Makes 6.

# CHEESE DANISH

for the pastry:

**a half quantity of processor Danish
    pastry pastry dough, rolled out, and ready
    to use, as above**

**2 baking sheets, oiled or lined**

for the filling:

**200g ricotta cheese**

**6 tablespoons caster sugar**

**pinch of salt**

**1 tablespoon lemon zest**

**1 large egg, beaten**

**3 tablespoons unsalted butter, melted
    and cooled**

the egg, clear and sugar glazes:

**as above**

Combine the cheese, sugar, salt, lemon zest, egg and butter to make the filling. Roll out the pastry into a big rectangle and cut it in half. Divide each half into 3 and place a tablespoon of cheese filling on each piece of dough. Fold the opposite corners up together and seal with a pinch.

Place on the baking sheets and brush with the egg glaze. Let them rise until they double in size, about 1½ hours; they should then feel like marshmallow. Meanwhile – about 30 minutes before they're ready to be cooked – preheat the oven to 180°C/gas mark 4. Pinch the corners back together if they have become unsealed, then put them on their baking sheets into the oven and bake for 15 minutes or until puffy and golden-brown.

Remove to a wire rack and make the two remaining glazes. To make the clear glaze, heat the caster sugar and water in a small saucepan. Bring to the boil, then take off the heat. To make the sugar glaze, add the water to the icing sugar a little at a time to make a runny icing; you should be able to ice the pastries in thin lines, running it off the prongs of a fork. So: let the Danish pastries cool slightly before brushing with the clear glaze, painting it on with a pastry brush, and then later, when they are more or less cold, zigzag the sugar glaze over them.

Makes 6.

# TARTE TATIN
## For Aunt Fel, 1934–2000

Tarte tatin is so overdone that I never thought I'd be including it in any book I wrote. And if tarte tatin is to be undertaken, it isn't, usually, with Danish pastry. But having made this Danish pastry, I knew instantly that it would be perfect in a tarte tatin. So I overruled myself.

I've relied a lot on my Aunt Fel's taste and judgement while working on this book, and indeed while cooking generally, and I invited her round to eat and give her comments on this. She loved it, and insofar as one can dedicate a recipe to someone's memory, I dedicate this to hers.

**100g unsalted butter**
**150g caster sugar**
**1kg Coxes apples, peeled, quartered**
**   and cored**

**half-measure Danish pastry, rolled**
**   out and ready to use, as above**
**22cm tarte-tatin dish, similar-shaped**
**   Le Creuset or cast-iron frying pan**

Preheat the oven to 200°C/gas mark 6 and put in a baking sheet at the same time.

Put the butter in the tarte-tatin dish or cast-iron frying pan on the hob. Let the butter melt and add the sugar. When it foams, add the prepared apples, arranging them in a circular pattern, hump-side down, in the dish. Cook on a high heat until the buttery, sugary juices turn a glorious caramel colour and the fruit has softened.

Take the pan off the heat, and leave it to stand for 10 minutes.

Roll the Danish pastry out thinly into a circle to fit the top of the dish, plus a bit of overhang. Lay it on top of the apples in the dish, tucking the edges down the sides under the apples, rather like tucking in a sheet. Transfer the dish to the baking sheet in the oven and cook for 20–30 minutes, until the pastry is golden-brown and the caramel syrup is bubbling.

Take the cooked tarte out of the oven, place a large plate on top of the dish and, wearing oven gloves and with great care, turn the whole thing the other way up. Remove the dish and, *voilà*, your tarte tatin, with its gloriously burnished crown of caramelized fruits. Pick up any apples which have stuck to the dish or that are otherwise out of position, and bring to the table with a small bowl of cold crème fraîche.

Serves 6.

## VARIATION
You can also use quinces, either by adding just a few, in among the apples (the most harmonious way, I think), or by substituting them entirely.

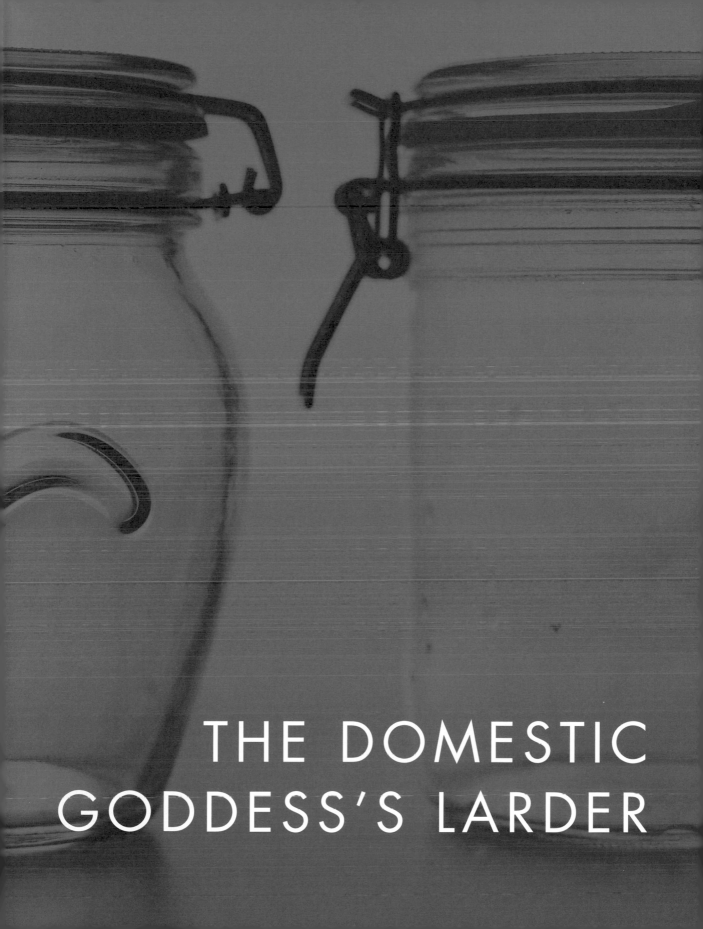

# THE DOMESTIC
# GODDESS'S LARDER

## THE DOMESTIC GODDESS'S LARDER

There are few things that make us feel so positively domestic as putting food in store. 'Putting up', it always used to be called, the canning and preserving of the fruits and vegetables presently in glut but soon to disappear. Life's not quite like that now, but I do preserve fruits and pickle vegetables for the simple reason that I love doing it. I feel I'm putting down roots, laying down a part of the foundation for living.

But please, I'm not getting into Mrs Bridges drag and don't suggest you do either. I'm not talking about buying bushels and pecks – whatever they may be – of produce and slaving over them for weeks on end. When I make jam, I sometimes make only one small pot at a time. For a start, it's much easier, and I suggest you begin your jam-making career just as sparsely. And few of us anyway have more than a scant shelf on which to store such things. But a few jars here and there are enough to adorn, give pleasure and be useful. It's true that we bought the house we now live in purely because I fell in love with the larder, had to have one, but I recognize that, in cities at any rate, certainly in any modern home, they no longer exist. A cupboard or a few centimetres' space on a counter top or shelf is fine, though. And in fact, many of the foods in this chapter actually need to be stored in the fridge.

I haven't forgotten the modern world; I wanted to concentrate on jams, chutneys, curds and pickles that were easy to make, required no expertise or experience and didn't take days or depend upon multi-staged procedures. I know the idea of being in the kitchen faffing around with bottles and jars and hot pans might seem confining to many, but honestly, I have found it liberating. The sense of connectedness you get, with your kitchen, your home, your food, is the very opposite of constraint. Just follow one suggestion, one recipe in this chapter and I promise you'll see what I mean.

## CLEAN JARS

Before you do anything, to store jams, chutneys, glazes, jellies, etc., you need sterilized jars. I have to say, I regard a dishwasher-cleaned jar as a sterilized jar, but you do have to use it straight away, while it's still warm from the machine. Otherwise, you can sterilize the jars in the microwave by filling them a quarter full with water and microwaving them on high for 10 minutes. Drain and use while still warm.

The conventional method for rigorous sterilizing of jars involves scrubbing them well in warm soapy water, rinsing them and then letting them dry off in a cool oven (140°C/gas mark 1). Again, you should put the jam in them while they're still warm, so you may as well leave the jars in the oven until you need them.

# VANILLA SUGAR

**750g caster sugar**                    **2 vanilla pods**

Fill a vacuum-sealable glass jar with the caster sugar and the vanilla pods, each cut into 3; after a week you will have sugar infused with the sort of domestically heady fragrance that seems as if it could only have come from the most well-stocked and well-ordered of Victorian larders. It's the aromatic equivalent of well-worn, ambrosially evocative, cream-painted tongue-and-groove panelling.

You can use it in place of ordinary sugar in cakes, pies, puddings – more or less anything sweet. You can even make this your kitchen-counter sugar pot, though have non-scented available for tea drinkers. This is good in coffee, and there's nothing nicer than mugs of vanilla-scented warm milk at bedtime.

## VARIATIONS
You can go quite to town with scented sugars. In place of the vanilla pods, use cinnamon sticks, unsprayed rose petals or dried tangerine peel, which you can find in Chinese and most Asian stores. I also keep a store of rosemary sugar, which is just caster sugar with a few sprigs of rosemary – the needles eventually fall off of their own accord – and use, sparsely, to sweeten meat or tomato sauces for pasta and on the rosemary loaf cake on p9.

# RHUBARB SCHNAPPS

In the middle of one night, I realized that, however great my love for rhubarb, I had never drunk a liqueur made from it. This, then, is my version. Use the measurements as guidance only. As with the quince brandy below, really it comes down to choosing quantities to fit into whatever jars or bottles you have available.

**approximately 1kg of rhubarb, to make 600g trimmed weight**
**300g caster sugar**

**1 litre vodka, plus more if needed**
**1 x 2-litre jar**
**1 x 1-litre bottle**

Chop the rhubarb and divide it between the two jars. Add 150g sugar to each jar, put the lids on and shake well. Unclip the lids and pour 500ml of vodka – and I use the cheapest I can find – into each to fill. If that doesn't fill them, then pour in more. But it should; the rhubarb takes up a lot of each jar.

Close the lids, put the rhubarb somewhere cool and dark for at least 6 weeks and up to 6 months. If you remember, shake the jars every day or every other day for the first month or so.

Strain into a jug, then pour into a bottle. There's your rhubarb schnapps.
Makes 1 litre.

# QUINCE BRANDY

To tell the truth I made this partly because I'd bought masses of quinces out of exuberance and excitement because they were in season and then felt increasingly guilty because I'd been too exhausted and busy to do anything with them. So I did this. Of course, now I'll do it every year: it is so peachily delicious. The quinces and the aromatic spices mellow the brandy, and their fragrances hover around just enough to let you know they're there. Use this for the quincemeat, and indeed the Christmas pudding, on pp265 and 256 – and in anything else that you think would benefit from it.

I don't bottle this: I leave it in its beautiful jar, like something you imagine William Morris dreaming of, and use a small, lipped ladle to spoon it out into shot glasses after dinner.

| | |
|---|---|
| **4–6 quinces** | **2 large or 4 small cinnamon sticks** |
| **approximately 4 bottles cheap brandy, or as needed to fill jar** | **4 star anise** |
| | **1 x 5-litre jar** |

Wipe your quinces with kitchen towels, then cut and quarter them; but don't peel them or core them. Put them in the bottom of a large, wide-mouthed bottle or jar and pour cheap brandy over to come to the top. Arrange the cinnamon sticks and star anise in this amber underwater scene and fasten the lid. Leave for at least 6 weeks before drinking.

Makes approximately 2 litres.

# QUINCE GLAZE

Quince jelly – which is the traditional use to which British quinces are put – seems to me to involve an exhausting and masochistic procedure. Take a tree of quinces, several days' dripping through elaborately suspended muslin, and what do you end up with? A bare pot's bottom of precious liquid, dotted with suicidally greedy ants and bugs.

This is the smarter alternative: if you're feeling domestically inclined you can use it to glaze fruit tarts or to sweeten and perfume apple pies and crumbles; if not, then use it as a stickily aromatic sauce over good bought ice cream (and over lemon or lemon meringue ice cream it's superb) or dribble in coral wreaths over cream-splodged meringues.

| | |
|---|---|
| **1 quince** | **750g caster sugar** |
| **750ml water** | **1 x 350ml jar** |

Roughly chop the quince (a cleaver is probably the best tool for this), put the pieces – peel, pips and all – in a medium-sized saucepan with the water and sugar, and bring to the boil. Let it bubble away for a good hour, or until the liquid seems reduced by half, and strain into the prepared jar, in which you can keep it pretty indefinitely in the fridge.

Makes 350ml.

# CURDS

Strictly speaking, a curd is not a larder item because it needs to be kept in the fridge, but that's irrelevant to my thesis: making a fruit curd is one of the simplest ways of making yourself feel like a provider of comforting domestic bounty.

## CRANBERRY CURD

There is only one word to describe the colour of this fabulous, astringent but velvety curd: magenta. Well, some would say cerise, but that, of course, would convey quite the wrong culinary connotations. Either way, you get the picture.

I've given enough quantities to make quite a bit, because it occurs to me that it would make a good Christmas present.

**500g cranberries**
**200ml water**
**100g unsalted butter**

**500g caster sugar**
**6 large eggs**
**5 x 250ml jars or equivalent**

Place the cranberries and water in a saucepan, cover them and cook on a low heat until tender and popped. Pass the cranberries through a food mill (or push through a sieve) and put the fruit purée back into a saucepan. Add the butter and sugar, melting them gently. Beat the eggs in a bowl and sieve them into the saucepan. Stir the curd constantly over a medium heat until it has thickened. This requires patience as you don't want to speed things up and curdle the mixture, but that's not particularly challenging. When it has thickened, it should coat the back of a spoon. Let cool a little before pouring into the jars. Keep in the fridge.

Makes 1¼ litres.

# PASSIONFRUIT CURD

As wonderful as this is to eat piled on top of fresh white bread, it is exceptional sandwiching a Victoria sponge, dolloped over muffins and pancakes, or poured into a cooked and cooled pastry case.

| | |
|---|---|
| **11 passionfruit** | **150g caster sugar** |
| **2 large eggs** | **100g unsalted butter** |
| **2 large egg yolks** | **1 x 350ml jar** |

Put the seeded pulp of 10 of the passionfruit into the processor and blitz just to loosen the seeds. Strain into a jug or bowl.

Beat the eggs, egg yolks and sugar together.

Melt the butter over a low heat in a heavy-based pan, and when melted stir in the sugar-egg mixture and the passionfruit juice, and keep cooking gently, stirring constantly, until thickened.

Off the heat, whisk in the pulp – seeds and all – of the remaining passionfruit, let cool slightly, then pour into the jar. Keep in the fridge.

Makes 350ml.

# LIME CURD

Flora Woods gave me this recipe when she blessed me with her famous courgette cake (pp18–19). I'll pass on your thanks to her.

| | |
|---|---|
| **75g unsalted butter** | **zest of 1 lime** |
| **3 large eggs** | **1 x 350ml jar** |
| **75g caster sugar** | |
| **125ml lime juice (of approximately** | |
| **4 limes)** | |

Melt the butter in a heavy-based saucepan, add all the other ingredients and whisk to a custard over a gentle heat. Let cool before filling a jar – or a cake – with it. Keep in the fridge.

Makes 350ml.

## JAMS AND JELLIES

I know the idea of making jam can seem off-putting, but let me tell you I never, or rarely with any success, use a sugar thermometer. I put a saucer into the deep freeze before I start, and while cooking I take the pan off the heat and splodge teaspoons of jam onto it. If the jam wrinkles when I push at it with a finger, it's ready.

Start by making small quantities, which are easier to keep under control and are anyway more useful. Always use a big pan to make jam, preferably a preserving pan, as the jam needs room to boil rapidly without boiling over.

## HANDS-FREE RASPBERRY JAM

This is the best jam to start with as it doesn't need any testing or temperature-taking or indeed anything much: you just put the fruit and sugar, separately, into the oven and then, on mixing together, you've made your jam. As you'd expect, it is intensely fresh-tasting, and indeed will spoil if you don't keep it in the fridge. It's the best jam to use, with sweet fresh cream, to sandwich a vanilla-scented, tender-crumbed Victoria sponge.

This is another recipe that comes from the movingly hand-scrawled book that belonged to Hettie's mother, Soot.

**250g raspberries**                         1 x 250ml jar
**250g caster sugar**

Preheat the oven to 180°C/gas mark 4.

Put the raspberries and sugar into two separate bowls; I use pie dishes, so the fruit will be spread out rather than piled up. Put the bowls into the oven for 20–25 minutes until they are really hot. Take them out of the oven carefully, and add the sugar to the raspberries. As you do so you'll find the fruit turns into a molten, ruby-red river. Pour this into the cleaned and waiting jar. Fasten it, and leave to cool before storing in the fridge.

Makes 250ml.

# STRAWBERRY JAM

It occurred to me when I was last making the strawberries in dark syrup from *How to Eat* that there was no reason why I couldn't use the balsamic vinegar – which provides the darkness and really does seem to make the strawberries strawberrier – when making jam. It was a good move.

I use preserving sugar here instead of jam sugar since the lemon provides enough pectin to make the jam set and the larger crystals of the preserving sugar make for a clearer, more jewel-like, jam.

**675g strawberries (buy 750g, since you will inevitably have to discard some)**

**700g preserving sugar**

**2 tablespoons lemon juice**

**1 teaspoon balsamic vinegar**

**4 x 200ml jars or equivalent**

Stick a saucer into the deep freeze.

Put all the ingredients into a wide saucepan and stir with a wooden spoon to make sure all the fruit is coated. I don't cut up the fruit, but you could if you wanted.

Put the pan on a low heat and, stirring every now and again, bring to the boil. Let boil for about 5–8 minutes, depending on the size of your pan, and start testing for setting point from 4 minutes, taking the pan off the heat and putting a scant teaspoon onto the saucer. Leave it to cool and then poke at it to see if it's ready.

When you've reached this point, leave the pan to cool for 20 minutes before decanting into the cleaned, prepared jars.

Makes 800ml.

## BLACKBERRY JAM

The first time I made this I used just the one punnet of blackberries I had in the house. It was a Saturday morning and I felt like some casual kitchen putskying. I used the same jam the next day to fill the crostata (p105) and I urge you, when you're in the mood, to do the same.

I've given quantities for quite an uncharacteristically large amount of jam because blackberries really are the one fruit – Bramleys aside – I find we do get a glut of here. But as you can see from the ratio of ingredients, you can work out what to do with less (or more) fruit casily cnough.

**1kg blackberries**
**1kg jam sugar**

**juice of 1 lemon**
**4 x 250ml jars or equivalent**

Place your testing saucer in the deep freeze.

Put the fruit, sugar and lemon juice into a preserving pan, or other large, wide pan, and let the sugar dissolve over a low heat. Turn the heat up and bring the jam to the boil. Keep the jam at a rolling boil until setting point is reached.

Makes 1 litre.

## GREENGAGE JAM

If blackberries are something we often have in excess, greengages I can never have enough of. Nothing can match their honeyed acidity or grapey fullness. Some years I worry that I'm never going to find them at all, and I would do anything to help preserve this increasingly unavailable fruit. I've done a small, selfish bit by planting a couple of trees, but I feel that more has to be done. In the meantime, keep your eyes peeled in August.

This is what you should do with any fruit you come across that is perhaps just too sour to eat – that sourness aids the setting. But don't use hard, bitter fruits that shouldn't even have found their way to market.

**1¹⁄2kg greengages, halved and stoned**
**250ml water**

**1kg jam sugar**
**4 x 350ml jars or equivalent**

Place a saucer in the deep freeze.

Get out a large pan, and gently simmer the greengages in the water for 15 minutes. Add the sugar, but don't boil until it has dissolved. Then boil until setting point is reached.

When the jam's at setting point, just, pour into warmed, cleaned jars and close.

Makes about 1½ litres.

## SOFT-SET PEACH AND REDCURRANT JAM

Not only does this look beautiful, the coral chunks of peach suspended in crimson jelly, but the tastes of these two very different fruits seem to set each other off particularly well.

Don't use those mean, hard little unyielding peaches, as unattractive as a bony bottom, but this jam is a good way of transforming fruit that might not be juicily rewarding to eat fresh.

| | |
|---|---|
| **8 peaches** | **250ml water** |
| **4 punnets redcurrants (600g)** | **juice of ½ a lemon** |
| **2kg preserving or caster sugar** | **5 x 350ml jars or equivalent** |

Put a saucer in the freezer, and get out a big pan or, ideally, a preserving pan, as the jam will need to bubble up a lot as it reduces.

Put everything in the pan, and let the sugar dissolve on a gentle heat. Then boil vigorously; it should reach setting point after about 20 minutes (and remember that this jam wants to be only just set; you need detect only the ghost of a wrinkle on the jam's surface).

Let the jam cool in the pan off the heat for 20 minutes before ladling into prepared jars and closing them.

Makes 1¾ litres.

Clockwise from top left: pink-grapefruit marmalade, greengage jam (p348) and soft-set peach and redcurrant jam (p349)

# PINK-GRAPEFRUIT MARMALADE

Please note the easy method for making this: no muslin bags or funny business with suspended cheesecloths involved.

**2 pink grapefruit, weighing**
   **approximately 800g**
**1kg preserving sugar**

**juice of 2 lemons**
**3 x 350ml jars or equivalent**

Place a saucer in the deep freeze.

Put the pink grapefruit into a large saucepan, fill with enough water so that they float freely, bring to the boil and simmer for about 2 hours, by which time the grapefruit should be very soft. Add more hot water from a kettle if the liquid's boiling away.

Drain, remove the fruit to a board and slice the cooked grapefruit thinly, and then chop a bit, using the whole fruit, pith and all (though remove any large pips). Put the grapefruit back into the saucepan, and add the sugar and lemon juice. Let the sugar dissolve over a gentle heat and then bring to the boil until setting point is reached, about 15 minutes.

Ladle into prepared jars and close the lids.

Makes just over 1 litre.

## VARIATIONS

To make ordinary orange marmalade, boil the same weight of Seville oranges for the same amount of time. When they're cooked and soft, take them out of the pan, reserving the liquid, cut them in half, scoop out the pips and put in a small pan, then chop up the oranges as finely or coarsely as you like and put them into a large pan.

Ladle some of the orange-cooking water over the pips in the small pan and put on the heat, bring to the boil and let boil for 5 minutes. Strain this over the chopped oranges in their pan, add the juice of 2 lemons and stir in 1.4kg sugar. Bring to the boil gently, so that the sugar dissolves before the jam actually starts boiling and then proceed as above.

To make ginger-orange marmalade, add about 1cm's worth of finely sliced or chopped ginger to the pips, and then push through 3cm's worth of ginger, in batches, through a garlic press to extract the juice over the pan of chopped oranges. Taste when you've reached setting point to see if you want to add more squeezed ginger.

I also love marmalade which is dark and treacly and especially aromatic: replace half the sugar with light muscovado (and add 1 tablespoonful of black treacle if you like this really dark) and pour in a slug of rum or bourbon, once with the chopped oranges and again after setting point is reached.

# MUSCAT JELLY

This is the easiest jelly in the world. And it is more than just easy: it's pure, golden pleasure. In France, Sauternes jelly is often eaten with foie gras, and feel free to use this the same way (indeed it would make a good present to accompany some at Christmas), but I love it with most cold meats, especially ham.

**350ml muscat**

**350g jam sugar**

**2 teaspoons orange-flower water**

**hand-squeezed juice of 1/2 a lemon, with pips**

**2–3 5cm-lengths orange peel**

**6 coriander seeds**

**pinch of salt**

**2 x 200ml jars or equivalent**

Put a saucer in the deep freeze.

Stir together all the ingredients in a medium-to-small saucepan, then put on the hob over a medium-to-high flame and stir no longer; any stirring now will make the jelly crystallize. Bring to the boil, boil for 10 minutes, then test a little on the cold saucer. When it's reached setting point, remove it from the heat.

If you've got a jelly bag, so much the better (it's finer), otherwise just strain it through a non-metallic sieve into a measuring jug and thence into the jars, waiting till the jelly's cool before putting on their lids.

Makes 400ml.

# FRUIT

## FIGS IN RUM SYRUP

Preserving figs is never going to have quite the same connotations for us as it does for Italians. They have, at the end of summer, an excess of them; for us they're nearly always imported, and therefore a luxury. But I still like to make these, if only because they're at their best about 3–4 months after bottling, which means that over Christmas you can eat them, glossy with dark, aromatic syrup, with vanilla ice cream or piled onto some toasted leftover panettone.

It occurs to me, too, that bottled in beautiful jars – and I use the very beautiful one you see, centrally, in the opening pages of this chapter – these would also make wonderful Christmas presents.

**1kg black figs (about 18)**
**500g caster sugar**
**500ml water**

**75ml white rum, plus 2 tablespoons**
**(30ml) and more as needed**
1 x 1-litre jar

Wash the figs and wipe dry with kitchen towels – gently so as not to break the tender skin – and set aside in a colander while you get on with the syrup.

Put the sugar and water in a large pan and bring slowly to the boil, so that the sugar's dissolved before the liquid reaches boiling point.

Let the syrup bubble away for 15 minutes – not too vociferously but don't, either, let it dwindle to a simmer. Take off the heat, add the 75ml of rum and, gently, the figs. Swill the pan so that the figs are more or less covered and cook at a simmer for about 1½ hours with the lid on at an angle, so that the heat doesn't build up too much, but not too much liquid evaporates. Every now and again, using wooden spatulas or some other tool that won't tear the figs' skin, turn the figs so that all parts are covered and cooked equally.

Remove the figs to the clean preserving jar, put the juices back on the heat, and let boil for 10 minutes to reduce further. Remove from the heat, add the 2 tablespoons of white rum, stir to combine and pour over the figs in the jar. If there's not enough syrup to cover them, pour in more rum.

Close the lid and leave in a dark, cool place for at least 6 weeks and not more than 6 months.

Makes enough to fill a 1-litre jar.

# PICKLED PLUMS

If you go into some health stores or specialist shops you will find Japanese plum seasoning. It's an intensely sharp, clear pink plum (*ume*) vinegar. It seemed obvious, therefore, to use this to pickle plums. Quite apart from how good these taste, they look so beautiful, the dark red of the fruit in the tawny pink of the pickling liquid.

Bring out to eat with cold meats and use within 3–4 months, not because they'll go off but because after a while the fruit goes a bit too mushy.

**500ml Japanese red-plum seasoning**

**375g caster sugar**

**2 star anise**

**25g fresh ginger, peeled and thinly sliced**

**1 tablespoon coriander seeds**

**2 cinnamon sticks, broken in half**

**3 strips of finely peeled orange zest**

**500g plums, halved and stoned**

**3 x 500ml jars or equivalent**

In a large saucepan, bring the Japanese plum seasoning to the boil with the sugar, star anise, ginger, coriander seeds, cinnamon sticks and orange zest. Stir well until all the sugar has dissolved and simmer for 15 minutes, then take off the heat and allow to cool a little.

Pack the plum halves into the sterilized jars, to come within 5cm of the top, while the jars are still warm. Now pour the vinegar over, covering the plums by about 2½cm. Tap the jars to make sure there are no air bubbles, then insert a long skewer down the sides of the jars to double-check (this works on the swizzle-stick principle, or so I like to think). Make sure the spices and orange zest are fairly evenly shared out and arranged so as to maximize aesthetic pleasure. Seal the jars well, and store in a cool, dark place for at least a week before eating. Keep in the fridge once opened.

Makes 3 x 500ml jars.

### VARIATION
Use red-wine vinegar (or any other vinegar you want) in place of the red-plum seasoning.

Clockwise from top: pineapple chutney (p358), spiced apple chutney and Chinese plum sauce (p363)

## CHUTNEYS AND PICKLES

Chutneys, you should know before reading further, are a breeze to make. You simply chuck everything in one pan and let it boil for about 30 minutes until you've got a pulpy mass.

## SPICED APPLE CHUTNEY

Well, all chutneys contain spices, but the intense, hot flavours in this chutney are the focus. I sneered when Hettie suggested this when we had a tree full of apples that I was letting rot, but she was right. The idea of apple chutney may seem unappealing – I just thought of it as grainy mush – but the taste is out of this world. I now cannot eat a Cornish pasty without it.

**500g cooking apples**
**1 medium onion**
**2 bird's-eye red chillies**
**250g demerara sugar**
**1 teaspoon ground allspice**
**1 teaspoon ground cloves**
**1/2 teaspoon sea salt**

**black pepper**
**1 heaped tablespoon chopped or**
  **grated fresh ginger**
**1 teaspoon turmeric**
**350ml cider vinegar**
**4 x 250ml jars or equivalent**

Peel and roughly chop the apples, and finely chop the onion. Seed the chillies and chop them finely (I'd advise you to put on washing-up gloves for this, especially if you wear contact lenses).

Put all the ingredients in a pan, and bring to the boil. Cook over a medium heat for 30–40 minutes, until the mixture thickens. Spoon into the cleaned jars and, when cool, place them, with great and warm satisfaction, in your store cupboard.

Makes 1 litre.

# PINEAPPLE CHUTNEY

This is fabulous with cold ham. And you can water it down and use it to glaze hams after you've poached them and before you've oven-blitzed them. And I adore it with cold turkey – along with some cold bread sauce and a spot of English mustard – in a Boxing-Day sandwich. Cold chicken and mayonnaise can always stand in.

1 ripe pineapple, peeled and chunked into bite-size pieces
juice of the pineapple (approximately 4 tablespoons)
1 medium cooking apple, peeled, cored and finely chopped
100ml rice (or cider) vinegar

150g demerara sugar
1 cinnamon stick, broken into pieces
3 cloves
2 star anise
1 teaspoon mustard seeds
1 teaspoon turmeric
2 x 250ml jars or equivalent

Put all the ingredients into a heavy-based saucepan. Bring to the boil, and simmer for 45 minutes or so, until you have a rough, jammy pulp.

Cool slightly and then ladle into the washed and sterilized jars.

Makes 500ml.

# PARADISE CHUTNEY

In a wonderful and instructive old book, Beryl Wood's *Let's Preserve It*, which I picked up at a second-hand bookshop in Falmouth, I read about a marvellous-sounding jelly, made of apples, quinces and cranberries, and called, evocatively, paradise jelly. So I thought I'd use the idea, and the name, to make something more plausible in the modern kitchen.

Since chutneys are – I think – at their best about a month after being made, it makes this perfect for adding a necessary jolt to a plateful of Christmas leftovers. For, since quinces are really only around in November, you can't make it at any other time of the year. And, you should know, it is excellent with blue cheese.

500g quince, peeled, cored and cut
    into chunks
750ml water
500g cooking apples, peeled, cored
    and cut into chunks
1 medium onion, chopped
250g fresh cranberries
150g dried cranberries
500g white sugar

4 cloves
2 cinnamon sticks, crumbled
1 tablespoon English mustard powder
Juice and zest of 1 orange
juice and zest of 1 lemon
350ml cider vinegar
350ml quince water (made from
    quince peel and the 750ml water)
4 x 500ml jars or equivalent

Save the peelings and cores from the quince, and put them into a saucepan with the water. Boil for about 10–15 minutes until you have about 350ml remaining.

Put all the ingredients, including the strained 350ml of quince-peelings liquid, in a large pan or preserving pan, and let the sugar dissolve over a low heat. Then bring it up to the boil and cook for about 1 hour. Try to keep the pan at a gentle boil, as you need everything to cook down and thicken slightly. When it's ready, all should be soft and fairly pulpy; only the pieces of quince should still be visible.

Ladle into sterilized jars.

Makes 2 litres.

# EDITH AFIF'S LIME PICKLES

I call these lime pickles because that's what my friend Steve, who gave me this recipe of his late mother's, calls them. But think, rather, of limes, salted, rinsed and preserved in aromatic oil. When the Edith of the title made these in her native Egypt, she dredged the limes with salt over days; only later did she adapt her method to what was then modern technology. People can get so precious about tradition that I love the proof that change and modernity can be progress: somehow, salting the limes and leaving them in the deep freeze – rather brilliant of her to come up with the idea – breaks down the fruit's fibres much more effectively.

You either have a sour tooth or you don't. I do, and love these pickles – with bread and cheese, aromatic stews, cold meats, anything.

10 limes

1kg coarse salt

approximately 500ml olive oil (not
   extra virgin)

1 tablespoon turmeric

1 teaspoon cumin seeds

3 dried red chilli peppers, crumbled

3 x 350ml preserving jars

30 x 20cm baking tray or Pyrex dish

Cut the limes into eighths lengthways and cover the bottom of your dish with them. Cover the limes with the salt and then put in the freezer overnight or for a day (12 hours should do it, but longer won't hurt).

Remove from the deep freeze and thaw thoroughly. Put into a colander and rinse under the cold tap. Shake dry. Put a third into each clean, waiting jar. Decant the oil into a measuring jug and stir in the turmeric, cumin seeds and crumbled pepper. Pour the oil to come to the very top of the jars (and if you need more than 500ml to do this then simply add more – if the limes aren't submerged you'll get mould). Close and put away in a dark place. Leave for at least 3 weeks before eating. The longer you leave them, the more tender and exquisite they are.

Makes 3 x 350ml jars.

# BROWN SAUCE

I know that the ingredients that follow hardly look like the stock constituents of brown sauce, and I should own up and say that this didn't start off life as brown sauce. It was conceived to be a rhubarb chutney, only I added too much liquid and what with one thing and another, I decided the only way to salvage it was to whizz it in the blender and turn it into a sauce. This isn't just a case of making the best of a bad lot: this is one of my favourite recipes in the whole book – for its depth of flavour, its full-toned tanginess – and a reminder that cooking is often about what you do, unplanned, in response to the here and now, not merely the careful application of culinary formulae.

**1kg rhubarb**

**500g red onions (about 5 small ones)**

**2 long red chillies, deseeded**

**2 garlic cloves**

**300g cooking apple (about 1 medium)**

**30g (about 3cm) fresh ginger, minced**

**1 tablespoon ground ginger**

**1 tablespoon paprika**

**150g sultanas**

**75g dried cherries**

**500ml red-wine vinegar**

**1 tablespoon salt**

**1kg demerara sugar**

**2 x 1-litre jars and 1 x 500ml jar, or equivalent**

Trim the rhubarb, chop it very roughly, put it into the food processor and chop finely, but don't turn it into a mush; you may want to do this in stages, or else just cut the trimmed rhubarb into ½cm slices by hand. Tip the chopped rhubarb into a large, heavy-bottomed pan. Now process the onions, chillies and garlic until finely chopped and transfer these to the pan with the rhubarb. Chop the apple the same way and add to the pan.

Stir in the minced fresh ginger (I use my fine Microplane grater which is peerless for this, but a garlic press would do just fine), the ground ginger, paprika, sultanas, dried cherries, red-wine vinegar, salt and sugar.

Bring to a boil, then lower the heat and simmer until everything has turned to an undulating but still just nubbly pulp – about 45 minutes.

Take the pan off the heat, let cool for about 10 minutes and then, a ladleful or so at a time, liquidize or process until smooth. Pour into the sterilized jars, let cool, cover and store away, with joy and satisfaction in your heart.

Makes 2½ litres.

# CHINESE PLUM SAUCE

Whether people from China would call this a Chinese plum sauce I can't honestly say, but let's not quibble about details. It's wonderful with pork, with sharp Cheddar, with, well, most things. And sometimes I stir a tablespoon or two of it into a winey beef stew while I'm making it. It's very addictive, which I guess has something to do with both the sugar and the chilli – and the fact that it tastes so good.

I made it last year from some plums in my garden, which was particularly satisfying, but it's certainly worth buying some expressly for this.

2kg plums, stoned and quartered

750g apples, peeled, cored and cut into 1cm chunks

1 medium red onion

4 cloves of garlic, minced

750ml rice vinegar

500g caster sugar

500g dark muscovado sugar (or light if you prefer)

2cm piece of ginger, peeled and sliced into fine splinters

2 long red chillies

2–4 dried red chillies (depending on how hot you want it), crumbled

2 teaspoons ground Chinese 5-spice

1 stick of cinnamon, broken into pieces

2 pieces dried orange peel, optional

5 x 550ml jars

Use a big pan, such as a preserving pan, so that it can boil well to reduce, and put all the ingredients in it.

Cook everything at a steady boil for 1–1½ hours. When it is ready, it will still be runny – remember it is sauce – but it will become firmer; both the apples and the plums will set more on cooling. However, it should have reduced to make a jam-like mixture with no obvious signs of the fruit still apparent.

Bottle in the sterilized jars.

Makes 2¾ litres.

# BIBLIOGRAPHY

Anderson, Pam, *The Perfect Recipe* (Houghton Mifflin, 1998)

Appel, Jennifer, and Allysa Torey, *The Magnolia Bakery Cookbook* (Simon & Schuster, 1999)

Bauer, Michael and Fran Irwin (eds), *The San Francisco Chronicle Cookbook* (Chronicle Books, 1997)

Bery, Odette J., *Another Season Cookbook* (The Globe Pequot Press, 1986)

Collister, Linda, *Sweet Pies and Tarts* (Ryland Peters & Small, 1997)

Colwin, Laurie, *Home Cooking* (HarperCollins, 2000)

Conte, Anna del, *The Gastronomy of Italy* (Bantam Press, 1987)

—— *Secrets from an Italian Kitchen* (Bantam Press, 1989)

Costa, Margaret, *Four Seasons Cookbook* (Grub Street, 1996)

Crawford-Poole, Shona, *Iced Delights* (Conran Octopus, 1986)

Farrow, Genevieve, and Diane Dreher, *The Joy of Muffins* (Golden West, 1989)

Fobel, Jim, *Jim Fobel's Old-Fashioned Baking Book: Recipes from an American Childhood* (Lake Isle Press, 1996)

Greenspan, Dorie, with Julia Child, *Baking with Julia* (William Morrow, 1996)

Greenstein, George, *Secrets of a Jewish Baker* (The Crossing Press, 1993)

Grigson, Jane, *Fruit Book* (Michael Joseph, 1982)

—— *English Food* (Ebury Press, 1992)

Kimball, Christopher, *The Yellow Farmhouse Cookbook* (Little, Brown, 1998)

Lawson, Nigella, *How to Eat* (Chatto & Windus, 1998)

Levy Beranbaum, Rose, *The Cake Bible* (William Morrow, 1988)

Machlin, Edda Servi, *The Classic Cuisine of the Italian Jews* (Giro Press, 1981)

McNair, James, *James McNair's Cakes* (Chronicle Books, 1999)

Ojakangas, Beatrice A., *The Great Scandinavian Baking Book* (University of Minnesota Press, 1999)

Ortiz, Joe, *The Village Baker* (Ten Speed Press, 1993)

—— and Gayle Ortiz, *The Village Baker's Wife* (Ten Speed Press, 1997)

Purdy, Susan G., *The Family Baker* (Broadway Books, 1999)

Rubinstein, Helge, *The Chocolate Book* (Macdonald & Co., 1981)

Schloss, Andrew, *One-Pot Cakes* (William Morrow, 1995)
Stavroulakis, Nicolas, *The Cookbook of the Jews of Greece* (Jason Aronson Inc., 1996)

Treuille, Eric and Ursula Ferrigno, *Bread* (Dorling Kindersley, 1998)

Willan, Anne, *Real Food: Fifty Years of Good Eating* (Macmillan, 1988)
Willard, Pat, *Pie Every Day* (Algonquin Books of Chapel Hill, 1997)
Wood, Beryl, *Let's Preserve It* (Souvenir Press, 1970)

# ACKNOWLEDGEMENTS

There are many people who have helped, either with ingredients or equipment, in the course of this book, and to whom I owe thanks, most notably the Conran Shop, Ecko Bakeware, Graham & Greene, Kitchen Ideas, Marks & Spencer together with W. Brice and Son of Mockbeggar Farm, Michanicou Brothers, Mortimer & Bennett, Selfridges, Somerill & Bishop, Tiffany & Co., Vessel and Wedgwood.

One wanders into the land of platitude in saying that no book is the product of only one person's effort, but it's true all the same. I am grateful to a number of people, Eugenie Boyd, Caz Hildebrand, Gail Rebuck, Alison Samuel, Petrina Tinslay and Ed Victor chief among them.

I could not even broach the subject of my own, overwhelming gratitude without mentioning my three graces: those domestic goddesses Lisa Grillo and Kate Mellor, who have made it possible for me to work, to write, indeed to live, and Hettie Potter, who came into my life at just the right time, and without whom this book could never have been written. She has cooked with me, taken notes for me, supported me and kept me sane.

# INDEX

**almonds and almond essence:**
  almond Danish 328
  cherry-almond loaf cake 28
  damp lemon and almond cake 12
  easy almond cake 6–8
  galette des rois 289
  ricciarelli 56
  Spanish macaroons 54
American breakfast pancakes 77
**apples:**
  apple and walnut cake 36
  apple kuchen 319–20
  apple-syrup upside-down pie 135
  blackberry and apple pie 118–19
  double apple pie 117–18
  spiced apple chutney 357
  tarte tatin 330
  toffee apples 226
  *see also* German plum tart (variations)
autumnal birthday cake 24

baby Bundts 26
bagels 304, 306
baklava 273
baklava muffins 73
**bananas:**
  banana bread 33
  banana, cherry and white-chocolate
    cupcakes 200
  banana muffins 218, 220
**birthday cakes:**
  autumnal birthday cake 24
  buttermilk birthday cake 210–11
**biscuits** 47
  butter cut-out biscuits 212
  Christmas decorations 270
  coffee and walnut splodge biscuits 62
  Granny Boyd's biscuits 204
  Halloween biscuits *see* Halloween
    cupcakes (variation)
  hot discs 64, 66
  Irish blue biscuits 64
  Italian biscuits 63
  lemon gems 61
  maple-pecan biscuits 59
  oatcakes 66
  rosebud madeleines 49
  snickerdoodles 58
  sweet and salty peanut biscuits 55
  white-chocolate and pistachio biscuits 205

*see also* macaroons
bitter-orange and blueberry tart 109–10
black and white tart 112
black cake 250–2
**blackberries:**
  baked summer-fruit tart 111
  black and white tart 112
  blackberry and apple pie 118–19
  blackberry galette 115
  blackberry jam 348
  crostata 105
  mini-pavlovas 239
blintzes, cheese 154–6
**blueberries:**
  baked summer-fruit tart 111
  bitter-orange and blueberry tart 109–10
  blueberry boy-bait 126–7
  blueberry muffins 72
  blueberry sauce 154
Boston cream pie 21–2
Boxing Day egg-and-bacon pie 278
brandy, quince 340
brandy butter 257
**breads** 292–4
  brown bread 297–8
  Finnish rye bread 299
  garlic and parsley hearthbreads 306–8
  lahmacun 312–13
  maple-pecan bread 303
  nigellan flatbread 311–12
  Norwegian mountain loaf 302
  potato bread 298
  schiacciata with Gorgonzola and pine
    nuts 309
  sourdough 300–1
  white loaf 296–7
**breakfast:**
  almond Danish 328
  American breakfast pancakes 77
  apple kuchen 319–20
  bagels 304, 306
  baklava muffins 73
  banana muffins 218, 220
  blueberry muffins 72
  cheese Danish 329
  Christmas-morning muffins 277
  jam-doughnut muffins 220–1
  johnnycakes 74–5
  lemon-raspberry muffins 74
  Norwegian cinnamon buns 322

rhubarb-crumble kuchen 321
schnecken 324–5
Snickers and peanut-butter muffins 218
Welshcakes 75
brown sauce 362
brownies 193
cream-cheese brownies 194
white-chocolate and macadamia brownies
194–5
buns:
Norwegian cinnamon buns 322
schnecken 324–5
burnt-butter brown-sugar cupcakes 41
butter cut-out biscuits 212
butterfly cakes 217
buttermilk birthday cake 210–11
butterscotch layer cake 20–1

cakes 2–3
almond cake 6–8
apple and walnut cake 36
apple kuchen 319–20
autumnal birthday cake 24
baby Bundts 26
banana bread 33
black cake 250–2
Boston cream pie 21–2
butterfly cakes 217
buttermilk birthday cake 210–11
butterscotch layer cake 20–1
certosino 255
cherry-almond loaf cake 28
chestnut ice-cream meringue cake 146–7
chocolate-chestnut cake 171
chocolate-marsala cake 183
chocolate mousse cake 176
chocolate-orange cake 170–1
chocolate-pistachio cake 174–5
Christmas cake 248–9
Coca-Cola cake 232–3
coconut cake 23
courgette cake 18–19
cranberry upside-down cake 284
damp lemon and almond cake 12
dense chocolate loaf cake 166
dolly-mixture fairy cakes 215
fairy cakes 39–40, 215
Flora's famous courgette cake 18–19
gâteau Breton 11
lemon-mascarpone sandwich cake 15–16
lemon-syrup loaf cake 13
marzipan fruit cake 34
mini lime-syrup sponges 242

molten chocolate babycakes 179
my mother-in-law's Madeira cake 5
rhubarb cornmeal cake 30
rosemary loaf cake 9
seed cakes see my mother-in-law's Madeira
cake (variations)
snow-topped spice cake 253
sour-cream chocolate cake with
sour-cream icing 169
sponge drops 43
torta alla gianduia 172
Victoria sponge 14–15
winter plum cake 37
see also cheesecakes; cupcakes
Calvados syllabub 139
cappuccino cupcakes 199
caraway seed cake see Madeira cake
(variations)
carrot cupcakes with cream-cheese icing 42
certosino 255
cheese:
cheese biscuits see maple-pecan biscuits
(variation)
cheese blintzes 154–6
cheese Danish 329
cheese, onion and potato pies 99
cheese scones see Lily's scones (variation)
Irish blue biscuits 64
pizza rustica 86–8
pizza rustica all'Inglese 89
schiacciata with Gorgonzola and pine nuts
309
see also cream cheese
cheesecakes:
chocolate cheesecake 175
London cheesecake 159
mini-cheesecakes 234
New York cheesecake 157
passionfruit cheesecake 160
Joe Dolce's Italian cheesecake 161
cherries:
cherry trifle 149–50
see also German plum tart (variations)
cherry-almond loaf cake 28
chestnuts/chestnut purée:
chestnut ice-cream meringue cake 146–7
chocolate chestnut cake 171
Mont Blanc 288
chick peas:
courgette and chick pea filo pie 93
children's food 209
banana muffins 218, 220
butter cut-out biscuits 212

butterfly cakes 217
buttermilk birthday cake 210–11
cinder toffee 229
Coca-Cola cake 232–3
cornflake crispies 217
dream bars 227
Easter nests 231
fairy cakes 215, *see also* cupcakes
fudge 228
gingerbread with lemon icing 236
Halloween cupcakes 216
jam-doughnut muffins 220–1
meringues 231
mini-cheesecakes 234
mini-pavlovas 239
mint dominoes 234
peanut-butter and jam jewels 221, 223
peanut-butter squares 223
rocky road 224
Roxanne's millionaire's shortbread 240
Snickers and peanut-butter muffins 218
Soot's flapjacks 232
toffee apples 226
Chinese plum sauce 363
chocolate 164–5
    banana, cherry and white-chocolate
      cupcakes 200
    brownies 193
    cappuccino cupcakes 199
    chocodoodles *see* snickerdoodles
      (variation)
    chocolate banana bread *see* banana bread
      (variation)
    chocolate cheesecake 175
    chocolate-cherry cupcakes 196
    chocolate-chestnut cake 171
    chocolate coffee volcano 181–2
    chocolate cupcakes 168
    chocolate icing 22
      all-purpose 195
    chocolate macaroons 186–7
    chocolate-marsala cake 183
    chocolate mousse cake 176
    chocolate-pistachio cake 174–5
    chocolate-raspberry tarts 187–8
    cream-cheese brownies 194
    dense chocolate loaf cake 166
    Easter nests 231
    espresso cupcakes 198
    florentines 203
    gooey chocolate stack 185–6
    Granny Boyd's biscuits 204
    mint dominoes 234

molten chocolate babycakes 179
night-and-day cupcakes 201
pain-au-chocolat pudding 190
peanut-butter squares 223
profiteroles (variation) 142–3
rocky road 224
Roxanne's millionaire's shortbread 240
sour-cream chocolate cake with
    sour-cream icing 169
store-cupboard chocolate-orange cake
    170–1
torta alla gianduia 172
white-chocolate and macadamia brownies
    194–5
white-chocolate and pistachio biscuits 205
white-chocolate rum custard 168
Christmas cake 248–9
    *see also* black cake; certosino
Christmas crème brûlée 287
Christmas cupcakes 267
Christmas decorations 270
Christmas-morning muffins 277
Christmas pavlova 283
Christmas pudding 256
chutneys 357
    paradise chutney 359
    pineapple chutney 358
    spiced apple chutney 357
cinder toffee 229
cinnamon:
    cinnamon sugar *see* vanilla sugar
      (variations)
    Norwegian cinnamon buns 322
clafoutis, red-gooseberry 136
Coca-Cola cake 232–3
coconut:
    coconut cake 23
    coconut macaroons 50
coffee:
    cappuccino cupcakes 199
    chocolate-coffee volcano 181–2
    coffee and walnut splodge biscuits 62
    coffee-butterscotch cake 20–1
    coffee sandwich cake *see* Victoria sponge
      (variations)
    espresso cupcakes 198
cornflake crispies 217
Cornish pasties 96–7
courgettes:
    courgette and chick pea filo pie 93
    Flora's famous courgette cake 18–19
cranberries:
    cranberry curd 343

cranberry upside-down cake 284
cream cheese:
    cream-cheese brownies 194
    cream-cheese icing 42
    night-and-day cupcakes 201
crème brûlée, Christmas 287
crème pâtissière 21, 22
crispies, cornflake 217
crostata 105
crumbles:
    gooseberry-cream crumble 129
    plum and pecan crumble 128
cupcakes 39
    banana, cherry and white-chocolate
        cupcakes 200
    burnt-butter brown-sugar cupcakes 41
    cappuccino cupcakes 199
    carrot cupcakes with cream-cheese icing
        42
    chocolate cupcakes 168
    chocolate-cherry cupcakes 196
    Christmas cupcakes 267
    Coca-Cola cupcakes see Coca-Cola cake
        (variations)
    espresso cupcakes 198
    Halloween cupcakes 216
    lavender cupcakes 40
    night-and-day cupcakes 201
curds 343
    cranberry curd 343
    lime curd 344
    passionfruit curd 344
custard 134
    Sauternes custard 258
    white-chocolate rum custard 168

damp lemon and almond cake 12
Danish pastry 327
    almond Danish 328
    cheese Danish 329
    tarte tatin 330
dolly-mixture fairy cakes 215
dream bars 227

Easter nests 231
Edith Afif's lime pickles 361
egg-and-bacon pie, Boxing Day 278
espresso cupcakes 198

fairy cakes 39–40, 215
    dolly-mixture fairy cakes 215
figs:
    figs in rum syrup 353

see also black and white tart (variation)
Finnish rye bread 299
flapjacks, Soot's 232
Flora's famous courgette cake 18–19
florentines 203
frangipane mince pies 263
fruit cakes:
    black cake 250–2
    Christmas cake 248–9
    marzipan fruit cake 34
    certosino 255
fudge 228

galette des rois 289
game pie 281–2
garlic and parsley hearthbreads 306–8
gâteau Breton 11
German plum tart 316–17
gin and tonic jelly 131
ginger-orange marmalade see grapefruit
    marmalade (variations)
gingerbread with lemon icing 236
glögg, Swedish 269
gooey chocolate stack 185–6
gooseberries:
    gooseberry-cream crumble 129
    gooseberry Victoria sponge see Victoria
        sponge (variations)
    red-gooseberry clafoutis 136
Granny Boyd's biscuits 204
greengage jam 348–9
grapefruit, pink:
    pink-grapefruit marmalade 351
    see also lemon-syrup loaf cake (variations)

Halloween cupcakes 216
Hanukkah:
    latkes 274
    loukamades 274, 275–6
hazelnuts:
    Nutella cake (torta alla gianduia) 172
hot discs 64, 66

iced rum sauce 258
icing:
    all-purpose chocolate 195
    butter 210, 211
    chocolate ganache 22
    cream-cheese 42
    lemon 236
    sour-cream 169
Irish blue biscuits 64
Italian biscuits 63

jam 346
    blackberry jam 348
    greengage jam 348–9
    peach and redcurrant jam 349
    raspberry jam, hands-free 346
    strawberry jam 347
    *see also* curds
jam-doughnut muffins 220–1
jars, sterilizing 335
jellies:
    gin and tonic jelly 131
    muscat jelly 352
    vodka and lime jelly *see* gin and tonic jelly
      (variations)
Joe Dolce's Italian cheesecake 161
johnnycakes 74–5

key lime pie 103–4
    mini key-lime pies 241

lahmacun 312–13
latkes 274
lavender cupcakes 40
lemons:
    baby Bundts 26
    damp lemon and almond cake 12
    lemon gems 61
    lemon mascarpone sandwich cake 15–16
    lemon poppyseed cake *see* Madeira cake
      (variations)
    lemon-raspberry muffins 74
    lemon-raspberry plate trifle 153
    lemon-syrup loaf cake 13
Lily's scones 67
limes:
    Edith Afif's lime pickles 361
    key lime pie 103–4
    lime curd 344
    mini key-lime pies 241
    mini lime-syrup sponges 242
    *see also* baby Bundts (variations)
London cheesecake 159
loukamades 274, 275–6

macaroons:
    chocolate macaroons 186–7
    coconut macaroons 50
    pistachio macaroons 53
    ricciarelli 56
    Spanish macaroons 54
Madeira cake, my mother-in-law's 5
madeleines, rosebud 49
maids of honour 268

manger mince pies 259–60
maple-pecan biscuits 59
maple-pecan bread 303
marmalade:
    marmalade sponge *see* steamed syrup
      sponge (variations)
    pink-grapefruit marmalade 351
marzipan:
    easy almond cake 6–8
    marzipan fruit cake 34
mascarpone:
    black and white tart 112
    lemon-mascarpone sandwich cake 15–16
    muscat-mascarpone cream 31
    passionfruit, mascarpone and meringue
      trifle 151
meringues 231
    chestnut ice-cream meringue cake 146–7
    Christmas pavlova 283
    mini-pavlovas 239
    Mont Blanc 288
    redcurrant meringue pie 121
mince pies:
    frangipane mince pies 263
    manger mince pies 259–60
    star-topped mince pies 260–2
mincemeat, Hettie Potter's suet-free 264
mint dominoes 234
molten chocolate babycakes 179
Mont Blanc 288
muffins:
    baklava muffins 73
    banana muffins 218, 220
    blueberry muffins 72
    Christmas-morning muffins 277
    jam-doughnut muffins 220–1
    lemon-raspberry muffins 74
    Snickers and peanut-butter muffins
      218
mulled wine 269
muscat jelly 352
muscat-mascarpone cream 31
muscat rice pudding 137
mushroom tarts, small 102
my mother-in-law's Madeira cake 5

New York cheesecake 157
nigellan flatbread 311–12
night-and-day cupcakes 201
Norwegian cinnamon buns 322
Norwegian mountain loaf 302
Nutella cake (torta alla gianduia) 172
nuts:
    dream bars 227

rocky road 224
sweet and salty peanut biscuits 55
white-chocolate and macadamia brownies
194–5
*see also* almonds; chestnuts; hazelnuts;
pecan nuts; pistachio nuts; walnuts

oatcakes 66
Om Ali 140
**onions:**
cheese, onion and potato pies 99
supper onion pie 85
*see also* German plum tart (variations)
**oranges:**
bitter-orange and blueberry tart 109–10
marmalade *see* grapefruit marmalade
(variations)
orange-syrup loaf cake *see* lemon-syrup
loaf cake (variations)

pain-au-chocolat pudding 190
**pancakes:**
American breakfast pancakes 77
johnnycakes 74–5
*see also* Welshcakes
paradise chutney 359
**passionfruit:**
passionfruit cheesecake 160
passionfruit curd 344
passionfruit, mascarpone and meringue
trifle 151
*see also* strawberry shortcakes (variation);
Victoria sponge (variations)
pasties, Cornish 96–7
**pastry:**
basic shortcrust 83
processor puff pastry 83
**pavlovas:**
Christmas pavlova 283
mini-pavlovas 239
**peaches:**
soft-set peach and redcurrant jam 349
*see also* black and white tart (variation)
**peaches, dried:**
peach cream pie 119–20
**peanuts/peanut-butter:**
peanut-butter and jam jewels 221, 223
peanut-butter squares 223
Snickers and peanut-butter muffins 218
sweet and salty peanut biscuits 55
**pecan nuts:**
maple-pecan biscuits 59
maple-pecan bread 303

plum and pecan crumble 128
peppermint creams *see* mint dominoes
(variation)
pickled plums 354
pickles, Edith Afif's lime 361
**pies and tarts** 80–1
*savoury:*
Boxing Day egg-and-bacon pie 278
cheese, onion and potato pies 99
Cornish pasties 96–7
courgette and chick pea filo pie 93
game pie 281–2
mushroom tarts 102
onion pie 85
pizza rustica 86, 88
pizza rustica all'Inglese 89
sausage and spinach pie 90
spinach, ricotta and bulgar wheat pie 91
steak and kidney pudding 94, 96
tomato tarts 100
*sweet:*
apple-syrup upside-down pie 135
baked summer-fruit tart 111
bitter-orange and blueberry tart 109–10
black and white tart 112
blackberry and apple pie 118–19
blackberry galette 115
chocolate-raspberry tarts 187–8
crostata 105
double apple pie 117–18
German plum tart 316–17
key lime pie 103–4
maids of honour 268
mini key-lime pies 241
peach cream pie 119–20
redcurrant meringue pie 121
rhubarb tart 107–8
tarte tatin 330
*see also* mince pies
pineapple chutney 358
**pistachio nuts:**
baklava 273
chocolate-pistachio cake 174–5
pistachio soufflés 145–6
white-chocolate and pistachio biscuits 205
pizza casareccia 315
pizza rustica 86–8
pizza rustica all'Inglese 89
**plums:**
Chinese plum sauce 363
German plum tart 316–17
pickled plums 354
plum and pecan crumble 128

winter plum cake 37
*see also* rhubarb tart (variation)
**pomegranates:**
Christmas pavlova 283
**potatoes:**
cheese, onion and potato pies 99
latkes 274
potato bread 298
profiteroles 142–3
**puddings** 124–5, *see also* cheesecakes; jellies;
pies and tarts, sweet; trifles
apple-syrup upside-down pie 135
blueberry boy-bait 126–7
Calvados syllabub 139
cheese blintzes 154–6
chestnut ice-cream meringue cake 146–7
chocolate-coffee volcano 181–2
Christmas crème brûlée 287
Christmas pavlova 283
Christmas pudding 256
galette des rois 289
gooey chocolate stack 185–6
gooseberry clafoutis 136
gooseberry-cream crumble 129
Mont Blanc 288
muscat-mascarpone cream (variation) 31
muscat rice pudding 137
Om Ali 140
pain-au-chocolat pudding 190
pistachio soufflés 145–6
plum and pecan crumble 128
profiteroles 142–3
rhubarb grunt 127
steamed syrup sponge 132–4
puff pastry, processor 83

**quinces:**
paradise chutney 359
quince brandy 340
quince glaze 342
quincemeat 265

**raspberries:**
baked summer-fruit tart 111
chocolate-raspberry tarts 187–8
hands-free raspberry jam 346
lemon-raspberry muffins 74
lemon-raspberry plate trifle 153
mini-pavlovas 239
**redcurrants:**
baked summer-fruit tart 111
redcurrant meringue pie 121
soft-set peach and redcurrant jam 349

**rhubarb:**
brown sauce 362
rhubarb cornmeal cake 30
rhubarb-crumble kuchen 321
rhubarb grunt 127
rhubarb schnapps 339
rhubarb tart 107–8
*see also* Victoria sponge (variations)
ricciarelli 56
rice pudding, muscat 137
**ricotta:**
spinach, ricotta and bulgar wheat pie 91
rocky road 224
rosebud madeleines 49
**rosemary:**
rosemary loaf cake 9
*see also* vanilla sugar (variations)
Roxanne's millionaire's shortbread 240
**rum:**
figs in rum syrup 353
iced rum sauce 258
white-chocolate rum custard 168
rye bread, Finnish 299

**sauces:**
blueberry sauce 154
brandy butter 257
brown sauce 362
Chinese plum sauce 363
iced rum sauce 258
sausage and spinach pie 90
Sauternes custard 258
schiacciata with Gorgonzola and pine nuts
309
schnapps, rhubarb 339
schnecken 324–5
scones, Lily's 67
seed cakes *see* my mother-in-law's Madeira
cake (variations)
shortbread, Roxanne's millionaire's 240
shortcakes, strawberry 69–70
shortcrust pastry 83
snickerdoodles 58
Snickers and peanut-butter muffins 218
snow-topped spice cake 253
Soot's flapjacks 232
soufflés, pistachio 145–6
sour-cream chocolate cake with sour-cream
icing 169
sourdough 300–1
spiced apple chutney 357
**spinach:**
sausage and spinach pie 90

spinach, ricotta and bulgar wheat pie 91
sponge drops 43
star-topped mince pies 260–2
steak and kidney pudding 94, 96
steamed syrup sponge 132–4
**strawberries:**
    strawberry jam 347
    strawberry shortcake 69–70
summer-fruit tart, baked 111
supper onion pie 85
Swedish glögg 269
syllabub, Calvados 139

tarte tatin 330
tarts *see* pies and tarts
toffee, cinder 229
toffee apples 226
tomato tarts, small 100
torta alla gianduia 172
**trifles:**
    cherry trifle 149–50
    lemon-raspberry plate trifle 153

passionfruit, mascarpone and meringue
    trifle 151

vanilla sugar 336
Victoria sponge 14–16
**vodka:**
    Swedish glögg 269
    vodka and lime jelly *see* gin and tonic
    jelly (variations)

**walnuts:**
    apple and walnut cake 36
    brownies 193
    coffee and walnut splodge biscuits 62
    *see also* maple-pecan biscuits (variations)
Welshcakes 75
white-chocolate and macadamia brownies
    194–5
white-chocolate and pistachio biscuits 205
white-chocolate rum custard 168
wine, mulled 269
winter plum cake 37